THE MODERN VERNACULAR LITERATURE OF HINDUSTAN

THE MODERN VERNACULAR LITERATURE OF HINDUSTAN

GEORGE A. GRIERSON

GYAN

Published by

GYAN

Gyan Publishing House
5, Ansari Road
Daryaganj, New Delhi-110002
Phone: 011-47034999, 9811692060
E-mail: books@gyanbooks.com

Distribution Network
gyanbooks.com
India, USA, Canada, UK, Australia

ISBN: 978-93-6780-201-4 (HB)

First Published, 1889

2nd Impression 2024

Printed at: Gyan Press, Delhi.

THE MODERN VERNACULAR LITERATURE OF HINDUSTAN
Author: GEORGE A. GRIERSON

Journal, As. Soc., Beng., Vol. LVII, Extra-Number, 1888.

Plate I.

Frontispiece.

Lichtdruck von E. Jaffé & A. Albert, Wien.

RĀMA'S CHILDHOOD.

THE MODERN VERNACULAR LITERATURE

OF

HINDUSTAN.

By GEORGE A. GRIERSON, B.A., B.C.S.

Wer den Dichter will verstehen,
Muss in Dichters Lande gehen.

[*Printed as a Special Number of the Journal of the Asiatic Society of Bengal, Part I, for 1888.*]

CALCUTTA:
Published by the Asiatic Society, 57, Park Street.
1889.

CONTENTS.

ILLUSTRATIONS.

PREFACE.

In the year 1886 it was my privilege to read, at the International Congress of Orientalists at Vienna, a paper on the Mediæval Vernacular Literature of Hindūstān with special reference to Tul'sī Dās. The preparation of this necessitated the arrangement of the notes on the entire vernacular literature of Northern India, which I had collected through a long series of years, although the essay itself dealt with only a portion of the literature which existed before the 17th century.

Encouraged by the attention with which this paper was received, I have endeavoured to give in the present work a more complete view of the vernacular literature of Hindūstān from the earliest times to the present day. It does not pretend to be more than a list of all the vernacular writers whose names I have been able to collect, nine hundred and fifty-two in number, of whom only some seventy have been previously noticed by Garcin de Tassy in his *Histoire de la litérature hindouie et hindoustanie.*

It will be observed that I deal only with *modern vernacular* literature. I therefore give no particulars concerning authors of purely Sanskrit works, and exclude from consideration books written in Prākrit, even when it may have been a vernacular, as not connoted by the term *modern*. Nor do I record the names of Indian writers in Arabic or Persian, or in the exotic literary Ūrdū, and

I have been the more willing to exclude these last from our present consideration as they have been already exhaustively dealt with by Garcin de Tassy. I may add that by Hindūstān I mean Rāj'putānā and the valleys of the Jamunā and of the Ganges as far east as the river Kōsī, and that I do not include under that term either the Pañjāb or Lower Bangāl. The vernacular languages dealt with may roughly be considered as three in number, Mār'wārī, Hindī, and Bihārī, each with its various dialects and sub-dialects. One omission must be mentioned with regret. I have refrained from including the large number of anonymous folk-epics and of folk-songs (such as *kaj'rīs*, *jat'sārs*, and the like) current throughout Northern India. These can only be collected on the spot from the mouths of the people, and, so far as I am aware, that has only been systematically done in the province of Bihār. I have therefore, after some hesitation, determined to exclude all mention of them from the work, as any attempt to describe them as a whole could only have been incomplete and misleading.

The introduction will explain the principle of arrangement adopted in this work. Many of the entries are mere names of authors and nothing more, which I have included to make the book as complete as possible. When any information was available, I have entered it against the author's name referred to; and in some cases I have, I believe, been able to present information which has not hitherto been placed at the disposal of European scholars. As examples of this, I would refer the reader to the articles on Sūr Dās (No. 37) and on Tul'sī Dās (No. 128). I do not pretend to have read all or even a considerable portion of the large body of literature catalogued in these pages, but I have seen and studied specimens of the works of nearly all the nine hundred and fifty-two authors whose names are mentioned. Nor do I pretend to have understood all I have studied; for many of the specimens are so difficult that it is hopeless to attempt their interpretation without the aid of a commentary, either oral or documentary. For this reason I do not venture to call this book a formal History of Literature. The subject is too vast, and the present state of our knowledge is too limited to allow such a task to be attempted. I therefore only offer it as a collection of *materials* which will form a foundation upon which others more fortunate than I am, and with more time at their disposal than a Bengal District Collector, may build.

Regarding the spelling of vernacular words, I have adhered to the system followed by Dr. Hoernle and myself in our *Comparative Dictionary of the Bihārī Language*, to which the reader is referred for particulars. It may be briefly stated as spelling every word rigidly as it is pronounced. I have only deviated from this rule in the case of the names of a few living gentlemen, natives of India. On the principle that every one has a right to spell his own name as he likes, I have spelt their names as they sign themselves when writing in the English character. The chief difficulty experienced has been in the division of groups of words forming proper names. It has been found by no means an easy task to secure uniformity without leading to results which were too strange and too variant from actual use to be adopted. Present custom in this respect, though convenient, has no system, and the adoption of any system must consequently lead to a certain amount of confusion. I have endeavoured to divide the same name in the same way whenever it occurred in the book, but I regret that amongst the four thousand and odd names which occur there have been some *lapsus calami*.

Apologies for dealing with the Neo-Indian vernaculars are not now so necessary as they would have been twenty years ago. At first, oriental scholars devoted themselves to Sanskrit alone, and then, under the guidance of Burnouf, attacked Pāli. In later years the classical Prākrits have attracted students, and thus the age of the object of our researches has become more and more modern in its character. I now ask my readers to take again one step over the very short gap which separates the latest Prākrit from the earliest Gaudian literature. Hēmachandra flourished about 1150 A.D.,[1] and Chand Bar'dāī, the first of the Gaudian poets of whom we have at present any certain remains, died in 1193.

It is possible, however, that some oriental students may still cling to the old love for Sanskrit, and these I must ask to test the rich ore found in the following pages, which contain the names of several vernacular commentaries on difficult Sanskrit books,[2] and of numerous technical works on such subjects as Grammar, Prosody, Vocabulary,[3] Composition, and the like. The student of inscriptions will also find a productive mine in the literature of Hindūstān, owing to the custom which vernacular poets had of dating their works and of naming their patrons. Besides this the muse

[1] He died 1172 A.D.

[2] For instance, Gumān Jī (No. 349) wrote a commentary of great reputation on the *Naiṣadha*. He lived early in the 18th century.

[3] For instance, Dayā Rām (No. 387) wrote a useful *anēkārthakōṣa*.

of History, so silent in Sanskrit literature, has been assiduously cultivated by these authors, and we have still extant historical works founded on materials which were written so far back as the ninth century. I therefore venture to put forward claims for attention not only from those scholars who have hitherto devoted themselves to Prākrit literature, but also from those who love to wander amid the intricacies of the *Naiṣadha*, or to apply themselves to the copper-plate grants of *The Indian Antiquary*.

There is another claim which I would mention, and that is the intrinsic merit of the Neo-Gaudian literature. After all that is said, the later Sanskrit and the Prākrit poems are but artificial productions, written in the closet by learned men for learned men; but the Neo-Gaudian poets wrote for unsparing critics,—the people. Many of them studied nature and wrote what they saw. They found 'tongues in trees,' and as they interpreted what they heard successfully or not, so was their popularity great or small, and so their works lived after them or not. Several works exist whose authors' names we do not even know; but they have remained living voices in the people's hearts, because they appealed to the sense of the true and of the beautiful.[1]

It is hoped that the three indexes will be found useful. Considerable trouble has been expended in order to make them as accurate as possible.

GEORGE A. GRIERSON.

[1] I refer to the folk epics, *bārā māsās* (songs of the seasons), *kajarīs*, and other songs current throughout India which are referred to above.

INTRODUCTION.

(*a.*) *The sources from which the information contained in this work is derived.*

THE work is founded in great measure on notes collected by myself from innumerable texts bought in the bazārs. It is derived almost entirely from native sources. Wilson's *Religious Sects of the Hindūs* and Garcin de Tassy's various works, especially his *History of Hinduī and Hindūstānī Literature,* have been frequently consulted as checks; and when the information given by them differed from that which I had collected, I have spared no trouble in order to ascertain the correct facts. The only English work which I have taken as an authority has been Tod's *Rājāsthān,* which contains much information not readily available elsewhere concerning the bards of Rāj'putānā. I have endeavoured to check Tod, as far as possible, by reference to competent native authorities, and in this respect I have specially to thank Paṇḍit Mōhan Lāl Viṣṇu Lāl Paṇḍiā, of Udaipur, for much assistance most kindly given to me.

A native work on which I have largely depended, and to which I am indebted for the information given regarding nearly all the minor poets, and many of the more important ones, is the very useful *Sib Siŋgh Sarōj,* by Sib Siŋgh Sēgar, published by Munshī Nawal Kishōr, of Lakh'naū (2nd edition, 1883). This is a compilation from former anthologies, including most of those named below. In addition to the *Sarōj,* I have myself consulted all the available anthologies which I have been able to collect, including many already worked through by Sib Siŋgh. When any poet's works are found in one or more of the principal of these, I have pointed out the fact against his name, by commencing the article with an abbreviation of the name of the anthology. I have not always done this in the case of minor anthologies, and in the case of one or two which came into my hands while the book was passing through the press. A work of this kind *crescit eundo.*

With regard to the dates given for the various authors, I have taken some trouble to verify them as far as I could. Vernacular poets had a laudable practice of dating their works, which has been useful in many cases. They also frequently mentioned their patrons;

and when these could be identified, they often gave a useful clue. When all other methods failed, I had in many cases the *Sarōj* as a guide. Sib Siŋgh continually gives dates, and I have generally found them fairly accurate,—with this proviso, that he always gives his date as that of the birth of the poet referred to, when in reality it is not seldom the date of his principal work.[1] The *Sarōj's* dates have, at any rate, this value, that, in default of any other authority, we may be pretty certain that the author referred to was alive on the date which Sib Siŋgh gives as that of his birth. In the present treatise any dates depending only on his authority have been printed in italics. I would draw attention to the addenda, which give some dates which I have been able to fix while the work was passing through the press.

The following is a list of the anthologies and other works which form the basis of this book :—

No.	Name of anthology.	Abbreviation.	Author's name.	Date.
1	Bhakt Mālā ...	Bhakt. ...	Nabhājī Dās (No. 51) ...	About 1550 A.D.
2	Gosāī Charitr' ...	Go. ...	Bēnī Mādhab Dās (No. 130).	About 1600.
3	Kabi Mālā ...	Māl. ...	Tul'sī (No. 153) ...	1655.
4	Hajārā ...	Haj. ...	Kālidās Tribēdī (No. 159)	1718.
5	Kābya Nir'nay ...	Nir. ...	Bhikhārī Dās (No. 344)	About 1725.
6	Sat-kabi-girā Bilās...	Sat. ...	Bal Dēb (No. 359) ...	1746.
7	List of poets praised by Sūdan.	Sūd. ...	Sūdan (No. 367) ...	About 1750.
8	Bidwan Mōd Taraŋginī.	Bid. ...	Subbā Siŋgh (No. 590)...	1817.
9	Rāg-Sāgarōdbhab Rāg-Kalpadrum.	Rāg. ...	Krish'nānand Byās Dēb (No. 638).	1843.
10	Sriŋgār Saŋgrah ...	Sriŋg. ...	Sar'dār (No. 571) ...	1848.
11	Ūrdū translation of Bhakt Mālā.	U. Bhakt.	Tul'si Rām (No. 640) ...	1854.
12	Ras Chandrōday ...	Ras. ...	Ṭhākur Par'sād Tripāṭhī (No. 570).	1863.
13	Dig-bijāī Bhūkhan...	Dig. ...	Gōkul Par'sād (No. 694)	1868.
14	Sundarī Tilak ...	Sun. ...	Harishchandr' (No. 581)	1869.
15	Kābya Saŋgrah ...	Kāb. ...	Mahēs Datt' (No. 696)...	1875.
16	Kabi Ratnākar ...	Kab. ...	Mātā Dīn Misar (No. 698).	1876.
17	Sib Siŋgh Sarōj ...	Sib. ...	Sib Siŋgh Sēgar (No. 595)	1883.
18	Bichitrōpadēs[2] ...	Bich. ...	Nak'chhēdī Tiwārī ...	1887.

[1] Sometimes, *e.g.* in the case of Mān Siŋgh (No. 599), he gives the date of the poet's death as that of his birth.

[2] This book is not mentioned in the body of the work, which only goes down to 1883. It is published at the Kāshikā Press, Banāras. The author's name is Nak'chhēdī Tiwārī *alias* Ajān Kabi, of Ḍum'rāw. He worked in collaboration with Sudhākar Kabi. It is an anthology of didactic pieces in a comic style. About fifty well-known poets are quoted.

It will be useful to insert here explanations of the Hindī terms corresponding to a few English technical terms used by me. The nine *rasas* or styles are as follows :—

1. *Sriṅgār Ras*,	translated by me as	"the erotic style."
2. *Hāsya Ras*,	ditto	"the comic style."
3. *Karunā Ras*,	ditto	"the elegiac style."
4. *Bīr Ras*,	ditto	"the heroic style."
5. *Raūdr' Ras*,	ditto	"the tragic style."
6. *Bhayānak Ras*,	ditto	"the terrible style."
7. *Bibhatsa*,	ditto	"the satiric style."
8. *Shānti Ras*,	ditto	"the quietistic style."
9. *Adbhut Ras*,	ditto	"the sensational style."

These translations do not pretend to be exact. Each is simply a convenient representation of one Hindī word by one English one.

An explanation of the terms *Nakh'sikh*, *Nāyak Bhēd*, and *Nāyikā Bhēd* will be found in the foot-note to No. 87.

The word *Sāmayik*, when used with reference to a work, I have, not without hesitation, rendered by "occasional." *Chetāonī* I have translated by "didactic." By "emblematic" verses (in Hindī *drishṭ kūṭ*) I mean those fanciful enigmatic *tours de force* which are familiar to Sanskrit scholars who have studied the *Nalōdaya* and the *Kirātārjunīya*.

(b.) *Principles of Arrangement of the Contents.*

Endeavour has been made to arrange the contents as much as possible in chronological order. This has not always been easy, and in some cases it has been found to be impossible. Hence those poets whose dates I have been unable to fix, ever so tentatively, I have grouped together in alphabetical order in the last chapter. While the work was passing through the press I found myself unexpectedly in possession of the approximate dates of a few of these when it was too late to introduce them into their proper places. They have therefore remained in the last chapter, but, to prevent mistakes, I have drawn attention to them in the addenda.

The work is divided into chapters, each roughly representing a period. The sixteenth and the seventeenth centuries, the Augustan age of Indian vernacular poetry, occupy six chapters, not strictly divided according to periods of time, but according to groups of poets, commencing with the romantic poetry of Malik Muḥammad, and including amongst others the Krisṇa cult of Braj, the works of Tul'sī Dās (to whom a special chapter has been allotted), and the technical school of poets founded by Kēsab Dās.

After each chapter are given addenda in small type, showing particulars of the minor poets belonging to the period or to the group dealt with. For most of the information contained in these addenda I am indebted to the *Sib Siŋgh Sarōj*.

(c.) *A Brief Account of the Vernacular Literature of Hindūstān.*

As far as my information goes, the earliest vernacular literature of Hindūstān is the bardic chronicles of Rāj'putānā. The first bard of whom we have any certain information was the well-known Chand Bar'dāī, who celebrated, towards the end of the twelfth century, the fortunes of Prithwī Rāj, the Chāūhān, of Dillī, in the famous *Prithī Rāj Rāy'sā*. Contemporary with him was the bard Jag'nāyak, who attended the court of Prithwī Rāj's great rival, Paramardī of Mahōbā, and who was probably the author of the *Ālhā Khanḍ*, a work equally famous in Hindūstān with the *Prithī Rāj Rāy'sā*, but which has had the misfortune of being preserved by oral tradition instead of in manuscript.

To continue the history of these bardic chronicles, we may mention Çārŋgadhara, or Sāraŋg Dhar, who sung, in the middle of the fourteenth century, the prowess of the heroic Hammīr of Ran'thambhōr (fl. 1300). Passing over Keh'rī (fl. 1580) of Bur'hān'pur, we come to two brilliant groups of bards who adorned the courts of Mēwār and Mār'wār in the 17th century. To these may be added names like that of Lāl (fl. 1650), who wrote a valuable history of Bundēl'khanḍ, and those of other minor poets. After the 17th century the Rāj'pūt bards lost their distinctive character, and while the greater number became merged in the sea of the other vernacular poets of India, the few that remained degenerated into mere compilers of facts derived from older records.

It is hardly necessary to do what Tod has already done in such glowing language, and to point out how completely these Rāj'pūt bards wash away the reproach so often levelled against Indian literature, that it contains no historical works. The value of these bardic chronicles, some of which are derived from older works dating as far back as the 9th century A.D., can hardly be over-estimated. It is true that they contain many legends which are of doubtful authenticity; but what contemporary European chronicle does not contain the same? They also embody the history of Rāj'putānā during the whole of the struggles between India and its Musalmān invaders, written by a series of contemporary authors extending over at least six centuries. Is it unreasonable to hope that some enlightened prince of Rāj'putānā will rescue these documents from the undeserved obscurity in which they lie, and publish the texts of all of them, with English translations?

Turning aside from these bardic historians we may now revert to the growth of vernacular literature in the Gangetic valley, coincident with the rise of the Vaishnava religion at the commencement of the 15th century. Rāmānand, the popularizer of the worship of Rāma, flourished about the year 1400; and even greater than he was his famous disciple Kabīr, who succeeded in founding a still existing sect, which united the salient points of Muhammadanism and Hinduism. Here we first touch upon that marvellous catholicity of sentiment of which the key-note was struck by Rāmānand, which is visible in the doctrines of all his successors, and which reached its truest height in the lofty teaching of Tul'sī Dās two centuries later. The worship of the deified prince of Āudh, and the loving adoration of Sītā, the perfect wife and the perfect mother, have developed naturally into a doctrine of eclecticism in its best form—a doctrine which, while teaching the infinite vileness of mankind before the Infinitely Good, yet sees good in everything that He has created, and condemns no religion and no system of philosophy as utterly bad that inculcates, Thou shalt love the Lord thy God with all thy heart, and with all thy soul, and with all thy strength, and with all thy mind; and thy neighbour as thyself.[1]

Far different has been the fate of that other great branch of the Vaishnava religion which is founded on mystic interpretations of the love which Kriṣṇa bare to Rādhā. Beautiful in itself, paralleled, also, by the teaching of many Christian doctors, and rendered more beautiful by the magic poetry of Mīrā Bāī (fl. 1420) in the west, and of Bidyāpati Ṭhākur (fl. 1400) in the east, its passionate adoration, whose inner meaning was too esoteric for the spirits of the common herd of disciples, in many cases degenerated into a poetry worthy of only the baser sorts of Tāntrik Çiva worshippers. But at its best the Kriṣṇa cult is wanting in the nobler elements of the teaching of Rāmānand. Its essence is almost selfish—a soul-absorbing, nay all-absorbing, individual love cast at the feet of Him who is Love itself.

[1] Mr. Growse (*e.g.* in the note to Rām. Bā. Dōhā, 24) has pointed out, in his translation of the *Rām-charit-mānas*, several points of resemblance between the doctrines of the Christian Church and those of Tul'sī Dās. There are hymns in our Church hymnals which might be literal translations of passages written by this great poet.

It teaches the first and great commandment of the Christian law, but the second, which is like unto it—Thou shalt love thy neighbour as thyself—it omits.

Leaving these two sects aside for a moment, we must pause at one remarkable man, who in some respects was an offshoot from the Răj'pūt bards, while on the other hand his writings bear strong marks of the influence of Kabīr's teaching. Malik Muḥammad (fl. 1540) studied under both Musalmān and Hindū doctors, and wrote, in the purest vernacular of his time, the fine philosophic epic entitled the *Padmāwat.* This work, while telling in vivid language the story of Ratan Sēn's quest for the fair Padmāwat, of Alāu'd-dīn's siege of the virgin city of Chitāūr, of Ratan's bravery, and of Padmāwat's wifely devotion which culminated in the terrible sacrifice of all in the doomed city that was true and fair, to save it from the lust of the conqueror, is also an allegory describing the search of the soul for true wisdom, and the trials and temptations which assail it in its course. Malik Muḥammad's ideal is high, and throughout the work of the Musalmān ascetic there run veins of the broadest charity and of sympathy with those higher spirits among his Hindū fellow-countrymen who were groping in the dark for that light of which so many of them obtained glimpses.

To the mere student of language the *Padmāwat* possesses, by a happy accident, inestimable value. Composed in the earlier portion of the 16th century, it gives us a representation of the speech and of the pronunciation of those days. Hindū writers, tied by the fetters of custom, were constrained to spell their words, not as they were pronounced, but as they were written in the old Sanskrit of their forefathers. But Malik Muḥammad cared not for Hindū customs, and wrote his work in the Persian character, thus giving necessarily a phonographic representation of every word he wrote. The system was not perfect, for, as was customary, vowels were seldom indicated, but in the *Padmāwat* we have the consonantal framework of each word put down as it was pronounced at the time of writing.

With Malik Muḥammad, the period of the apprenticeship of vernacular literature in Hindūstān may be said to have come to a close. The young giant had bestirred himself, and found that he was strong; and, young and lusty as an eagle, he went forth rejoicing to run his course. The earlier Răj'pūt bards wrote in a time of transition, in a language which it would be difficult to define accurately, either as a late Prākrit or as an old form of the modern language of

Rāj'putānā. This was the period of infancy. Then came that of youth, when, with the revival of a popular religion to fill the place once taken by Buddhism, the teachers of the new doctrine had to write in a tongue 'understanded of the people.' Malik Muḥammad and the apostles of the two Vaishnava sects had to feel their way, and walked with uncertainty. When they wrote, the language spoken was practically the same as that spoken now in the rural parts of India, and they must have felt the same hesitation which Spenser and Milton felt in writing in their vernacular. Spenser chose the wrong method and cast his Faërie Queene into an antique mould, but Milton, though he once thought of writing his Paradise Lost in Latin, dared to be right, and thenceforward the English language was made. So was it in India,—the first vernacular authors dared greatly, and succeeded.

The 16th and 17th centuries form the Augustan age of Hindūstanī vernacular literature. Nearly every great writer of the country lived during this period. Its greatest writers were contemporaries with our masters of the reign of Elizabeth, and, to us English, it is interesting to note that when our country first came into contact by its ambassadors with the Mughal court, and when the East India Company was first founded, each of the nations, separated so widely by sea and land, was at its culminating point of literary glory. We must consider separately the various groups of authors who flourished during this age.

It was in Braj, the country of the cowpens and the scene of the childhood of Kriṣṇa and of his early amours with the herdmaidens of Gokula, that the Kriṣṇa cult naturally took its strongest root; and during the 16th century it was the home of a school of poets devoted to the worship of that god, founded by the great apostle Ballabhāchār'j and his son Biṭṭhal Nāth. Of their eight principal disciples, grouped under the name of the *Ashṭa Chhāp*, Krish'n Dās and Sūr Dās were the ones most celebrated. The latter is considered by his fellow-countrymen to share with Tul'sī Dās the throne of absolute perfection in the art of poesy; but European critics will be inclined to award the latter poet alone the supreme crown, and to relegate the blind bard of Āg'rā to a lower, though still an honourable, place. One more poet of this group may here be noticed for his fame as a singer. I allude to Tān Sēn, who besides being an author was chief court-singer to the Emperor Ak'bar. The principal native authority for the Kriṣṇa poets of the 16th century is the enigmatical *Bhakt Mālā* of Nābhā Dās, with its various commentaries.

While the successors of Ballabhāchār'j were filling Braj with their music, the not distant Mughal Court at Dillī had collected a group of state poets, some of whom were of no mean reputation. Ṭōḍar Mall, who besides being a great finance minister was the immediate cause of the acceptance of the Ūrdū language, Bīr'bal, Ak'bar's friend and author of many witty impromptus, 'Abdu'r Raḥīm Khān'khānā, and Mān Siŋgh of Amēr, were more famous as the patrons of authors than as vernacular writers themselves; but Nar'harī, Hari Nāth, Karan, and Gaŋg, are justly celebrated as poets of a high rank.

Tul'sī Dās (fl. 1600, d. 1624), the greatest poet of the deeds of Rām, occupies a position amongst these authors peculiar to himself. Far different from the founders of the Braj school, who were surrounded by numerous imitators and successors, he lived in Banāras, unapproachable and alone in his niche in the Temple of Fame. Disciples he had in plenty,—to-day they are numbered by millions,—but imitators, none. Looking back along the vista of centuries we see his noble figure standing in its own pure light as the guide and saviour of Hindūstān. His influence has never ceased—nay, it has increased and is still increasing; and when we reflect on the fate of Tantra-ridden Bengal or on the wanton orgies which are carried out under the name of Kriṣṇa worship, we can justly appreciate the work of the man who first in India since Buddha's time taught man's duty to his neighbour and succeeded in getting his teaching accepted. His great work is at the present day the one Bible of a hundred millions of people; and fortunate has it been for them that they had this guide. It has been received as the perfect example of the perfect book, and thus its influence has not only been exercised over the unlettered multitude, but over the long series of authors who followed him, and especially over the crowd who sprung into existence with the introduction of printing at the beginning of the present century. As Mr. Growse well says in the introduction to his translation of the *Rāmāyan* of this author, "the book is in every one's hands, from the court to the cottage, and is read or heard and appreciated alike by every class of the Hindū community, whether high or low, rich or poor, young or old." For further particulars concerning him the reader is referred to the body of this work.

This Augustan age was not only a period of the erotic poetry of Sūr Dās and of the nature-poetry of Tul'sī, but was also signalized by the first attempts to systematize the art of poetry itself. The young growth had shown a tendency to shoot forth too luxuriantly, and even Malik Muḥammad wrote verses which were quaintly unmusical. Sūr Dās and Tul'sī Dās possessed the strength of giants, and were far beyond their contemporaries in polish and in a sense of proportion; but the works of the other early writers of this period jarred upon the senses of scholars brought up in the strictly classical schools of Sanskṛit philology. So, after one or two earlier attempts by minor authors, such as the poet Khēm (No. 87), Kēsab Dās (fl. 1580) stepped forward and settled for ever the canons of poetic criticism. A romantic story connects him with the poetess Par'bīn Rāī, and it is said that it was for her sake that he composed his great work the *Kabi-priyā*. Seventy years later, in the middle of the seventeenth century, Chintāmanī Tripāṭhī and his brothers amplified and developed the rules laid down by him. This group of critical poets is fitly closed at the end of the 17th century by Kālidās Tribēdī, the author of the *Hajārā*, the first great anthology of extracts from the works of the Augustan age of Hindūstān.

The latter half of this period, that is to say the 17th century, saw the rise of some remarkable religious sects, which gave birth to a considerable body of literature. The principal reformers who may be mentioned were Dādū (fl. 1600), founder of the Dādū Panthī sect; Prān Nāth (fl. 1650), the founder of the Pran'nāthīs; and Gōbind Siŋgh (fl. 1698), the founder of the militant Sīkh religion and compiler of the *Granth*, or holy book of that sect.

The Rāj'pūt bards of this Augustan period have been already referred to, and, passing by the lubric but popular Naẕīr, the only other great poet of the time who need be mentioned is the graceful Bihārī Lāl Chaūbē (fl. 1650), nick-named "the mine of commentators." Never was a description more accurate. He was the author of seven hundred verses, for each of which he received a gold *ashrafi* as a reward from his patron Jāī Siŋgh. Each verse is a perfectly polished jewel, designedly made as artificial as possible and capable of a double meaning. The greatest authors have not disdained to write commentaries elucidating the marvellous difficulties of this *tour de force*.

With this graceful writer our survey of the Augustan age of Hindūstānī vernacular literature is concluded. From the early years of the 18th century commences a comparatively barren period. It was the period of the decline and fall of the Mughal empire and of the supremacy and fall of the Marāṭhā power. Rāj'putānā itself was torn by intrigues, prince struggling with prince to rob his neighbour in the general loss of authority coincident with the cessation of Mughal supremacy. Bards there were few, and, as these could only sing of bloodshed and treachery, they preferred to remain silent. In other branches of literature there was a similar decay. No original authors of the first rank appeared, and the only great names we meet are those of commentators on the works of the preceding two centuries, and of men who further developed the critical laws founded by Kēsab Dās. Of the last, the best known were Uday Nāth Tribēdī and Jas'want Siŋgh, the authors of the *Ras-chandrōday* and of the *Bhākhā Bhūkhan* respectively. Similarly there appeared a number of anthologies, such as the *Sat-kabi-girā Bilās* of Bal Dēb, the *Kābya Nir'nay* of Bhikhārī Dās, and others. The end of the century is redeemed from barrenness by the *Prēm Ratna*, the work of one of the few poetesses of India—Bībī Ratan Kũar.

The first half of the 19th century, commencing with the downfall of the Marāthā power and ending with the Mutiny, forms another well-marked epoch. It was the period of renascence after the literary dearth of the previous century. The printing-press now for the first time found its practical introduction into Northern India, and, led by the spirit of Tul'sī Dās, literature of a healthy kind rapidly spread over the land. It was the period of the birth of the Hindī language, invented by the English, and first used as a vehicle of literary prose composition in 1803, under Gilchrist's tuition, by Lallū Jī Lāl, the author of the *Prēm Sāgar*. It was also a period of transition from the old to the new. The printing-press had not yet penetrated to Central India, and there the old state of affairs continued. Poets, of whom Padmākar Bhaṭṭ was the most famous, not unworthily wore the mantle which had descended from Kēsab Dās and Chintāmani Tripāṭhī, while Bikram Sāhi wrote an ingenious *Sat Saī* in imitation of the more famous one of Bihārī Lāl.

In Banāras, on the contrary, the art of printing gave a new audience to the learned; and to supply the demand thus created, several works of the first importance appeared. The chief of these was the translation of the *Mahābhārata* into Hindī by Gōkul Nāth. Critical writers of a new school also came to the front, of whom the best, *longo intervallo*, was Harishchandr', the author of the *Sundarī Tilak* and many other excellent works; while in Rājā Śiva Prasād the cause of education received an enlightened friend, and a pioneer in that most difficult work, the writing of good school-books. Lallū Jī Lāl, the author of the *Prēm Sāgar*, has already been mentioned;

and another product of Calcutta civilisation, of a very different kind, was the huge anthology of Krish'nānand Byās Dēb, called the *Rāg-Sāgarōdbhab Rāg-Kalpadrum,* written in emulation of the better known Sanskrit lexicon, the *Çabda-Kalpadruma.*

The same period saw the rise of the Hindī drama,[1] which is now firmly established, and gives a hope of achieving considerable excellence in the near future.

The post-Mutiny days this sketch will not touch upon. A brief imperfect account will be found in the body of this work. It may further be noted that more extended reviews of the literature of the principal periods will also be found in the introductions to chapters VII to XI. All that has been attempted in the present note has been to show the most salient points of a not inglorious past in the vernacular literary history of Hindūstān.

(*d.*) *Description of the Plates.*

The frontispiece represents Rāma's childhood in Kāūsalyā's house. I am indebted for it to the kindness of Rājā Śiva Prasād, C.S.I., who procured the original photograph of one of the illustrations in the magnificently-illuminated M.S. belonging to the Mahārāj of Banāras.

To the kindness of the same gentleman I am indebted for the other plates, which are photographs of ten pages of the *Rāj'pur Rāmāyan,* described on page 45, believed to be in the poet's handwriting, of three pages of the old Banāras M.S. referred to on the same page, and of a deed of arbitration said to be in the poet's own handwriting. A transliteration and translation of the first two will be found on page 51 of this work, and of the last in the Addenda.

The frontispiece has already appeared, I believe, in one edition of Mr. Growse's excellent translation of the *Rāmāyan;* but as this work appeals to quite a different class of readers, and as the picture is itself a worthy specimen of Hindū art, I do not hesitate to give it here again.

[1] See also section 706 in the body of the work.

ADDENDA ET CORRIGENDA.

NOTE.—In pointing out misprints, I have not taken the trouble to correct instances of unsystematic division of compound words. Such mistakes will in no case lead to difficulty, and they will be found corrected in the indices.

4. *Kumār Pāl* reigned 1088—1172 A.D. The famous *Hēmachandra* flourished at his court.

20. *Mīrā Bāī*. Note[1]. *Read* Tod, ii, 21.

23. *Charan Dās*.' *Read Gyān Swarōday*.

34. *Ballabhāchār'j*. *P*. 19, *l*. 6 *from bottom, read* Harishchandr'; *p*. 20, *l*. 9, *read Aṇubhāṣya*. *Add* 'This work is being published in the *Bibliotheca Indica*.'

37. *Sūr Dās*. *Read* सूर दास, *not* सूरदास.

51. *Nābhā Dās*. *P*. 28, *l*. 8, *read Hitōpadēça*.

54. *Byās Swāmi*. *Read Sukal*. *So also in* 56, *Hit Haribans*.

70. *Keh'rī*. *Read* Tod, ii, 76.

71. *Ās'karan Dās*. *Read* Tod, ii, 353.

72. *Chētan Chandr'*. The *Ashwa Binōd* is dated *Sambat* 1616 (1559 A.D.), which Sib Siŋgh gives as the date of the poet's birth.

73. *Prithwī Rāj*. *Read* Tod's *Rājāsthān*, i, 343.

76. *Uday Siŋgh*. *Read* and ii, 29.

92. *Read* घन स्याम सुकल *Ghan Syām Sukal*.

105. *Ṭōḍar Mall, see* addenda to No. 128, below.

106. *Bīr'bal*. *P*. 35, *l*. 11 *from bottom, read Bijāur*.

108. *Khān'khānā*. He patronised the poet *Gaŋg* (No. 119). The latter in one of his works praises him and his son *Turāb Khān*.

119. *Gaŋgā Par'sād*, or *Gaŋg*. A verse of the poet *Khūb Chand* (No. 809) states that on one occasion *Khān'khānā* (No. 108) made *Gaŋg* a present of 36 lākhs. Khān'khānā was certainly praised by Gaŋg in one of his works.

127. *Mukund Siŋgh*. *Read* Tod, ii, 506.

128. *Tul'sī Dās, p*. 43, *last line, read Rājāpur and Bāndā ; p*. 44, *l*. 7, *add a comma after Kuru Chhēttr' ; p*. 45, *l*. 15, *read Rājāpur ; so also elsewhere ; p*. 46, *l*. 11 *from bottom, read Kuṇḍaliyā*.

As promised in the Introduction, I here give a transliteration and translation of the deed of arbitration in the handwriting of Tul'sī Dās, dated Sam. 1669 (A.D. 1612). I take this opportunity of expressing my acknowledgments to my old friend and teacher Mīr Āulād 'Alī, Professor of Arabic, Persian, and Hindūstānī at Trinity College, Dublin, for much assistance rendered in transcribing and translating the Persian and Arabic portions of the deed.

TRANSLITERATION.

Çrī-Jānakī-vallabhō vijayatē.

Dviç çaraṁ nābhisaṁdhattē dvis sthāpayati nāçritān | Dvir dadāti na . . . 1
chārthibhyō Rāmō dvir nāiva bhāṣatē || 1 || Tulasī jānyō Daçarathahī dha- . . . 2
ramu na satya samāna || Rāmu tajō jehi lāgi binu Rāma pariharē prāna || 1 || . . . 3
Dharmō jayati nādharmas satyaṁ jayati nānṛitaṁ | Kshamā jayati na krōdhō . . . 4
Viṣṇur jayati nāsurāḥ || 1 || . . . 5

Allāhu Akbar.

Chū Anad Rām bin Tōdar bin Dēō Rāy wa Kanhāē bin Rām Bhadar bin Tōdar mazkūr . . . 6
dar ḥuzūr āmada qarār dādand ki dar mawāẓi'i matrūka ki tāfṣīli ā dar Hindwī mazkūr ast . . . 7
bilmunāṣafa batarāẓī i jānibāin qarār dādēm. Wa yak ṣad ō pinjāh (?) bīghā zamīn ziyāda (?) qismati munāṣafa khūd [1] . . . 8
dar māuẓa'i Bhadāinī Anand Rām mazkūr ba Kanhāē bin Rām Bhadar mazbūr tajwīz namūda . . . 9
barī ma'anī rāẓī gashta i'tirāf ṣaḥīḥ shar'ī namūdand banābari ā 10
muhr karda shud. . . . 11

(Seal) ? Sādullāh bin * * * . . . . .

Qismati Anad Rām.		Qismati Kanhāē.		
Qariyā	*Qariyā*	*Qariyā*	*Qariyā*	12
Bhadāinī, dō ḥiṣṣa,	Lahartārā, darōbast	Bhadāinī, sih ḥiṣṣa.	Shiūpūr. darōbast.	13
Qariyā	*Qariyā*	*Qariyā*		
Nāīpūra, ḥiṣṣa i Tōdar tamām.	Chhitūpūra, ḥiṣṣa i Tōdar tamām.	Nadēsar ḥiṣṣa i Tōdar tamām (?) Iṭṭala'a'alāh (illegible).		14

Srī Paramēswar.

Sambat 1669 samae, kuār sudi tērasī, bār subh dīnē likhatiṁ (*sic*) patra Anand . . . 15
Rām tathā Kanhaīā. Ans bībhāg purbak āgē kāī āgya dunahu janē māgā . . . 16
Jē āgya bhāī sē pramān mānā. Dunahu janē bīdīt taph'sīlu. Ans Ṭōḍar Malu . . . 17
kē mah jē bibhāg padu hōt rā (? hā) * * * . 18

---

[1] Or (?) az ḥiṣṣa qismati munāṣafa.

Ans Āannd Rām. Mãũjē Bhadãĩnī mah an-
-s pā̃ch, tehī mah ans dui Ānand Rāmu.
Tathā Lahar'tārā sagarē u. Tathā Chhītu-
-purā ans Ṭōḍar Malu ka. Tathā Nãĩpurā an
-s Ṭōḍar Malu ka. Hīl(ā) hujatī nāstī
Līkhītaṁ Anand Rām, jē upar līkhā, sē sahī.

Ans Kanhaï. Mãũjē Bhadãĩnī mah ans pā̃ch, tehī . . 19
mah tīnī ans Kanhaï. Tathā mãũjē Sīpurā . . . 20
Tathā Nades'rī ans Ṭōḍar Malu ka. Hīl(ā) . . 21
hujatī nāstī 22
23
Līkhītaṁ Kanhaï, jē upar līkhā sē sahī . . . 24

(Here follow the witnesses' signatures, ending—)

Shahada
bimāfīhi Jalāl Maqbūlī.
bikhaṭṭihi.

Shahada 25
bimāfīhi Ṭāhir ibni Khwāja 26
Dãũlatī Qānūngōī. . . 27

TRANSLATION.

(*Sanskrit.*) Victory to the lord of Çrī Jānakī.

Two arrows cannot be shot at one time. Twice one does not support refugees. Twice over benefits are not given to applicants. Rāma does not speak in two ways.

(*Old Bais'wārī.*) O Tul'sī, Das'rath knew no virtue equal to the truth. He gave up Rām for it, and without Rām he gave up his life.

(*Sanskrit.*) Virtue conquers and not vice ; truth and not falsehood. Mercy conquers and not anger. Viṣṇu conquers and not the Asuras.

(*Persian.*) God is great.

Whereas Anand Rām, son of Tōdar, son of Dēō Rāy, and Kanhāē, son of Rām Bhadar, son of Tōdar aforesaid, appeared before me and acknowledged that with their mutual consent the inheritance, viz. the villages as detailed in Hindwī, have been equally divided, and the said Anand Rām has given to the said Kanhāē, son of Rām Bhadar, 150 *bighās* of land in village Bhadãĩnī more than his own half share ; they are satisfied, and have made correct acknowledgment according to law. Their seals have been affixed hereto.

Share of Anand Rām.

Village Bhadãĩnī, 2 shares.
Village Lahar'tārā, whole.
Village Nãĩpūra, the whole of Tōdar's share.
Village Chhitūpūra, the lesser, the whole of Tōdar's share.

Share of Kanhāē.

Village Bhadãĩnī, 3 shares.
Village Shiūpūr, the whole.
Village Nadēsar, the whole of Tōdar's share.
(?) I am informed of this (?) (illegible).

(*Old Bais'wārī.*) To The Most High God.

In the Sambat year 1669, on the 13th of the bright half of Kuār, on the auspicious day of the week, was this deed written by Anand Rām and Kanhaīā. By way of partition of shares, we two formerly asked for a decision (*translation doubtful*), and the decision which has been passed, that we recognise as authoritative. Both parties admit the list. The division of the share of Ṭōḍar Mal, which has been made . . . .

The rest is unintelligible, and partly illegible.

Share of Anand Rām.—In village Bhadāīnī, out of five shares, two to Anand Rām. Also the whole of Lahar'tārā. Also Ṭōḍar Mal's share in Chhitūpūrā and in Nāīpūrā. There is no evasion or reservation. Signed Anand Rām. What is written above is correct.

Share of Kanhaī.—In village Bhadāīnī, out of five shares, three to Kanhaī. Also the village of Sīpūrā; also Ṭōḍar Mall's share in Nades'rī. There is no evasion or reservation. Signed Kanhaī. What is written above is correct.

Witnesses (to Anand Rām's signature): Rāghab Rām, son of Rām Dat; Rām Sēnī, son of Ūdhab; (U)dāī Karn, son of Jagat Rāy; Jamunī Bhān, son of Paramānand; Jānakī Rām, son of Srī Kānt; Kāwalā Rām, son of Bāsudēb; Chand Bhān, son of Kēsāū Dās; Pāṇḍē Harīballabh, son of Purusōtam; Bhāwarī, son of Kēsāūu (*sic*) Dās; Jadu Rām, son of Nar'harī; Ājodhyā, son of Lachhī; Sabal, son of Bhīkham; Rām Chand, son of Bāsudīw (*sic*); Pītāmbar Das'wadhī, son of Puran; Rām Rāī and Garīb Rāī (?), sons of Makuṭirī Karn (?). (*Arabic*) Witness to whatsoever is in this, Jalāl Maqbūlī, by his own hand.

Witnesses (to Kanhaī's signature): Rām Sīgh, son of Uddhab; Jādāū Rāē, son of Gahar Rāē; Jagadīs Rāē, son of Mahōdadhī; Chakrapānī, son of Sīwā; Mathurā, son of Pīthā; Kāsī Dās, son of Bāsudēwā (by the hand of Mathurā); Kharag Bhān, son of Gosāi Dās; Rām Dēw, son of Bisa(m)-bhar; Srī Kānt Pāṇḍē, son of Rāj'baktra (?); Bīṭhal Dās, son of Harihar; Hīrā, son of Das'rath; Lōhāg, son of Kīshnā; Man(ī) Rām, son of Sītal; Krishn Dat, son of Bhag'wan; Bin'rāban, son of Jāī; Dhanī Rām, son of Madhu Rāē. (*Arabic*) Witness to whatsoever is in this, Ṭāhir, son of Khwājah Dāūlatī, the Qānūngōī.

In connexion with the above it is interesting to speculate who this *Tōḍar Mall*, the father of Anand Rām and grandfather of Kanhaī, was. Can he have been Ak'bar's great Finance Minister (No. 105)? He died in 1589, and his son might well be alive in 1612. He was born at *Lāhar'pur*, in Audh, and one of the villages above mentioned, *Lahar'tārā*, has a somewhat similar name. In India contiguous villages have often very similar names.

128—133 Add., p. 57. Other versions of the Rāma legend.

(9) *Read Īswarī Par'sād Tripāṭhī* (712).

(10) *For 686 read* 702.

(11) *For 689 read* 695.

(12) *For 711 read* 725.

(13) *For 829a read* 858.

134. *Kēsab Dās.* The *Bigyān Gītā* was written in Sambat 1600 (1543 A.D.) and was dedicated to *Madhukar Shāh.* The *Rasik-priyā* is dated *Sambat* 1648 (1591 A.D.).

142. *Sundar Dās.* The *Sundar Sriŋgār* is dated *Sambat* 1688 (1631 A.D.).

145. *Bhūkhan Tripāṭhī.* From a short poem of *Mati Rām Tripāṭhī* (No. 146), the name of the Rājā of Kumāō appears to have been *Udōt Chand.*

146. *Mati Rām Tripāṭhī. Read* Tod, ii, 481 *and Fat'ḥ Sāhī.*

149. *Par'tāp Sāhī.* I know of two rājās called *Ratān* or *Rat'nēs* in *Bundēlkhaṇḍ.* One is praised by *Bhikhārī Dās* (No. 344) in the preface to the *Prēm Ratnākar,* which was written in 1685 A.D. This may possibly be the father of *Par'tap Sāhī.* The other succeeded *Bikram Sāhī* (No. 514) as Rājā of *Char'khārī* in 1829 A.D. He was born 1816 A.D. and died 1860. He is referred to in Nos. 519—522 and 524. Bikram Sāhī was born 1785 and died 1828 A.D.; and if Par'tāp Sāhī was the son of this Rat'nēs, he would probably be Bikram Sāhī's grandson, but could not have been his contemporary, for his father was only twelve years old at the latter's death. Yet, again, I hear from Char'khārī (though on what authority I cannot ascertain) that a Par'tāp Sāhī did live in Char'khārī in Bikram Sāhī's reign. Regarding the Bhākhā Bhūkhan, which is usually considered as written at the end of the eighteenth century, I find a Bombay edition of the work identifying *Jaswant Siŋgh,* its author, with *Jas'want Siŋgh* (1638—1681) of *Mār'wār.* This would tally with the date given in the body of the work; but on the whole I am inclined to reject Sib Siŋgh's statement that this poet attended Chhattr' Sāl's court, and would place him as flourishing about the year 1830 A.D., after No. 518. His relationship to the Rat'nēs of No. 519 must remain an open point. There was also a poet called *Ratan.* See No. 155.

152. *Sib Nāth. Read* Tod's *Rājāsthān,* ii, 481.

159. *Kalidās Tribēdī.* In his *Badhū-binōd,* which he dates *Sambat* 1749 (1692 A.D.), he mentions that *Jōgājīt Siŋgh's* father was *Britti Siŋgh.*

160. *Sukh Dēb Misar. Read Ar'jun Singh and Britt Bichār.*

164. *Sundar Dās. Read Sundar Saŋkhyā.*

171. *Najīr. Reaa Naẓīr, not Naẓīr, throughout.*

173. *Ṭhākur. Read* Gosāī.

177. *Read Īswar.*

195. *Ajīt Siŋgh. For* 91*n read* 89*n.*

196. *Bihārī Lāl Chaūbē. P.* 76, *l.* 4, *for* 364 *read* 355. *Also read Ẓū'lfaqār.*

199. *Rat'nēs. See* No. 149, Add. Cf. No. 155.

213. *Chandr'. Read Sul'ṭān.*

226. *Bihārī Dās. Read* बिहारी.

251. *Read Par'bīn.*

326. *Sūratī Misar.* The *Alaŋkār Mālā* is dated *Sambat* 1766 (1709 A.D.).

331. *Bhōj Misar. Read Sriŋgār.*

344. *Bhikhārī Dās. Read Chhandārnab.* The *Prēm Ratnākar* is dated *Sambat* 1742 (1685 A.D.) and the *Chhandārnab Sambat* 1799 (1742 A.D.). In the former work he praises a Rājā *Rat'nēs.* Cf. No. 519. *See* also No. 149, Add.

346. *Karan*. His *Sāhitya Chandrikā* is dated *Sambat* 1794 (1737 A.D.), which the Sib Siŋgh Sarōj gives as the date of his birth. With regard to Hir'dai Sāhi, see also No. 503.

349. *Gumān Jī Misar*. *Read* *Naiṣadha*. The *Kalā Nidhi* is dated *Sambat* 1805 (1848 A.D.). The work is rather a translation than a commentary.

351. *Prēm Nāth*. *Read* *Khīrī*.

355. *Hari Nāth*. The *Alaŋkār Dar'pan* is dated *Sambat* 1826 (1796 A.D.), which Sib Siŋgh gives as the date of the poet's birth.

357. *Sambhu Nāth*. The *Rām Bilās* is dated *Sambat* 1798 (1741 A.D.).

361. *Kēsab*. *Read* *Nārāyan*.

664. *Haṭhī*. The date of his birth (1830 A.D.) given by Sib Siŋgh is certainly wrong, for the *Rādhā Satak* is dated *Sambat* 1847 (1790 A.D.).

THE MODERN VERNACULAR LITERATURE

OF

HINDŪSTĀN.

CHAPTER I.

THE BARDIC PERIOD. [700—1300 A.D.]

1. पुष्य कवि, the poet *Puṣya,* of *Ujāin*. Fl. 713 A.D.

This is the earliest vernacular poet of whom I have found any mention in Native authors. The *Sib Siŋgh Sarōj* states that he flourished in the year 713, and that he is the "root of the vernacular" *bhākhā kī jaṛ*. It is not clear from this account whether his name was *Puṣya, Puṣpa,* or *Puṇḍa*. It states categorically that he wrote both in Sanskrit and in the vernacular, and that he is mentioned by Col. Tod in his *Rājāsthān*. If by vernacular we are to understand a stage of language later than that of the Prākṛits, this seems a most improbable statement; nor can I find that it is borne out by Tod. The only allusion apparently bearing on this point in the *Rājāsthān* is a reference (i, 229; Calcutta edition, i, 246) to a *Puṣya,* the author of an inscription (translated i, 799). I can find no mention in Tod regarding the language in which he wrote.

2. खुमान सिङ्घ, *Khumān Siŋgh alias Khumān Rāut Guh'lāut,* king of *Chitāur,* in *Mēwār*. Fl. 830 A.D.[1]

In his honour was written the *Khumān Rāy'sā*. This is the most ancient poetic chronicle of *Mēwār,* and was written in the ninth

[1] See Tod's *Rājāsthān,* i, 240; Calc. ed., i, 258.

century.[1] It gives a history of *Khumān Rāut* and of his family. It was recast during the reign of *Par'tāp Siŋgh* (fl. 1575), and, as we now have it, carries the narrative down to the wars of that prince with Ak'bar, devoting a great portion to the siege of *Chitāūr* by *Alāu'd-dīn Khiljī* in the thirteenth century.[2] We may therefore presume that the copies now extant are in a dialect of Mēwār not later than the end of the sixteenth century.

3. केदर कवि, the poet and bard *Kēdar*. Fl. *1150* A.D.

Mentioned in the *Sib Siŋgh Sarōj* as attending the court of *Alāu'd-dīn Ghōrī*. He therefore flourished about 1150 A.D., and if any of his works can be found, they will probably be the oldest specimens of vernacular literature obtainable. I have never seen any of his writings, and I fear they are lost, unless they have been preserved in the Tod manuscripts. He is possibly mentioned by Tod, but I have not been able to find his name.

4. कुमार पाल, king *Kumār Pāl*, of *An'hal*. Fl· 1150 A.D.

Towards the end of the same century an anonymous poet of *Rāj'putānā* wrote a bardic chronicle, entitled the *Kumār Pāl Charitra*,[3] detailing the line of descent of the Buddhist[4] Rājā *Kumār Pāl*, of *An'hal*, from *Brahmā* downwards. The manuscript exists in the Tod collection, being No. 31 in the Royal Asiatic Society's list.

We now come to the time of *Pithāūrā* or *Prithwī Rāj*, the *Chāūhān*, of *Dillī*, who was born 1159 A.D. and died 1193 A.D. He was not only a valiant hero,[5] but was a great patron of literature. If we may believe Sib Siŋgh, the works of two at least of the bards who attended his court have come down to us. These were Nos. 5 and 6.

5. अनन्य० दास, *Ananya Dās*, of *Chaked'wā*, district *Gōḍā*. B. *1148* A.D.

The only authority for this poet is the *Sib Siŋgh Sarōj*, which states that he was author of a work called *Ananya Jōg*, from which

[1] Tod, ii, 757; Calc. ed., ii, 814.

[2] Tod, i, 214; ii, 757; Calc. ed., i, 231; ii, 814.

[3] Tod, i, 81, 80n, 241n, 256; ii, 242n; Calc. ed., i, 86, 87n, 259n, 275; ii, 266.

[4] See Tod, i, 98; Calc. ed., i, 106.

[5] For a history of his life and times, see Tod, i, 95, 256; Calc. ed., 102, 275.

it gives an extract. I suspect that he was really a contemporary of another *Prithwī Rāj* (of *Bīkānēr*), who lived in the sixteenth century (Tod, i, 343 and ff.; ii, 186; Calc. ed., i, 363 and ff.; ii, 203). See No. 73.

6. **चन्द्र कवि**, the poet and bard *Chandr'* or *Chand Bar'dāī*. Fl. 1191 A.D.

Rāg., ? Sun. He belonged to the family of an ancient bard named *Bīsal Dēb*, the *Chāuhān* (cf. Tod, ii, 447 and ff.; Calc. ed., ii, 492 and ff.), of *Ran'thambhōr*, and, according to the account of his descendant, the poet *Sūr Dās*, belonged to the *Jagāt* clan.[1] He came to *Prithwī Rāj's* court and was appointed his minister and poet-laureate (*kavīçvara*). His poetical works were collected by *Amar Siŋgh* (cf. No. 191), of *Mēwār*,[2] in the early part of the seventeenth century. They were not improbably recast and modernised in parts at the same time, which has given rise to a theory[3] that the whole is a modern forgery. His principal work is the famous *Prithī Rāj Rāy'sā* (Rāg.), or life of his patron. According to Tod[4] it is a universal history of the period in which he wrote, and is in 69 books, comprising 100,000 stanzas, of which Tod has translated 30,000—certainly more than any other European has succeeded in doing. *Chand* and *Prīthwī Rāj* were both killed in battle fighting against the Muhammadans in the year 1193. As already mentioned, one of his descendants was the poet *Sūr Dās*, and another was the poet *Sāraŋg Dhar* (No. 8), who is said to have written the *Hammīr Rāy'sā* and the *Hammīr Kābya*.[5] A portion of the text of the *Prithī Rāj Rāy'sā* has been edited by Mr. Beames, and another portion edited and translated by Dr. Hoernle. The excessively difficult character of the task has prevented both scholars from making much progress. Pandit *Mōhan Lāl Viṣṇu Lāl Paṇḍiā* has just commenced editing a critical edition of the whole text, of which the first two fasciculi have been published (Medical Hall Press, Banāras, 1887). The *Mahōbā*

---

[1] See the account of Sūr Dās's genealogy given in No. 37.

[2] Reigned 1597—1621. See Tod, i, xiii (Introd.); 350 and ff.; Calc. ed., i, xii; 371 and ff.

[3] See J. A. S. B., 1886, p. 5, "On the antiquity, authenticity, and genuineness of *Chand Bar'dāī's* epic the *Prithirāj Rāsāū*," by Kavirāj *Syāmal Dās*, in which our poet is attacked, and "The Defence of *Prithirāj Rāsā* of *Chanda Bar'dāī*" by Pandit *Mōhan Lāl Viṣṇu Lāl Paṇḍiā* (Banāras, Medical Hall Press, 1887), which is a reply to the former paper.

[4] Tod, i, 254; Calc. ed., i, 273.

[5] Tod, ii, 452n; Calc. ed., ii, 497n.

Khaṇḍ of the poem, which, however, is probably spurious, or at least not by *Chand*, has been more than once translated into Hindī.[1] It deals with the famous heroes *Ālhā* and *Ūdan* (or *Ālhā* and *Rūdal*, according to the tradition of Eastern Hindūstān), and the translation with which I am best acquainted (without, however, being in a position to vouch for its accuracy) is that by *Ṭhākur Dās*, of *Fatihgaṛh*, under the name of the *Ālkhaṇḍ*. This is not the same as the *Ālhā Khaṇḍ* which will be found described under the head of the poet *Jag'nik* (No. 7), though it deals with the same heroes. According to Garcin de Tassy (Histoire, etc., i, 138), a Russian *savant*, Robert Lenz by name, translated a portion of Chand's poem, which he intended to have published in 1836 on his return to St. Petersburg, but the premature death of this scholar deprived orientalists of this interesting work. Col. Tod printed a translation of an episode under the title of 'The Vow of *Sanjogta*'[2] in the 25th volume of the Asiatic Journal, pp. 101—112, 197—211, 273—286.

My own studies of this poet's work have inspired me with a great admiration for its poetic beauty, but I doubt if any one not perfectly master of the various Rāj'putānā dialects could ever read it with pleasure. It is, however, of the greatest value to the student of philology, for it is at present the only stepping stone available to European explorers in the chasm between the latest Prākṛit and the earliest Gauḍian authors. Though we may not possess the actual text of Chand, we have certainly in his writings some of the oldest known specimens of Gauḍian literature, abounding in pure Apabhraṁça Çaurasēnī Prākṛit forms.

According to Garcin de Tassy (l.c.), we owe to this poet another work, entitled *Jāī Chandra Prakās*, or history of *Jāī Chand*, which is written in the same dialect as the Rāy'sā, and is quoted by Ward.

7. जग॰निक, the bard *Jag'nik* or *Jag'nāyak*, of *Mahōbā*, in *Bundēl'khaṇḍ*. Fl. 1191 A.D.

Contemporary with *Chand* was the bard *Jag'nik*. I am not certain that I have ever seen any of this poet's works. He attended the court of *Par'māl* (*Paramardī*), of *Mahōbā*, in Bundēl'khaṇḍ, and chronicled the wars of that prince with *Prithwī Rāj*. There is a not impossible

[1] For an English translation of an episode in the Mahōbā Khaṇḍ, see Tod, 614 and ff.; Calc. ed., i, 648 and ff.

[2] Cf. Tod, i, 623 and ff.; Calc. ed., i, 657 and ff.

tradition that the *Ālhā Khaṇḍ,* of which we possess many versions, and which has sometimes been described as a spurious canto of *Chand's* epic, was originally written by this poet. The *Ālhā Khaṇḍ* is, so far as I am aware, only current in oral versions sung all over Hindūstān by professional singers. As might be expected, these versions differ considerably in language, and each is modernised to suit the dialect of the reciter. For a full account of the *Ālhā Khaṇḍ,* see *Indian Antiquary*, vol. xiv, pp. 209, 255. For an account of Ālhā's share in the war between Prithwī Rāj and Par'māl, see *Report of the Arch. Sur. Ind.*, vii, pp. 13—20.

The *Mahōbā Khaṇḍ* has already been mentioned under the head of *Chand* (No. 6). It and other Western recensions of the poem give the names of the heroes as *Ālhā* and *Ūdal* or *Ūdan,* the latter being short for *Uday Siŋgh;* but the Eastern recensions give the names as *Ālhā* and *Rūdal.* Two versions of the Western recension have been printed—one edited by Chaūdh'rī *Ghāsī Rām,* of *Bhaṭipurā,* and the other, under the supervision of Sir C. (then Mr.) Elliott, by *Ṭhākur Dās,* of *Fatihgaṛh,* already mentioned. The latter edition was, I believe, taken down[1] by him as recited by three illiterate professional bards of *Kanaūj,* being respectively by caste a Jōsī, a Tēlī, and a Brāhman, and pieced together with additions of his own and some extracts or adaptations from different manuscripts that he borrowed. It is thus rather a heterogeneous composition. Portions of this recension have been translated into English ballad metre by Mr. Waterfield in vols. lxi, lxii, and lxiii of the *Calcutta Review* under the title of "The Nine-Lākh Chain, or the *Mārō* feud." The Eastern recension only exists in the mouths of itinerant singers, and is nearly always couched in the Bhoj'pūrī dialect of Bihārī. According to the tradition of Eastern Hindūstān, the poem was originally written by *Jag'nik* in the Bundēl'khaṇḍī dialect. Mr. Vincent Smith has presented me with a number of short poems in that dialect, many of which appear to be fragments of a larger work. In them the second hero is called *Ūdal.*

8. सारङ्ग धर कवि, the poet and bard *Sāraŋg Dhar,* of *Ran'thambhōr.* Fl. 1363 A.D.

We have now a gap of a century and a half, and in the year 1363 find flourishing the *Sāraŋg Dhar* already mentioned as a descendant of *Chand.* According to Tod, he attended the court of the heroic Rājā

[1] I am indebted to Mr. Growse for this information.

Hammīr Dēb (Fl. 1300 A.D.), the *Chāuhān,* of *Ran'thambhōr,* who belonged to the family of *Bīsal Dēb,* the ancestor of *Chand. Hammīr's* dogged valour and heroic death at the hands of *Alāu'd-din Khiljī* have given rise to innumerable proverbs, and have been celebrated in poetical works in many languages of India. None, however, is so popular as *Sāraŋg Dhar's* two works known as the *Hammīr Rāy'sā* and the *Hammīr Kābya.*[1] M. Barth has suggested to me that this poet is the same as the *Çārŋgadhara,* author of the Sanskṛit anthology entitled the *Çārŋgadhara Paddhati,* described by Mr. FitzEdward Hall in the preface to his edition of the Vāsavadattā, and by Prof. Aufrecht in ZDMG., xxvii, 2. A reference to Paṇḍit *Mōhan Lāl Viṣṇu Lāl Paṇḍiā* has confirmed the accuracy of this suggestion, and I am indebted to this gentleman for quotations showing that it was not *Sāraŋg Dhar* or *Çārŋgadhara,* but his grandfather *Raghu Nāth,* who was spiritual guide to *Hammīr.* The *Çārŋgadhara Paddhati* was written in 1363 A.D.

I have only seen detached extracts from this poet's works, and hence am unable to say whether the other two poems were certainly by him or not. What gives rise to doubt is the existence [in the J. A. S. B., vol. xlviii (1879), p. 186] of a translation of a *Hammīr Rāsā,* or "History of Hammīr, Prince of Ran'thambhōr," by Bābū *Brajanātha Bandhōpādhyāya,* of *Jāipur.* According to the Introduction of this work, the original was written by one *Jōdh*[2] *Rāj,* of *Nim'rānā,* in Al'wār. He attended the court of a *Chāuhān* prince named *Chandr' Bhān,* a descendant of *Prithwī Rāj,* and was by birth a Gāuṛ Brāhman, born at *Bijāwar.* There is a copy of the *Çārŋgadhara* (or *Sāraŋg Dhar*) *Paddhati* in the Tod collection of manuscripts (No. 32) in the Library of the Royal Asiatic Society. I have only had an opportunity of a very cursory examination of the work, which is 299 fol. long. Prof. Peterson has published an edition of it in Bombay. No. 42 in the same collection is entitled the *Hammīra Charitra,* but I am unable to say if it is the same as any of the works above mentioned.

9. **जोध राज,** the poet *Jōdh Rāj,* of *Nim'rānā* in *Al'wār.* Fl. 1363 (?) A.D. See No. 8 above.

---

[1] Tod, ii, 452n, 472n; Calc. ed., ii, 497n, 517n.

[2] There was a *Jōdh* Kabi (No. 118) who attended the court of the Emperor *Ak'bar,* who may be the same as this author.

CHAPTER II.

THE RELIGIOUS REVIVAL OF THE FIFTEENTH CENTURY.

10. रामानन्द स्वामी, the master *Rāmānand.* Fl. c. 1400 A.D.

Rāg. We now leave the era of the bards, and, emerging from the mists of antiquity, come upon a great revival of literature coincident with the rise of the Vaishnava religion, at the commencement of the fifteenth century. The first name we meet is that of *Rāmānand* (fl. cir. 1400 A.D.). He was much more of a religious reformer (see Wilson, *Religious Sects of the Hindūs*, i, 47) than an author, but I have collected hymns written, or purporting to have been written, by him, which had travelled in the people's mouths as far east as *Mithilā.*

11. भवानन्द, *Bhawānand.* Fl. c. 1400 A.D.

One of *Rāmānand's* immediate disciples (Wilson, *Religious Sects of the Hindūs*, i, 56). He is the reputed author of an explanation in Hindī of the Vēdānta system of philosophy in fourteen chapters, entitled *Amrit Dhār.* See *Mack. Cat.* ii, 108, quoted by Garcin de Tassy, i, 140.

12. सेन कवि, the poet *Sēn*, of *Bāndhō.* Fl. c 1400 A.D.

Haj. One of *Rāmānand's* immediate disciples, a barber by caste. Poems by him are also in the Sīkh *Granth.* He and his descendants were for some time the family gurus of the Rājās of *Bāndhō (Rīwā̃).* See Wilson, *Religious Sects of the Hindūs*, i, 118, for a legend concerning him.

13. कबीर दास, *Kabīr Dās*, the *Jolāhā* (weaver) of *Banāras.* Fl. c. 1400 A.D.

Haj., Rāg. He was the most famous of *Rāmānand's* disciples. His principal works are included in the well-known *Sabdābalī, Ramāīnīs, Sākhīs*, and the *Sukh Nidhān*, which are everywhere known and quoted at the present day. According to tradition, he was the son of a virgin Brāhman widow. He was exposed by her, and was found on a lotus in *Lahar Talāo*, a pond near *Banāras,* by the wife of a Jolāhā or Musalmān weaver named *Nīmā,* who with her husband *Nūrī* was there in attendance on a wedding procession. He is said to have lived 300 years, or from 1149 to 1449 A.D., and in fact he flourished about the beginning of the fifteenth century.[1]

A complete list of a voluminous mass of writings attributed to Kabīr, as preserved in the collection called the *Khās Granth,* will be found in Wilson, *Religious Sects of the Hindūs*, i, 76, and is here reproduced for ready reference. Cf. also Garcin de Tassy (Histoire, etc. i, 274).

(1) *Sukh Nidhān.*

(2) *Gōrakh Nāth kī Gōshṭhī.*

(3) *Kabīr Pāñjī.*

(4) *Balakh kī Ramāinī.*

(5) *Rāmānand kī Gōshṭhī.*

(6) *Ānand Rām Sāgar.*

(7) *Sabdābalī,* containing 1,000 *sabdas,* or short doctrinal expositions.

(8) *Maṅgal,* 100 short poems, amongst which is the account of *Kabīr's* discovery given as above.

(9) *Basant,* 100 hymns in that *Rāg.*

(10) *Hōlī,* 200 of the songs called *Hōlī.*

(11) *Rēkh'tās,* 100 odes.

(12) *Jhūl'nās,* 500 odes in a different style.

(13) *Khas'rā,* 500 odes in a different style.

(14) *Hiṇḍōls,* 12 ditto. The subject of all these odes or hymns is always moral or religious.

(15) *Bārah Māsā,* the 12 months from a religious point of view, agreeably to Kabīr's system.

(16) *Chañchars,* 22.

(17) *Chaũtīsās,* 2; the 34 letters of the Nāgarī alphabet, with their religious signification.

(18) *Alifnāmah,* the Persian alphabet in the same manner.

(19) *Ramāinīs,* short doctrinal or argumentative poems.

(20) *Sākhīs,* 5,000. These may be considered as texts, consisting of one stanza each.

(21) The *Bījak* (Rāg) (the greater and the lesser), in 654 sections.

There is also a variety of stanzas, called *Āgams, Bānīs,* etc., composing a very formidable course of study to those who wish to go deep into the doctrine of this school.

---

[1] For further particulars see Wilson, *Religious Sects of the Hindūs*, i, 73.

14. भगो दास, *Bhagō Dās.* Fl. 1420 A.D.

One of *Kabīr's* immediate disciples, and author or compiler of the shorter *Bījak*. See Wilson, *Religious Sects of the Hindūs*, i, 79; Garcin de Tassy, i, 118.

15. स्रुत गोपाल, *Srut Gōpāl.* Fl. 1420 A.D.

Another of *Kabīr's* immediate disciples, and author of the *Sukh Nidhān*. See Wilson as above, page 90.

16. कमाल कवि, the poet *Kamāl*, of *Banāras*. Fl. 1450 A.D.

Haj., Rāg. He was *Kabīr's* son. He spent his time making couplets in refutation of his father's sayings. Hence the proverb बूड़ा बन्स कबीर के कि उपजा पूत कमाल,—An unlucky family was Kabīr's, in which the son Kamāl was born. See Fallon's *Hd. Dy.* s.v. *Upaj'nā*, page 13.

17. बिद्यापति ठाकुर, *Bidyāpati Ṭhākur*, of *Bisapī*, in *Dar'bhaṇgā* district. Fl. 1400 A.D.

Rāg. Retracing our steps, and leaving for a time the Central Hindūstān, made famous by *Rāmānand* and *Kabīr*, we find flourishing in the year 1400 one of the most famous of the Vaishnava poets of Eastern India. *Bidyāpati Ṭhākur* was founder of the school of master-singers, which in after years spread over the whole of Baṇgal, and his name is to the present day a household word from the *Kar'm'nāsā* to *Calcutta*. He has been translated into and imitated in most of the dialects falling between these limits. Little is known of his life. He was the son of *Gan'pati Ṭhākur*, who was the son of *Jāi Datt' Ṭhākur*. The founder of the family was *Viṣṇu Çarman*, who lived seven generations before *Bidyāpati* in the village of *Bisapī*, the modern *Bis'phī*. This village was given to the poet as a rentfree gift by king *Sib Siṇgh* (then heir apparent) of *Sugāonā* in the year 1400 A.D. The deed of endowment is still extant. *Bidyāpati* was author of many Sanskrit works, the principal of which are the well-known *Puruṣa Parīkṣa*, the *Durgābhakti Taraṇgiṇī*, the *Dānavākyāvali*, the *Vivāda Sāra*, and the *Gayā Pattana*; but his chief glory consists in his matchless sonnets (*pada*) in the Maithilī dialect dealing allegorically with the relations of the soul to God under the form of the love which Rādhā bore to Krish'n. These were adopted and recited enthusiastically by the celebrated Hindū reformer *Chaitanya,* who flourished at the beginning of the sixteenth century (b. 1484 A.D.), and, through him, became the house-poetry of the Lower Provinces. Numbers of imitators sprung up, many of whom wrote in Bidyāpati's name, so that it is now difficult to separate the genuine from the imitations, especially as the former have been altered in the course of ages to suit the Baŋgālī idiom and metre. *Bidyāpati* was a contemporary of the Baŋgālī poet *Chaṇḍī Dās,* and of *Umāpati* and *Jāī Dēb,* and was, we know, on terms of intimate friendship with the first. He was, we have seen, a famous poet in A.D. 1400, and a copy of the *Bhāgavata Purāṇa* in his handwriting, dated L.S. 349 (A.D. 1456), still exists, so that he lived to a good old age. These are the only two certain dates we have in his life. The following dates depend upon the dates mentioned in *Ajodhyā Par'sād's Gulzār-Bihār* as those of the accessions of the various kings. *Ajodhyā Par'sād's* dates are as follows:—King *Dēva Siṁha* (*Dēb Siŋgh*) came to the throne A.D. 1385; *Çiva Siṁha* (*Sib Siŋgh*) 1446; two queens reigned 1449—1470; *Nara Siṁha Dēva* (*Nar Siŋgh Dēb*) 1470; *Dhīra Siṁha* (*Dhīr Siŋgh*) 1471.

Now the *Puruṣa Parīkṣa* was according to its colophon written during the lifetime of *Dēb Siŋgh, i.e.* before 1446, and the *Durgābhakti Taraŋgiṇī* was written during the reign of *Nar Siŋgh Dēb, i.e.* in the year 1470. We therefore can arrange the dates which we have of *Bidyāpati Ṭhākur's* life as follows, giving those which depend upon *Ajodhyā Par'sād* in italics:—

	A.D.
Granted the village of *Bisapī*, and therefore already a learned man	1400
Wrote *Puruṣa Parīkṣa* before	*1446*
Wrote the numerous songs dedicated to *Sib Siŋgh* before	*1449*
Copied the *Bhāgavata Purāṇa*	1456
Wrote *Durgābhakti Taraŋgiṇī*	*1470*

Assuming the above dates to be correct, he must have been at least ninety years old when he completed his last work. Rājā *Sib Siŋgh,* Bidyāpati's great patron, was also named *Rūp Nārāyan,* which seems to have been a general title of many members of the family. He had several wives, of whom the poet has immortalised *Lakhimā Ṭhakurāīn,*

Prān'batī, and *Mōd'batī*. There is a tradition that the emperor *Ak'bar*[1] summoned *Sib Siŋgh* to *Dillī* for some offence, and that Bidyāpati obtained his patron's release by an exhibition of clairvoyance. The emperor locked him up in a wooden box and sent a number of courtezans of the town to bathe in the river. When all was over he released him and asked him to describe what had occurred, when Bidyāpati immediately recited impromptu one of the most charming of his sonnets which has come down to us, describing a beautiful girl at her bath. Astonished at his power, the emperor granted his petition to release king Sib Siŋgh. Another legend is that the poet, feeling his end approaching, determined to die on the banks of the holy Ganges. On the way he remembered that the stream was the child of the faithful, and summoned it to himself. The obedient flood immediately divided itself into three streams, and spread its waves up to the very spot where Bidyāpati was sitting. Joyfully gazing on its sacred waters, he laid himself down and died. A Çiva *liŋga* sprang up where his funeral pyre had been, and it and the marks of the river are shown there to the present day. It is close to the town of *Bāzit'pur,* in the *Darbhangā* district. Such is the fitting legend of the passing away of the great old master-singer.

Bidyāpati's influence on the history of the literature of Eastern Hindūstān has been immense. He was a perfect master of the art of writing those religious love-sonnets which have since become in a much degraded form the substance of the Vaishnava bibles. Subsequent authors have never done anything but, *longo intervallo,* imitate him. But while the founder of the school never dealt with any subject without adorning it with some truly poetical conceit, his imitators have too often turned his quaintness into obscurity, and his passionate love-songs into the literature of the brothel.

18. उमापति, *Umāpati*. Fl. 1400 A.D. He was one of the great poets of Mithilā, and according to tradition he attended the court of king *Sib Siŋgh* and was a contemporary of *Bidyāpati*. See J. A. S. B., vol. liii, page 77. Cf. ZDMG, vol. xl, page 143, where Professor Aufrecht fixes the date of an Umāpati, whom Maithil tradition claims as being the same as the one mentioned, as in the first half of the eleventh century.

---

[1] It is hardly necessary to point out that the real hero of this story (if it is to be believed) cannot have been *Ak'bar,* who lived in the latter half of the sixteenth century.

19. जैदेब, *Jāideb.* Fl. 1400 A.D.

A Maithil poet, said to be distinct from *Jayadēva,* author of the *Gīta Gōvinda.* He attended the court of *Sib Siŋgh,* of *Sugāonā,* and was a contemporary of *Bidyāpati.* See J. A. S. B., vol. liii, page 88.

20. मीरा बाई, *Mīrā Bāī,* the Mār'wārī. Fl. 1420 A.D.

Rāg. Leaving *Bidyāpati* and his successors, we may now turn to the extreme west of Hindūstān, where, in Mēwār, *Mīrā Bāī,* the one great poetess of Northern India, was pouring forth her passionate hymns to *Krish'n Ran'chhōṛ.* This remarkable woman, who flourished in the year 1420 A.D., was the daughter of Rājā *Ratiyā Rānā,*[1] the *Raṭhāūr,* of *Mer'tā,* and was married in Sambat 1470 (A.D. 1413) to Rājā *Kumbh'karan* (No. 21), son of *Mōkal Dēb,* of *Chitāūr.*[2] Her husband was killed in Sambat 1534 (A.D. 1469) by his son *Ūdā Rānā.* Her great work is the *Rāg Gōbind,* and she also wrote a much-admired commentary on the *Gītā Gōvinda* of *Jayadēva.* She was devoted to that form of the god Krish'n known as *Ran'chhōṛ,* and the tradition is that she worshipped his image with such fervour that it came to life, and the god, descending from his shrine, embraced her, crying 'Welcome Mīrā." On hearing these words, overcome with rapture, she died in his arms. According to Wilson[3] she was much persecuted by her husband's family on account of her religious principles. She became the patroness of vagrant Vāishnavas, and visited in pilgrimage *Brindābān* and *Dwārikā.* Previous to leaving the latter place she visited the temple of her tutelary deity to take leave of him, when on the completion of her adoration the image opened, and Mīrā leaping into the fissure it closed and she finally disappeared. Some idea of the popularity of her writings may be gained from the fact that I have collected from the mouths of the people of Mithilā songs purporting to be by her.[4]

21. कुम्भकरन, *Kumbh'karan,* king of *Chitāūr* (*Mēwār*), husband of *Mīrā Bāī.* Fl. 1419 A.D.

---

[1] According to Tod, ii, 23 (Calc. ed. ii, 24) her father's name was Dūdoh (?).

[2] According to Wilson, *Udāipur.*

[3] *Religious Sects of the Hindūs,* p. 137.

[4] Cf. Tod, i, 289; ii, 760; Calc. ed. i, 309; ii, 818.

? Rāg. He came to the throne about 1400 A.D., and was killed by his son *Ūdā* in the year 1469 A.D. According to Tod (i, 289; Calc. ed. i, 308,) he was a skilled poet, and wrote a commentary to the *Gītā Gōvinda*. He is said to have been originally instructed in poetry by his wife, the famous *Mīrā Bāī* (No. 20).

22. **नानक,** *Nānak* the Bēdīkhatrī, of *Til'waṛī* (see Wilson, *Essays*, ii, 123) in the Panjāb. B. 1469 A.D.; d. 1539 A.D.

Rāg. The celebrated founder of the *Nānak-panthī* sect, and part author of the *Granth* (Rāg.) (see No. 169). The Granth (see Wilson, l. c.) is said by Sib Siŋgh to contain poems by (1) *Nānak,* (2) *Aŋgad,* (3) *Amar Dās,* (4) *Rām Dās,* (5) *Hari Rām Dās,* (6) *Tēg Bahādur,* (7) *Gōbind Siŋgh,* (8) *Kabīr Dās,* (9) *Trilōchan Dās,* (10) *Dhanā Bhagat,* (11) *Rāy Dās,* (12) *Sēn,* (13) *Shēkh Farīd,* (14) *Mīrā Bāī,* (15) *Nām Dēb* (Rāg.), (16) *Balibhadr'.* (Cf. Wilson, *Religious Sects of the Hindūs*, i, 274, for a different list.)

The first seven of these names are the names of seven of the ten *gurus* or apostles of the religion. The other three apostles were, (8) *Hari Gōbind,* (9) *Hari Rāy,* (10) *Hari Kishun.* Some idea of Nānak's popularity may be gathered from the fact that I have collected unwritten songs purporting to be by him in the heart of Mithilā. (See also Garcin de Tassy, i, 385.)

ADDENDA TO CHAPTER II.

23. **चरन दास,** *Charan Dās,* the Brāhman of *Paṇḍit'pur,* district *Faiz-ābād.* B. *1480* A.D.

Rāg. The author of a work entitled the *Gyān'swarōday.*

24. **अजबेस प्राचीन,** *Ajabēs,* the old poet of that name. B. *1513* A.D.

Sun. He attended the court of king *Bīr Bhān Siŋgh* (1540—1554), of *Bāndhō* (*Rīwā*),[1] and seems to have resided as a professional bard in that country. Cf. No. 530.

[1] The *Sib Siŋgh Sarōj* gives Jōgh'pur, which is apparently a misprint for Jōdh'pur; but I can find no reference to a prince of Jōdh'pur named Bīr Bhān. Ajabēs in one of his poems states that this prince protected Ak'bar when a child. Bīr Bhān was, therefore, the prince of that name in *Bāndhō* (*Rīwā*), with whom *Humāyūn* took refuge. See art. Rewah in *Imperial Gazetteer of India*, where the dates are given incorrectly, and *Rep. Arch. Sur. Ind.* xvii, 101, and xxi, 109. Cf. Nos. 113 and 530.

25. **गदा धर मिसर,** *Gadā Dhar Misar*, of *Braj*. B. *1523* A.D.

Rāg.

26. **माधब दास,** *Mādhab Dās*, the Brāhman. B. 1523.

Rāg. He was father of *Bhag'wat Ramit* (No. 61). He is probably the same as a *Mādhō Dās*, the author of a song in praise of the Ammonite, which I collected in Mithilā.

27. **गोपा कबि,** the poet *Gōpā*. B. *1533* A.D. He wrote the *Rām Bhūkhan* and the *Alaṅkār Chandrikā*.

28. **नरमिया कबि,** the poet *Naramiyā alias Naramī*, of *Jūnāgaṛh*, in *Guj'rāt*. B. *1533* A.D.

Rāg.

29. **भगन्वान दास,** *Bhag'wān Dās*, of *Mathurā*. B. *1533* A.D.

Rāg.

30. **मोती लाल कबि,** the poet *Mōtī Lāl*, of *Bāsīrāj*. B. *1533*.

Rāg. He translated the *Gaṇēça Purāṇa* into the vernacular.

CHAPTER III.

THE ROMANTIC POETRY OF MALIK MUHAMMAD. [1540 A.D.]

31. मलिक मुहम्मद जायसी, *Malik Muhammad*, of *Jāyas*, in *Audh*. Fl. 1540 A.D.

He flourished under *Shēr Shāh* in the year 1540 A.D. He was the author of the *Padmāwat* (Rāg.), which is, I believe, the first poem and almost the only one written in a Gaudian vernacular on an original subject. I do not know a work more deserving of hard study than the Padmāwat. It certainly requires it, for scarcely a line is intelligible to the ordinary scholar, it being couched in the veriest language of the people. But it is well worth any amount of trouble, both for its originality and for its poetical beauty.

Malik Muhammad was a Musalmān *faqīr* of great sanctity. The rājā of *Amēṭhī*, who believed that he owed a son and his general prosperity to the saint, was one of his principal devotees. When the poet died he was buried at the gate of the rājā's fort at *Amēṭhī*, where his tomb is still worshipped. He tells us himself, in the introduction to his poem, that he was a disciple of Sayyad *Ashraf Jahān'gīr* and of Shekh *Bur'hān*,[1] and that he subsequently studied under Hindū pandits. He is said not to have been a man of great learning, but was famed for his wisdom, and for the fact that he wrote for the people in the people's tongue. According to the text of the Banāras edition of the *Padmāwat*, which is very incorrect,[2] the poet commenced to write it in A.H. 927 (A.D. 1520); but this is probably a misreading, for he says in the preface that *Shēr Shāh* of the *Sūr* dynasty, who

---

[1] Shekh *Bur'hān* resided at *Kāl'pī*, in *Bundēl'khaṇḍ*, and is said to have died at 100 years of age in A.H. 970, or A.D. 1562-63. See *Rep. Arch. Sur. Ind.* xxi, 131.

[2] My friend Pandit *Chhōṭū Rām Tiwārī*, Professor of Sanskrit at *Bāṅkīpur* College, has undertaken to translate and edit a correct text of this important work for the *Bibliotheca Indica.* (Alas, since the above was written, a learned and humble scholar, who never said an unkind word of anyone, and one of the most upright gentlemen with whom it has been my privilege to be on terms of intimacy, has gone to his long home. By his untimely death I have lost a true friend and a respected teacher.)

came to the throne in A.H. 947 (A.D. 1540), was then the ruling king. 927 is therefore probably incorrect for 947.

The outline of the story of Padmāwat is as follows:—There was a king named *Ratan Sēn*, of *Chitāūr*, who was informed by a parrot of the great beauty of *Padmāwat* or *Padminī*, daughter of the king of *Siŋghal Dīp* (Ceylon). He journeyed to Ceylon as a mendicant, married her there, and returned with her to Chitāūr. After this one *Rāghō*, a dismissed astrologer of Ratan's court, informed *Alāu'd-dīn Khiljī*, then reigning at Dillī, of the great beauty of *Padminī*. *Alāu'd-dīn* in consequence attempted, but unsuccessfully, to capture Chitāūr in order to obtain possession of her. He nevertheless, by a stratagem succeeded in capturing *Ratan's* person, and held him as a hostage for her surrender. During her husband's imprisonment proposals of an insulting nature were made to her by one *Dēb Pāl*, Rājā of *Kambhal'nēr*, which she repelled with scorn. Ratan was subsequently released from his dungeon by the valour of two heroes, *Gōrā* and *Bādal*, the former being killed fighting bravely in the battle which ensued. As soon as Ratan was again seated on his throne, he attacked Kambhal'nēr in revenge for the insult offered to his wife, and killed Dēb Pāl. He was, however, himself sorely wounded, and only arrived at Chitāūr in time to die. His two wives *Padminī* and *Nāg'matī* became *satī* for him, and while their ashes were still warm the advance guard of Alāu'd-dīn's army appeared at the gates of the city. It was nobly defended by Bādal, who fell fighting in the gate, but was finally taken and sacked, "and Chitāūr became *Islām*." In the final verses of his work the poet says that it is all an allegory. By *Chitāūr* he means the body of man; by *Ratan Sēn* the soul; by the parrot the *guru* or spiritual preceptor; by *Padminī* wisdom; by *Rāghō* Satan; by *Alāu'd-dīn* delusion, and so on.

The story of the Padmāwat is founded on the historical facts of the siege of Chitāūr, which is described by Tod [*Rājāsthān* i, 262 (Calc. ed. i, 281), and ff.]. The substance is as follows:—*Lakam'sī*, the minor king of *Chitāūr*, came to the throne A.D. 1275. His uncle *Bhīm'sī* ruled during his minority. He had espoused *Padminī*, the daughter of *Hammīr Saŋkh* (*Chāūhān*), of Ceylon. *Alāu'd-dīn* besieged the city in order to obtain possession of her, and after a long and fruitless siege he restricted his desire to a mere sight of her extraordinary beauty, and acceded to the proposal of beholding her through the medium of mirrors. Relying on the faith of the Rāj'pūt he entered Chitāūr, slightly guarded, and having gratified his wish returned.

The Rāj'pūt, unwilling to be outdone in confidence, accompanied the king to the foot of the fortress. Here Alā had an ambush waiting. Bhīm'sī was made prisoner, and his liberty made to depend on the surrender of Padminī. She being informed of this, agreed to give herself up as a ransom for her husband; and having provided wherewithal to secure her from dishonour, she designed, with two chiefs of her own kin of Ceylon—her uncle *Gōrā* and her nephew *Bādal*—a plan for the liberation of the prince without hazarding her life and fame. She was accompanied into Alā's camp by a procession of litters, borne by, and filled with, armed men disguised as females and handmaids, some of whom returned, taking Padminī and Bhīm'sī with them in disguise; the rest remained in the enemy's camp till the *ruse* was discovered, when they covered the retreat of their master and were cut down to a man in doing so. Bhīm'sī and Padminī escaped into Chitāūr, and after an unsuccessful attempt at storming the citadel (in which Gōrā was killed) Alāu'd-dīn raised the siege. He returned again to the siege in 1290 (Firishta says thirteen years later), and one by one eleven out of twelve sons of Bhīm'sī were slain. Then, having made arrangements for the escape of *Ajāīsī*, his second son, to continue the family line, the Rānā himself, calling around him his devoted clans, for whom life had no longer any charms, threw open the portals and carried death into, and met it in the crowded ranks of Alā. 'But another awful sacrifice preceded this act of self-devotion, in that horrible rite the *Jāūhar*, where the females are immolated to preserve them from pollution or captivity. The funeral pyre was lighted within the great subterranean retreat, in chambers impervious to the light of day, and the defenders of Chitāūr beheld in procession its queens, their own wives and daughters, to the number of several thousands. The fair Padminī closed the throng, which was augmented by whatever of female beauty or youth could be tainted by Tatar lust. They were conveyed to the cavern, and the opening closed upon them, leaving them to find security from dishonour in the devouring element.' The Tatar conqueror took possession of an inanimate capital, strewed with the bodies of its brave defenders, the smoke yet issuing from the recesses where lay consumed the once fair object of his desire.

Malik Muḥammad has changed the name of the hero from *Bhīm'sī* to *Ratan*, the name of the king of *Mēwār* who ruled at *Chitāūr* at about the time that the poem was written (Tod, i, 309; Calc. ed. i, 328).[1]

[1] It is worthy of note that the second sack of Chitāūr, that by Bahādūr of Guj'rāt, took place in 1533 (Tod, i, 311; Calc. ed. 331).

He has also borrowed part of his story from that of another *Padmāwat*, the *Padmāvatī* of *Udayana* and the *Ratnāvalī*. He makes his hero turn a mendicant devotee in order to gain his beloved, and the scene of the burning together of the two queens, though suggested by the terrible real tragedy, seems also to bear marks of the somewhat similar situation in the Ratnāvali.

From the date of the Padmāwat the literature of Hindūstān became, so to speak, crystallised into two grooves. This was due to the Vaishnava reformation of *Rāmānand* and *Ballabhāchār'j*. The first of these, who has been already mentioned, founded the modern worship of Viṣṇu in his incarnation of Rām (Rāma), and the other the worship of the same god in his incarnation of Krish'n (Kṛiṣṇa). From this date all the great poetical works of the country were devoted to either one or other of these two incarnations, and Malik Muḥammad's work stands out as a conspicuous, and almost solitary, example of what the Hindū mind can do when freed from the trammels of literary and religious custom. It is true that there are examples of didactic, grammatical, and medical works in the long roll of authors which follows; but the fact remains that from the middle of the sixteenth century to the present day all that was great and good in Hindustānī[1] literature was bound by a chain of custom or of impulse, or of both, to the ever-recurring themes of Rām and Krish'n. Rāmānand has already been dealt with, and his only conspicuous follower was Tul'sī Dās, concerning whom I shall hereafter deal at length. Before considering *Ballabhāchār'j* and the great school of *Braj* authors founded by him, it will be convenient to clear the way by enumerating two minor writers.

ADDENDA TO CHAPTER III.

---

32. **दील्ह कवि**, the poet *Dīlh* (?). B. *1548* A.D. No particulars.

33. **नरोत्तम दास**, *Narōttam Dās*, the Brāhman of *Bāṛī*, district *Sītāpur*. B. *1553* A.D.

Rāg. The author of the *Sudāmā Charitr'* (Rāg.).

---

[1] I use this word here, as elsewhere, as the adjective corresponding to the substantive Hindūstān, and not as meaning the so-called Hindūstānī language.

CHAPTER IV.

THE KṚIṢṆA-CULT OF BRAJ. [1500—1600.]

34. बल्लभाचार॰ज, *Ballabhāchār'j*, of *Gōkul*, in *Braj*. B. 1478 A.D.

Rāg. Although *Ballabhāchār'j* was more of a religious reformer than a literary character, I shall deal with him at greater length than I have done with Rāmānand, both because of his greater importance, and because I am able to give some particulars concerning him which have not hitherto been made available to European scholars. *Ballabhāchār'j* (*Vallabhāchārya*) was the celebrated founder of the *Rādhāballabhī* sect.[1] According to *Harishchandr'*,[2] his father's name was *Lachhman Bhaṭṭ* (a Tailiŋga Brāhman of *Madras*) and his mother's name was *Illamgārū*. His father had three sons—*Rām Krish'n, Ballabhāchār'j*, and *Rām Chandr'*. Both his brothers were Vaishnava authors of repute. *Lachhman Bhaṭṭ* lived at *Ajodhyā*, and was paying a visit to *Banāras* when on the way, near the village of *Chāūrā*, in the vicinity of *Betiyā*, in the district of *Champāran*, in *Bihār*, on Sunday, the 11th of the dark half of Bāīsākh, Sambat 1535 (A.D. 1478), Ballabhāchār'j was born.[3] At Banāras he commenced studying under the celebrated *Mādhi'wāchār'j* (Rāg.) at the age of five years, and remained there till the death of his father, after which he led a wandering life and visited the court of *Krish'n Dēb*, king of *Bijāīnagar*, apparently the same as *Krish'n Rāyalū*, who reigned about the year 1520 A.D. Here he overcame the Smārta Brāhmans in controversy (see Wilson, *Religious Sects of the Hindūs*, p. 120). According to Harischandr', however, this took place before Sambat 1548 (A.D. 1491), when he was only thirteen years of age. In this year he made a tour to *Braj*, where he studied the *Bhāgavata Purāṇa*, and subsequently returned to *Banāras*, preaching Vaishnava doctrines as he went along. From *Banāras* he went to *Gayā, Jagannāth*, and the *Deckan*, spreading his doctrines

[1] See Wilson, *Religious Sects of the Hindūs*, p. 120.

[2] *Prasiddh Māhātmāō kā Jīban Charitr'*, ii. 28.

[3] See the third khaṇḍ of the *Ballabh Digbijāī*, सम्बत १५३५ शाके १४४० बैसाख मास कृष्ण पक्ष रविवार मध्यान. See also a hymn by *Dwārikēs* quoted by Harishchandr', l.c.

everywhere. He finished his first tour (technically called his *Digbijāi*, or conquest of the world) in Sambat 1554 (A.D. 1497) at the age of nineteen.[1] He then made *Braj* his head-quarters and established an image of *Shrī Nāth* at *Gōbardhan*. From this as his head-quarters he made his second missionary tour throughout India. He died in *Banāras* in Sambat 1587 (A.D. 1530) at the age of fifty-two years, leaving two sons—*Gōpī Nāth* and *Biṭṭhal Nāth*. He was a voluminous author. His most admired works are a commentary on the *Bhāgavata Purāṇa* entitled *Subōdhanī*,[2] the *Anubhāṣya*, and the *Jaiminīya Sūtra Bhāṣya*. The two latter are in Sanskrit. Harishchandr' (l.c.) gives a complete list of his works. The authorship of a vernacular work of considerable authority, the *Bishnu Pad*, or stanzas in honour of Viṣṇu, is also attributed to him. Many verses by him are included in the anthology entitled *Rāg-Sāgarōdbhab* of *Krishnānand Byās Dēb*. For further particulars see No. 35.

35. **बिट्ठल नाथ गोसाँईं**, the holy master *Biṭṭhal Nāth*, of *Braj*. Fl. 1550 A.D.

Rāg. *Ballabhāchār'j* was succeeded as leader of the *Rādhāballabhī* sect by his son *Biṭṭhal Nāth*, of *Braj* (Fl. 1550). *Biṭṭhal Nāth* had seven sons, all of whom became *Gosāīs*, or leaders of the sect. The descendants of two of these (*Gir'dhar* and *Jadunāth*)[3] still exist in *Gōkul*.[4] Many of his verses are included in the *Rāg-Sāgarōdbhab*, and he is possibly the same as a *Biṭṭhal Kabi* mentioned in the *Sib Siṅgh Sarōj* as an erotic poet.

Ballabhāchār'j had four famous pupils, viz. *Krish'n Dās Pay Ahārī* (No. 36), *Sūr Dās* (No. 37), *Par'mānand Dās* (No. 38), *Kumbhan Dās* (No. 39); and *Biṭṭhal Nāth* had also four pupils, named *Chatur'bhuj Dās* (No. 40), *Chhīt Swāmī* (No. 41), *Nand Dās* (No. 42), *Gōbind Dās* (No. 43). The first four may be considered as flourishing in the year 1550, and the second four as flourishing about 1567 A.D. These eight all lived in *Braj* and wrote in Braj Bhākhā, and are named the *Ashṭa Chhāp*, or eight acknowledged masters of the literature of that dialect. Wilson and others speak of a work entitled the *Ashṭa Chhāp*, giving the lives of these poets; and I once believed in the existence of such

---

[1] This is the date quoted by Harishchandr'.

[2] According to Wilson, *Subōdhinī*.

[3] See Harishchandr' (l.c.), ii, 36.

[4] For further information cf. Wilson, *Religious Sects of the Hindūs*, i, 125, where he is wrongly called *Vitala Nāth*.

a work myself, but I now know that by the term *Ashṭa Chhāp* is simply meant this list, which, so far as I can make out, was first given and so named in some verses of Sūr Dās (translated in No. 37) and next noted by me in a work entitled the *Tul'sī Sabdār'th Prakās*, by *Gōpal Siṇgh*, of *Braj*, whose date I have been unable to give.

I now proceed to mention these eight authors in detail.

36. **क्रिश्नन्न दास पय अहारी,** *Krish'n Dās*, surnamed *Pay Ahārī*, or 'he whose food was milk,' of *Gōkul*, in *Braj*. Fl. 1550 A.D.

Rāg. He was a disciple of *Ballabhāchār'j* and a member of the *Ashṭa Chhāp*,—see No. 35. He was a graceful and sweet poet, many of whose verses will be found in the *Rāg Sāgarōdbhab*. There is a legend that *Sūr Dās* in his poetry had exhausted all that could possibly be said concerning the god Krish'n, and that hence, when *Krish'n Dās* wrote anything, it was always found to be identical with something that Sūr Dās had already written. One day the latter challenged him to produce a single stanza which did not comply with this disagreeable necessity, and he failed to do so. He then promised to bring an original verse next day, and going away spent the whole night in vain endeavouring to concoct one. In the morning he found a verse mysteriously written upon his pillow, which he took to Sūr Dās, who at once identified it as one which had been written by their master, *Ballabhāchār'j*. In spite of this legend, which seems to point to a rivalry between the two poets, *Krish'n Dās* is always graceful and as original as his subject will admit. His best known work is the *Prēm-ras-ras*. His most famous disciples were *Agr' Dās* (No. 44), *Kēwal Rām* (No. 45), *Gadā Dhar* (No. 46), *Dēbā* (No. 47), *Kalyān* (No. 48), *Haṭī Nārāyan* (No. 49), and *Padum Nāth* (No. 50). *Agr' Dās* had *Nābhā Dās* (No. 51), the author of the *Bhakt Mālā*, of whom more anon, for his disciple.

37. **सूरदास,** *Sūr Dās*, the Bhāṭ, of *Braj*. Fl. 1550 A.D.

Nir., Rāg. Sūr Dās deserves a more extended notice. He was, with his father Bābā *Rām Dās* (No. 112), a singer at the court of the emperor *Ak'bar* (see *Āīn-i-Akbarī*, Blochmann's translation, p. 612). He and *Tul'sī Dās* are the two great stars in the firmament of Indian vernacular poetry. Tul'sī was devoted to Rām (*ēkānt Rām-sēbak*), while Sūr Dās was devoted to Krish'n (*ēkānt Krish'n-sēbak*), and between them they are considered to have exhausted all the possibilities of poetic art.

According to a tradition preserved in the glosses of the *Bhakt Mālā* and to the *Chaūrāsī Bārtā,* he was a Sāraswat Brāhman, and his father and mother were beggars who lived at *Gaū Ghāṭ* or at *Dillī.* The fact that books of the authority of these two works countenance this theory is typical of the tendency of mediæval Indian authors to trust to tradition instead of to independent research. Subsequent writers, English and foreign, have followed the *Bhakt Mālā,* and have all been led wrong in consequence, for we have the very best authority, that of *Sūr Dās* himself, that he was not a Sāraswat Brāhman, and that his father was not a beggar and did not live at *Gaū Ghāṭ.*[1]

Sūr Dās wrote a collection of emblematic verses (*drishṭ kūṭ*) with the accompanying necessary commentary,[2] and in the latter the author gives the following account of himself[3] :—

'The founder of my family was *Brahm Rāō,*[4] first of the *Jagāt* (or of the *Prath Jagāt*)[5] clan. In his famous family was born the handsome famous *Chand.*[6] To him *Prithwī Rāj* (Fl. 1190 A.D.) gave the country of *Jwālā.* He had four sons, of whom the eldest succeeded him as king (*narēs*). The second was *Gun Chandr',* whose son was *Sīl Chandr',* whose son was *Bīr Chandr'.* This last used to sport with *Hammīr,*[7] king of *Ran'thambhōr.* In his family was born *Hari Chandr',* who dwelt at *Āg'rā. Hari Chandr's* heroic[8] son dwelt in *Gōp'chal* and had seven sons, viz. (1) *Krish'n Chand,* (2) *Udār Chand,* (3) *Jurup Chand* (or possibly *Rūp Chand*), (4) *Buddhi Chand,* (5) *Dēb Chand,* (6) (?) *Sansrit Chand,* and (7) myself *Sūraj Chand.* My six brothers were

---

[1] It must not be forgotten that *Priyā Dās,* the author of the gloss to the *Bhakt Mālā,* collected the traditions more than a century after *Sūr Dās's* death.

[2] The work has been printed at the Light Press, Banāras.

[3] The late lamented *Harishchandr',* of *Banāras,* the greatest, I had almost said the only, critic of Hindūstān, was the first to draw attention to this in his magazine the *Harishchandra Chandrikā,* vol. vi, No. 5, pp. 1—6. The article has been subsequently reprinted in the collection known as *Prasiddh Mahātmāō kā Jīban Charitr'.* (Bankipur. Sāhib Prasād Siṇgh. Khaḍg Bilās Press. 1885.)

[4] The title Rāō renders it probable that he was either a rājā (of royal stock) or a Bhāṭ or panegyrist.

[5] This clan is not mentioned in the list of clans of Sāraswat Brāhmans drawn up by Paṇḍit *Rādhēs Misar. Jagāt* or *jagatiyā* means a panegyrist.

[6] Or perhaps *Bhāō Chand,* if we take *bhāū* (= *huā,* 'was') as a contraction of *bhāō.*

[7] The famous king of *Ran'thambhōr,* who was attacked by *Alāu'd-dīn Khiljī,* and for whom 1,000 wives became *satī.* The date of his death was about 1300 A.D.

[8] His son's name was probably *Rām Chandr',* which he subsequently changed, according to Vaishnava custom, to *Rām Dās.* But a possible translation of the passage gives his name as *Bīr* (*Chandr'*).

killed in battle with the Musalmāns; I alone, *Sūraj Chand,* blind[1] and worthless, remained alive. I was fallen into a well,[2] and though I called for help, no one saved me. On the seventh day Jadupati (Krish'n) came and pulled me out[3] and, making himself visible to me (or giving me my eyesight), said "Son, ask what thou desirest as a boon." I said, "Lord, I ask for the boon of perfect devotion, for the destruction of the enemy,[4] and that now that I have seen the form of my God, mine eyes may never see aught else." As the Ocean of Compassion heard me, he said. "So let it be. Thine enemy will be destroyed by a mighty Brāhman of the *Deckan.*" Then named he me *Sūraj Dās, Sūr,* and *Sūr Syām,* and disappeared, and thereafter all was darkness to me.[6] I then went to live in *Braj,* where the holy master (*Biṭṭhal Nāth*) entered my name in the *Ashṭa Chhāp.*"[7] We thus get the following genealogy:—

Brahm Rāō, the *Jagāt.*
|
Chandr'. (Fl. 1190 A.D.)
|
Second son, *Gun Chandr'.*
|
Sīl Chandr'.
|
Bīr Chandr'. (Fl. 1300 A.D.)
|
Hari Chandr' (of *Āg'rā*).
|
Descendants unknown.
|
Rām Chandr' (of *Gōp-chal*).
|
Sūraj Chand (Fl. 1550) and six others.

It is evident that he was not of a Brāhman, but of a royal stock.[8] According to tradition he was born about Sambat 1540 (1483 A.D.),

---

[1] Either literally or figuratively. Owing to the undoubted fact of his blindness, every blind singing mendicant is nowadays called a *Sūr Dās.*

[2] This may by taken literally, *i.e.* fallen into a dry well (*andhā kūā*), or figuratively that he was a sinner.

[3] Or, taken figuratively, after seven days of internal conflict I became converted and obtained salvation.

[4] *I.e.* of his evil passions, or perhaps of the Musalmāns.

[5] *I.e. Ballabhāchār'j.*

[6] *I.e.* he became literally blind,—the fulfilment of his third request, *dusarō nā dēkhō rūpa, dēkhī Rādhā-Syāma.* The line may also be translated, 'he disappeared in the last watch of the night.'

[7] The list of the eight great poets of Braj. See No. 35.

[8] He calls Chand'r's eldest son *narēs.*

and was instructed by his father at *Āg'rā* in singing, in Persian, and the vernacular. On his father's death he took to writing hymns (*bhajans*), and gained many disciples. At this time he signed his verses *Sūr Swāmī*, and under that title wrote a poem dealing with the story of *Nala and Damayantī*.[1] He was then in the prime of his youth, and is said to have lived at *Gaū Ghāṭ*, a village nine *kōs* from *Āg'rā* on the road to *Mathurā*. About this time he himself became a disciple of *Ballabhāchār'j*, and signed his poems with the name of *Sūr Dās*, *Sūr*, *Sūraj Dās*, or, as before, *Sūr Syām*.[2] At this time he translated the *Bhāgavata Purāṇa* into verse in the vernacular, and he also collected his hymns into the compilation entitled the *Sūr Sāgar* (Rāg.).[3] In his old age his fame reached the ears of the emperor *Ak'bar*, who summoned him to his court. He died in *Gōkul* about Sambat 1620 (1563 A.D.). The above tradition is certainly wrong so far as regards dates and as regards *Sūr Dās's* father, for the *Āīn-i-Akbarī*, which was completed in 1596-97 A.D., mentions both *Sūr Dās* and *Bābā Rām Dās* as (apparently) then alive. *Abū'l Faẓl* says that *Rām Dās* came from *Gwāliyar*, but *Badāonī* (ii, 42) says he came from *Lakh'naū*.

Another legend current throughout India concerning Sūr Dās may be mentioned. Subsequently to his becoming blind, during the absence of his amanuensis, Krish'n came himself and wrote down for him the words which welled forth from the unsuspecting poet's mouth. At length Sūr Dās perceived that the writer was outstripping his tongue, and was writing down his thoughts before he had uttered them. Recognising the *Antarajāmī* God by this, Sūr Dās seized him by the hand, but Krish'n thrust him away and disappeared. Sūr Dās then uttered a poem still extant, and in my opinion by far his highest flight, the leading idea of which is that though a mortal might thrust him away, no one but God could tear himself from the poet's heart.[4]

Regarding Sūr Dās's place in literature, I can only add that he justly holds a high one. He excelled in all styles. He could, if occasion required, be more obscure than the Sphynx and in the next verse be as

---

[1] No copies of this are known to exist.

[2] Also possibly *Sant Das*. (See No. 235.)

[3] Said to contain 60,000 verses.

[4] *Kara chhaṭakāī jātu hāū, durabala jānī mōhi*
Hiradaya sē jāū jāhugē, marada bakhānō tōhi.

Thou thrustest away my hand and departest, knowing that I am weak (and pretending that thou art but a man),
But not till thou depart from my heart will I confess thee to be a mortal.

clear as a ray of light. Other poets may have equalled him in some particular quality, but he combined the best qualities of all.[1] Natives of India give him the very highest niche of fame, but I believe the European reader will prefer the nobility of character of all that *Tul'sī Dās* wrote to the often too cloying sweetness of the blind bard of Āg'rā.

38. परमानन्द दास, *Par'mānand Dās,* of *Braj.* Fl. 1550 A.D.

Rāg.

39. कुम्भन दास, *Kumbhan Dās,* of *Braj.* Fl. 1550 A.D.

Rāg. These two were pupils of *Ballabhāchār'j* (No. 34), and are included in the *Ashṭa Chhāp.*

40. चतुरभुज दास, *Chatur'bhuj Dās.* Fl. 1567.

Rāg. He is included in the *Ashṭa Chhāp* as a pupil of *Biṭṭhal Nāth,* of *Gōkul* (No. 35). He is probably the same as another *Chatur'-bhuj* mentioned by Sib Siŋgh. Garcin de Tassy (i, 142), quoting the preface to the *Prēm Sāgar,* mentions a *Chatur'bhuj Misar,* author of a Braj translation of the 10th book of the *Bhāgavata Purāṇa* in *dōhās and chaupāīs.*

41. छीत स्वामी, *Chhīt Swāmī.* Fl. 1567 A.D.

Rāg. He is included in the *Ashṭa Chhāp* as a pupil of *Biṭṭhal Nāth* (No. 35). He is possibly the same as a *Chhīt Kabi* included in Haj., whom Sib Siŋgh dates as 1648 A.D.

42. नन्द दास, *Nand Dās* the Brāhman, of *Rām'pur.* Fl. 1567.

Rāg. He was a pupil of *Biṭṭhal Nāth* (No. 35), and his name is included in the *Ashṭa Chhāp.* A proverb about him is और सब गढ़िया, नन्द दास जड़िया,—All others are simply founders (or melters),

[1] As an anonymous poet of Ak'bar's court says, "*Gaŋg* excels in sonnets and *Bīr'bal* in the *Kabitta* metre. *Kēsab's* meaning is ever profound, but *Sūr* possesses the excellences of all three."

but Nand Dās is the artificer (who joins the pieces of cast metal into a composite whole). His principal works are (1) *Nām Mālā,* (2) *Anēkārth,* (3) *Pañchādhyāyī* (Rāg.) (printed. It is a poem in imitation of the *Gīta Gōvinda,* see Garcin de Tassy, i, 387), (4) *Rukmīnī Maŋgal* (Rāg), (5) *Dasam Skandh,* (6) *Dān Līlā,* (7) *Mān Līlā.* He is also the author of numerous detached verses.

43. **गोविन्द दास,** *Gōbind Dās,* of *Braj.* Fl. 1567 A.D.

Rāg. He was a disciple of *Biṭṭhal Nāth* (No. 35) and a member of the *Ashṭa Chhāp.*

44. **अग्र॰ दास,** *Agr' Dās,* of *Gal'tā,* in *Amēr* (*Jaipur*). Fl. 1575 A.D.

Rāg. He was a disciple of *Krish'n Dās Pay Ahārī* (No. 36), who together with *Sūr Dās* was a disciple of *Ballabhāchār'j.* He himself was preceptor of *Nābhā Dās* (No. 51), the celebrated author of the *Bhakt Mālā.* Many of his songs are included in Rāg. He is possibly the same as another poet mentioned by Sib Siŋgh as being born in 1569 A.D., and the author of *Kuṇḍaliyā, Chhappāi,* and *Dōhā* verses on morals.

45. **केवल राम कवि,** the poet *Kēwal Rām,* of *Braj.* Fl. 1575 A.D.

Rāg. Mentioned in the *Bhakt Mālā.* A disciple of *Krish'n Dās Pay Ahārī* (No. 36).

46. **गदा धर दास,** *Gadā Dhar Dās.* Fl. 1575 A.D.

He was a pupil of *Krish'n Dās Pay Ahārī* (No. 36). He is probably the same as a *Gadādhar* mentioned by Sib Siŋgh as a quietistic (शान्ति रस) poet.

47. **देवा कवि,** the poet *Dēbā* of *Udāipur* (*Mēwār*). Fl. 1575 A.D.

48. **कल्यान दास,** *Kalyān Dās,* of *Braj.* Fl. 1575 A.D.

Rāg.

49. हटी नारायन, *Haṭī Nārāyan*, of *Braj*. Fl. 1575 A.D.

50. पदुम नाभ, *Padum Nābh*, of *Braj*. Fl. 1575 A.D.

Rāg. These four were all disciples of *Krish'n Dās Pay Ahārī* (No. 36).

51. नाभा दास कबि, the poet *Nābhā Dās alias Nārāyan Dās*, of the Deccan. Fl. 1600 A.D.

We shall now anticipate the course of time a little in order to complete the history of this famous group of *Braj* poets. *Krish'n Dās Pay Ahārī* (No. 36) had a pupil, *Agr' Dās* (No. 44), of *Gal'tā*, who in turn was preceptor of *Nābhā Dās alias Nārāyan Dās*, of the *Deckan*, who flourished about 1600 A.D. and was a Ḍōm by caste. According to tradition he was born blind, and when but five years old was exposed by his parents, during a time of scarcity, to perish in the woods. In this situation he was found by *Agr' Dās* and another Vaishnava named *Kīl*. They had compassion upon his helplessness, and Kīl sprinkled his eyes with the water of his *kamaṇḍal*, or water-pot, and the child saw. They carried Nābhā to their *Maṭh*, where he was brought up and received the initiatory *mantra* from Agr' Dās. When arrived at maturity, under the direction of *Agr' Dās* he wrote the *Bhakt Mālā* (Rāg.) or "Legends of the Saints," consisting of 108 verses in Chhappāī metre.[1] It is one of the most difficult works in the Braj dialect, and, as we have it now, was avowedly edited, and perhaps rewritten, by a disciple (?) of *Nābhā Dās* entitled *Nārāyan Dās* who lived in the reign of *Shāh Jahān* (1628—1658). Mr. Growse, to whom I am indebted for this last piece of information, adds :—'A single stanza is all that is ordinarily devoted to each personage, who is panegyrised with reference to his most salient characteristics in a style that might be described as of unparalleled obscurity were it not that each separate portion of the text is followed by a gloss written by one *Priyā Dās* (No. 319) in the Sambat year 1769 (1712 A.D.), in which confusion is still worse confounded by a series of most disjointed and inexplicit allusions to different legendary events in the saint's life.' *Priyā Dās's* gloss is in the *Kabitta* metre. He was followed by *Lāl Jī* (No. 322), a Kāyasth of *Kādhalā*, who in Hij'rī 1158 (A.D. 1751) wrote a further commentary, entitled *Bhakt Urbasī*. In the year 1854 *Tul'sī Rām*

[1] The above is mainly taken from Wilson, *Religious Sects of the Hindūs*, i, 60. Cf. Garcin de Tassy, i, 378.

Agar'wālā (No. 640), of *Mīrāpur,* translated the *Bhakt Mālā* into Ūrdū, calling his translation the *Bhakt Māl Pradīpan.*

The name *Nārāyan Dās,* which Mr. Growse attributes to a disciple of *Nābhā Dās,* was, according to Native writers, really the actual name of Nābhā Dās, the latter being his *nom de guerre.* *Nābhā Dās* is possibly the same as a *Nārāyan Dās* Kabi mentioned in the *Sib Siŋgh Sarōj* as born in 1558 A.D. and author of a translation of the *Hitōpādēça* and *Rājanīti* into the vernacular, and as another *Nārāyan Dās,* a Vaishnava author of an undated prosody describing 52 metres, entitled *Chhand Sār.*

52. **कान्हर दास कबि,** the poet *Kānhār Dās,* of *Braj.* Fl. 1600 A.D.

Rāg. He was son of *Biṭṭhal Dās Chaūbē,* of *Mathurā.* At a meeting held at his house *Nābhā Dās* (No. 51) received the title of *Gosāī.*

53. **स्री भट्ट कबि,** the poet *Srī Bhaṭṭ.* B. *1544* A.D.

Rāg. He is said to have excelled in describing the actions of a lover and his beloved. Possibly the same as *Kēsab Bhaṭṭ* (see Wilson, *Religious Sects of the Hindūs,* i, 151), one of the pupils of *Nīmāditya.*

54. **ब्यास स्वामी,** *Byās Swāmī alias Hari Rām Suk'l,* of *Uṛ'chhā,* in *Bundēl'khaṇḍ.* Fl. 1555 A.D.

Rāg. He was a Gaūṛ Brāhman of Dēb'band, and joined the *Rādhāballabhī* sect. In the year 1555 A.D., when he was forty-five years of age, he settled in *Brindāban* and founded a new Vaishnava religion, entitled the *Haribyāsī* sect. According to Wilson (*Religious Sects of the Hindūs,* p. 151), he and *Kēsab Bhaṭṭ* were pupils of *Nīmāditya* (Rāg.), the founder of the *Nimāwat* sect.

55. **परसु राम** *Parasů Rām,* of *Braj.* B. *1603* A.D.

Rāg., Dig. He was a follower of *Srī* (*Kēsab*) *Bhaṭṭ* and *Haribyās* (see Wilson, *Religious Sects of the Hindūs,* p. 151). It is not certain that the poets quoted in Rāg and Dig. are the same person.

56. **हित हरिबन्स स्वामी गोसाँईं,** the very holy master *Hit Haribans.* Fl. 1560 A.D.

Rāg. His father was *Byās Swāmī alias Hari Rām Suk'l* (No. 54). He is a much esteemed author. In Sanskrit he wrote the *Rādhā Sudhānidhi*, and in the vernacular the *Hit Chaũrāsī Dhām*. Amongst his pupils was the poet *Nar Bāhan* (No. 57). See Wilson, *Religious Sects of the Hindūs*, p. 177, and Growse, J. A. S. B., vol. xlvii (1878), p. 97, where specimens of both his works are given and translated.

57. नर बाहन जी कवि, the poet *Nar Bāhan Jī*, of *Bhaũgãw*. Fl. 1560 A.D.

He was a disciple of *Hit Haribans* (No. 56). He is mentioned in the *Bhakt Mālā*.

58. ध्रुव दास, *Dhrub Dās*. Fl. 1560 A.D.

Rāg. A pupil of *Hit Haribans* (No. 56), and a voluminous writer. A complete list of his works is given by Mr. Growse in J. A. S. B., vol. xlvii (1878), p. 113.

59. हरि दास स्वामी, the master *Hari Dās*, of *Brindāban*, in *Braj*. Fl. 1560 A.D.

Rāg. His Sanskrit works are considered equally good with those of *Jayādēva*, and his vernacular poems rank next after those of *Sūr Dās* and *Tul'sī Dās*. His best known works are the *Sādhāran Siddhānt* and the *Ras kē pad*. He had many celebrated pupils, amongst whom may be mentioned *Tān Sēn* (No. 60), *Bipul Biṭṭhal* (No. 62) (his uncle), and *Bhag'wat Ramit* (No. 61). He is said by Wilson to have been a pupil of *Chaitanya*, who disappeared about A.D. 1527 (*Religious Sects of the Hindūs*, p. 159). This, however, is doubtful. See Growse, J. A. S. B., vol. xlv (1876), p. 317, where the matter is discussed at length, and where (p. 318) the text of the Sādhāran Siddhānt is given and translated.

60. तान सेन कवि, the poet *Tān Sēn*, of *Gwāliyar*. Fl. 1560.

Rāg. He was son of *Mak'rand Pā̃ṛē*, a Gaũṛ Brāhman. He was a disciple of *Hari Dās* (No. 59), from whom he learned the art of poetry. He then repaired to Shēkh *Muḥammad Ghaũs*, of *Gwāliyar*, a famous teacher of singing. The legend is that Muḥammad Ghaũs simply touched Tān Sēn's tongue with his own, and thenceforth Tān Sēn became the most famous singer of his age.

He became enamoured of *Daulat Khān*, son of the famous *Shēr Khān*, and wrote many poems in his honour. When Daulat Khān died he went to the court of *Rām Chand Singh*, the Baghēlā king of *Bāndhō* (*Rīwā̃*). From thence he was summoned (A.D. 1563) by the emperor *Ak'bar*, where he became one of the court singers and a close friend of *Sūr Dās* (see *Āīn-i-Akbarī*, Blochmann's translation, pp. 403, 612). The first time that Tān Sēn performed at court the emperor is said to have made him a present of two *lākhs* of rupees. Most of his compositions are written in Ak'bar's name, and his melodies are even nowadays everywhere repeated by the people of Hindūstān. His most famous work on music is the *Sangīt Sār* (Rāg.).

61. भगवत रमित, *Bhag'wat Ramit*, of *Brindāban*, in *Braj*. Fl. 1560 A.D.

He was son of *Mādhab Dās* (No. 26) and pupil of *Hari Dās* (No. 59). He is the author of some admired *Kundaliyās*.

62. बिपुल बिट्ठल, *Bipul Biṭṭhal*, of *Gōkul*, in *Braj*. Fl. 1560 A.D.

Rāg. He was uncle and pupil of *Hari Dās* (No. 59). He attended the court of the rājā of *Madhuban*, and many of his verses are included in Rāg.

63. केसव दास, *Kēsab Dās*, of *Kāshmīr*. Fl. 1541 A.D.

Rāg. After acquiring a great reputation he came to Braj, and was conquered in discussion by *Krish'n Chaitanya*.

64. अभय राम कबि, the poet *Abhay Rām*, of *Brindāban*, in *Braj*. B. *1545* A.D.

Haj., Rāg.

65. चतुर बिहारी कबि, the poet *Chatur Bihārī*, of *Braj*. B. *1548* A.D.

Rāg. He is probably the same as two other poets, *Chatur Kabi* and *Chatur Bihārī*, mentioned by Sib Singh without dates.

66. **नारायन भट्ट,** the master *Nārāyan Bhaṭṭ,* of *Ũch Gā̃w Bar'sānā,* in *Braj.* B. *1563* A.D.

Rāg. He was a very holy man.

67. **इब्राहीम,** Sayyad *Ibrāhīm alias* the poet *Ras Khān,* of *Pihānī,* district *Har'dōī.* B. *1573* A.D.

Sun. He was originally a Musalmān, but turned a Vaishnava and dwelt in *Braj.* He is mentioned in the *Bhakt Mālā.* His poems are said to be full of sweetness. One of his pupils was *Qādir Bakhsh* (No. 89).

68. **नाथ कबि,** the poet *Nāth.* B. *1584* A.D.

Rāg., ? Sun. He was son of *Gōpāl Bhaṭṭ,* and dwelt in *Braj.* Poems by him on the seasons and other subjects are included in Rāg.

69. **बिद्या दास,** *Bidyā Dās,* of *Braj.* B. *1593* A.D.

Rāg.

ADDENDA TO CHAPTER IV.

70. **केहरी कबि,** the poet *Keh'rī.* B. *1553* A.D.

He attended the court of king *Ratan Siŋgh,* and was a skilled poet. This was probably *Rāw Ratan,* of *Bur'hān'pur,* district *Nimār,* who flourished A.D. 1579. (See Tod, ii, 485; Calc. ed. ii, 522.)

71. **आसकरन दास,** *Ās'karan Dās,* the Kachh'wāhā Rāj'pūt of *Nar'war Gaṛh,* in *Gwāliyar.* Fl. c. 1550 A.D.

Rāg. He was son of king *Bhīm Siŋgh.* See Tod, ii, 362; Calc. ed. ii, 390.

72. **चेतन चन्द्र कबि,** the poet *Chētan Chandr'.* B. *1559* A.D.

He wrote a treatise on veterinary surgery (शालि-होत्र) entitled *Ashwa Binōd* for king *Kusal Siŋgh,* of the *Sēgar* family.

73. **प्रिथ्वी राज कबि,** the poet and prince *Prithwī Rāj.* Fl. 1567 A.D.

Haj., Rāg. He was prince of *Bīkānēr,* and wrote both in Sanskrit and in the vernacular. He was son of *Kalyān Siŋgh* and brother of Rājā *Rāy Siŋgh.* See Tod's *Rājāsthan,* i, 337 and ff.; ii, 186; Calc. ed. i, 363 and ff.; ii, 203.

74. **परबत कबि,** the poet *Par'bat.* Fl. *1567* A.D.

Haj.

75. **छत्त्र कबि,** the poet *Chhattr'.* B. *1568* A.D.

The author of a work entitled the *Bijāī Muktābalī,* which is an abstract of the *Mahābhārata* in verse. It is extremely condensed, being little more than a table of contents. He is possibly the same as a *Chhattr' Patī Kabi* mentioned by Sib Siŋgh.

76. उदय सिङ्घ, Mahārāj *Uday Siŋgh,* of *Mār'wār.* Fl. 1584 A.D.

In his name an unknown bard wrote a work called *Khyāt,* in which are detailed the histories of *Uday Siŋgh,* of his grandson *Gaj Siŋgh,* and of his great grandson *Jas'want Siŋgh.* See Tod, ii, 4 (where Gaj is incorrectly called Uday's son), and ii, 30; Calc. ed. ii, 32.

77. जीवन कवि, the poet *Jīban.* B. *1551* A.D.

Haj., Rāg.

78. मानिक चन्द कवि, the poet *Mānik Chand.* B. *1551* A.D.

Rāg.

79. ऊधो राम कवि, the poet *Ūdhō Rām.* B. *1553* A.D.

Haj., ? Rāg. Cf. No. 495.

80. नन्द लाल कवि, the poet *Nand Lāl.* B. *1554* A.D.

Haj.

81. गनेस जी मिसर, *Ganēs Jī Misar.* B. *1558* A.D.

82. जलाल उद्दीन कवि, the poet *Jalālu'd dīn.* B. *1558* A.D.

Haj.

83. ओली राम कवि, the poet *Ōlī Rām.* B. *1564* A.D.

Haj.

84. दामोदर दास, *Dāmōdar Dās,* of *Braj.* B. *1565.*

Rāg. Possibly the same as a *Dāmōdar Kabi* mentioned by Sib Siŋgh, without date.

85. जमाल उद्दीन, *Jamālu'd dīn,* of *Pihānī,* district *Hardōī.* B. *1568* A.D.

No particulars. He is possibly the same as a *Jamāl Kabi,* whom Sib Siŋgh gives as born in 1545 A.D., and as being skilled in emblematic verses (कूट).

86. नन्दन कवि, the poet *Nandan.* B. *1568* A.D.

Haj.

87. खेम कवि the poet *Khēm,* of *Braj.* B. *1573* A.D.

Rāg. He wrote on lovers.[1] He is possibly the same as a poet *Chhēm,* of the *Dōāb,* mentioned by Sib Siŋgh. Cf. Nos. 103 and 311.

88. सिव कवि, the poet *Sib.* B. *1574.*

Haj., Sun.

89. कादिर बखस, *Qādir Bakhsh,* the Musalmān, of *Pihānī,* district *Har'dōī.* B. *1578* A.D.

A skilled poet. He was a pupil of the elegant author Sayyad *Ibrāhīm,* of Pihānī (No. 67).

90. अम॰रेस कवि, the poet *Am'rēs.* B. *1578* A.D.

Reputed as a very excellent poet, many of whose poems are in Haj.

---

[1] When it is said that a poet wrote on lovers, it is to be understood as a translation of a statement made by a Native authority that he wrote a *Nāyak Bhēd* or a *Nāyikā* [or *Nāyakā* (*sic*)] *Bhēd.* These are technical names for those works in which the various kinds of heroes (*nāyak*) or heroines (*nāyikā*) are described and classified to an extreme, and often absurd, minuteness. A further development is the *Nakh'sikh,* which will be frequently met with further on, in which all the portions of the body and features of a possible hero or heroine, from the toe-nails (*nakh*) to the top-knot (*sikh*), are similarly classified.

91. निहाल, *Nihāl*, the elder. B. *1578* A.D.

92. घन स्याम सुकन्ल, *Ghan Syām Suk'l*, of *As'ni*, district *Fatih'pur*. B. *1578* A.D.

Haj., Sun. He attended the court of the king of *Bāndhō* (*Rīwā̃*).

93. चन्द सखी, *Chand Sakhī*, of *Braj*. B. *1581* A.D.

Rāg. He is possibly the same as a *Chand Kabi* mentioned by Sib Singh and included in Haj., and as a *Chand Kabi* quoted in Sun.

94. मुबारक अली, Sayyad *Mubārak 'Alī*, of *Bil'grām*, district *Har'dōī*. B. *1583* A.D.

Sun. He is the well-known author of hundreds of short verses current in the mouths of the people.

95. नागर कबि, the poet *Nāgar*. B. *1591* A.D.

Haj. Possibly the same as a *Nāgarī Dās* mentioned in the preface to Rāg.

96. दिलन्दार कबि, the poet *Dil'dār*. B. *1593* A.D.

Haj.

97. दौलत कबि, the poet *Daūlat*. B. *1594* A.D.

98. जगन कबि, the poet *Jagan*. B. *1595* A.D.

An erotic writer.

99. ताज कबि, the poet *Tāj*. B. *1595*.

Haj.

100. लालन दास, *Lālan Dās* a Brāhman of *Ḍal'maū*, district *Rāy Barēlī*. B. *1595*.

Haj. A quietistic (शान्ति रस) poet.

101. बारक कबि, the poet *Bārak*. B. *1598* A.D.

102. बिस्व नाथ कबि, the poet *Biswa Nāth* the elder. B. *1598*.

CHAPTER V.

THE MUGHAL COURT.

103. छेम कवि, the poet and bard *Chhēm,* of *Ḍal'maū,* district *Rāy Barēlī.* Fl. 1530.

He attended the court of the emperor *Humāyūn* (1530—1540). He is possibly the same as a poet *Khēm* of *Bundēl'khaṇḍ* mentioned by Sib Siṅgh. Cf. Nos. 87 and 311.

104. अक॰बर बाद॰शाह, the emperor *Ak'bar.* Reigned 1556 to 1605 A.D.

We may now glance at the brilliant court of the emperor *Ak'bar* (B. 1542) and the constellation of poets which shone there. Most of the foregoing authors, from *Malik Muḥammad* (No. 31) downwards, were contemporaries of this king, who was so celebrated a patron of learning. It may be noted that the reign of the emperor Ak'bar nearly coincided with that of the English queen Elizabeth, and that the reigns of both these monarchs were signalised by an extraordinary outburst of literary vigour; nor, indeed, if *Tul'sī Dās* and *Sūr Dās* were compared with Shakespeare and Spenser would the Indian poets be found very far behind. In addition to the following poets, *Tān Sēn* (No. 60) and *Sūr Dās* (No. 37) also attended his court. Particulars about them have been given in the previous chapter.

Ak'bar's claim as a Hindī author is founded only on a few detached verses, in which he signs himself as *Akabbar Rāy.* Possibly these were really written by Tān Sēn. (See No. 60.)

105. टोडर मल खत्री, Rājā *Ṭōḍar Mal,* the *Khattrī.* B. 1523.

The celebrated minister of the emperor *Ak'bar.* He is wrongly called a Pañjābī, because the Ma'āsiru'l Umarā says he was born at Lahāūr. He was, however, really born at Lāhar'pur, in Āudh. (See *Āīn-i-Akbarī*, Blochmann's translation, p. 620.)

He translated the *Bhāgavata Purāṇa* into Persian. His best known vernacular verses are on morals (नीति). He died in Hij'rī 998 (1589 A.D.). For his life see *Āīn-i-Akbarī*, p. 351. His influence in making Hindūs learn Persian is especially noteworthy, as it accounts for the formation and acceptance of Ūrdū.

106. **बीर॰बल**, Rājā *Bīr'bal, alias Bīr'bar, alias Mahēs Dās, alias Brahm Kabi, alias Kabi Rāy*. Born cir. 1528 A.D.

Nir., Sun. The celebrated minister and poet-laureate (Kabi Rāy) of *Ak'bar's* court. He was as much renowned for his liberality as for his musical skill and poetical talent. His short verses, *bon-mots*, and jokes, are still in the mouths of the people of Hindūstān. He was much hated by pious Musalmāns, owing to the belief that he had influenced Ak'bar to abjure Islām. According to Sib Singh he was born in Sambat 1585 (A.D. 1528), but Blochmann in the *Āīn-i-Akbarī* (p. 404 and ff.) leaves the matter in obscurity. His original name was *Mahēs Dās*, and he was a Kanaūj Dūbē Brāhman of *Kāl'pī*, in the district of *Hamīr'pur*. He was at first one of the court poets of *Bhag'wān Dās*,[1] Rājā of *Amēr*, who gave him as a *nazar* to Ak'bar shortly after the latter's accession. At this time he used to sign himself in his poems as *Brahm Kabi*. At Ak'bar's court he was at first very poor but quick-headed, and remarkable for his powers of apprehension. His *bon-mots* in a short time made him a general favourite. His Hindī verses were also much liked, and Ak'bar conferred on him the title of *Kabi Rāy* (above mentioned), and gave him other important state offices near his person. *Nagar'kōṭ* was given to him as his *jāgīr*, but it is doubtful if he ever really got it. In A.H. 990 (A.D. 1583) Bīr'bal was sent by Ak'bar to reinforce *Zaīn Khān Kōkah* at *Bijāūr* against the Yūsufzaīs, and was there killed in battle. *Badāonī* (translation of *Āīn-i-Akbarī*, l.c., and p. 204) says 'Bīr'bal also, who had fled from fear of his life, was slain, and entered the row of the dogs in hell, and thus got something for the abominable deeds he had done during his lifetime. * * * His Majesty (Ak'bar) cared for the death of no grandee more than for that of Bīr'bal. He said, "Alas! they could not even get his body out of the pass, that it might have been burned." But at last he consoled himself with the thought that Bīr'bal was now free and independent of all earthly fetters, and as the rays of the sun were sufficient for him, there was no necessity that he should be cleansed by

[1] Tod, ii, 362; Calc. ed. ii, 390.

fire. * * * Among the silly lies—they border on absurdities—which during this year (A.D. 1588) were spread over the country was the rumour that Bīr'bal, the accursed, was still alive, though in reality he had then for some time been burning in the seventh hell. The Hindūs, by whom his Majesty is surrounded, saw how sad and sorry he was for Bīr'bal's loss, and invented the story that Bīr'bal had been seen in the hills of Nagar'kōṭ walking about with Jōgīs and Sannyāsīs. His Majesty believed the rumour, thinking that Bīr'bal was ashamed to come to court on account of the defeat which he had suffered at the hands of the Yūsufzaīs ; and it was, besides, quite probable that he should have been seen with Jōgīs, inasmuch as he had never cared for the world. An Ahadī was therefore sent to Nagar'kōṭ to inquire into the truth of the rumour, when it was proved that the whole story was an absurdity. Soon after his Majesty received a report that Bīr'bal had been seen at Kāliñjar (which was the jāgīr of this dog), and the Collector of the district stated that a barber had recognised him by certain marks on his body, which the man had distinctly seen when one day Bīr'bal got him to rub his body with oil. From that time, however, Bīr'bal had concealed himself. His Majesty then ordered the barber to come to court, and the Hindū Krōrī (Collector) got hold of some poor innocent traveller, charged him with murder, and kept him in concealment, giving out that he was Bīr'bal. The Krōrī could of course send no barber to court. He therefore killed the poor traveller to avoid detection, and reported that it was Bīr'bal in reality, but that he had since died. His Majesty went actually through a second mourning, but he ordered the Krōrī and several others to come to court. They were for some time tortured as a punishment for not having informed his Majesty before, and the Krōrī had, moreover, to pay a heavy fine.'

Bīr'bal founded the town of *Ak'bar'pur* and dwelt there, and in the *Nār'nāul* quarter of that town his descendants still exist.

No complete work by Bīr'bal has come down to us, but numerous verses and *bon-mots* attributed to him are still in every Hindū's mouth. An anonymous work, entitled the *Bīr'bar-nāmā,* can be bought for a few pice in any Bihār bazār. It is a collection of facetious tales, of which the heroes are Ak'bar and Bīr'bal, and in which the latter always gets the better by some witty or indecent retort. It is, in fact, the Indian Joe Miller's Jest Book. Some of the stories are the common property of all nations.

107. मनोहर दास कबि, the poet and Rājā *Manōhar Dās*, the Kachh'wāhā. Fl. 1577 A.D.

He was son of Rājā *Lōŋkaran*, the Kachh'wāhā, and was one of *Ak'bar's* commanders of 400. (See *Āīn-i-Akbarī*, trans., p. 494.) He wrote in Persian, in Sanskrit, and in the vernacular. In the first language he wrote under the name of *Tōsanī*.

108. अबदुल रहीम, *'Abdu'r Rahīm Khān'khānā Nawāb*, commonly called *Khān'khānā*, the son of *Bairam Khān*. B. 1556.[1]

Nir. He was not only learned in Arabic, Persian, Tur'kī, etc., but also in Sanskrit and Braj Bhākhā. He was much loved by *Ak'bar*. (See Blochmann's translation of *Āīn-i-Akbarī*, p. 334 and ff. He wrote under the *nom de guerre* of *Rahīm*, *ib.* p. 338.) His father was the famous Bairam Khān, to whom may justly be ascribed Humāyūn's conquest of India. (See Blochmann, p. 315.) Full particulars of his life will be found in the places above cited. Sib Siŋgh adds that he was not only a great patron of poets himself, but that also he wrote extremely learned (and difficult) çlōkas in Sanskrit, and that his *kabittas* and *dōhās* in all styles in the vernacular are admirable. Best of all are his *dōhās* on morals (नीति). Here his Persian works are not dealt with. It will be sufficient to mention his best known Persian work, a translation of Bābar's Chaghtāi Memoirs (*Wāqi'āt-i-Bābarī*). Amongst the poets who attended his court may be mentioned *Lachh'mī Nārāyan* (No. 124), of Mithilā.

109. मान सिङ्घ, Mahārāj *Mān Siŋgh*, the Kachh'wāhā of *Amēr*. B. 1535.

He was a great patron of learned men, and used to give *Hari Nāth* (No. 114) and other poets a lākh of rupees for a single verse. He was son of *Bhag'wān Dās*. (See *Āīn-i-Akbarī*, translation, p. 339, where a full account of his life is given.) He was a general of *Ak'bar's*, at first on the Kābul frontier, and subsequently in Bihār. He died in the Deccan in 1618 A.D., when sixty of his fifteen hundred wives burned themselves. The ground on which the Tāj at Āg'rā stands belonged to Mān Siŋgh.

---

[1] *I.e.* A.H. 964, which is the date given by Blochmann in passage cited below. Sib Siŋgh gives the date Sambat 1580, *i.e.* A.D. 1523.

The poets at his court wrote the *Mān Charitr'*, which is a very full account of his life and times. (See also Tod's *Rājasthan*, i, xv, and ii, 353; Calc. ed. ii, 390.)

110. अबुल फैज, *Abū'l Faiz alias Faizī*. B. 1547 A.D.

This is the famous son of Shekh *Mubārak*, brother of *Abū'l Fazl* and friend of *Ak'bar*. He was born A.H. 954 (A.D. 1547). See Blochmann's translation of the *Āīn-i-Akbarī*, p. 490.

He was an excellent Sanskrit scholar, and is the author of many detached verses (*doh'rā*) in the vernacular.

111. फहीम, *Fahīm*. B. cir. 1550 A.D.

According to Sib Siṅgh he was a younger brother of *Faizī* and *Abū'l Fazl*. I can, however, find no mention of him in the *Āīn-i-Akbarī*. He is the author of many detached verses (*doh'rā*) in the vernacular.

112. राम दास, Bābā *Rām Dās*, of *Gōp'chal*. Fl. 1550 A.D.

Rāg. He was father of *Sūr Dās* (No. 37), and was one of the court singers to the emperor *Ak'bar*. See *Āīn-i-Akbarī* (Blochmann's translation), p. 612. According to *Badāonī* he came from *Lakh'naū*. He appears to have been with *Bairām Khān* during his rebellion, and he received once from him one *lākh* of *tānkahs*, empty as Bairām's treasure chest was. He was first at the court of *Is'lēm Shāh*, and he was looked upon as second only to *Tān Sēn* (No. 60,) the most celebrated singer of Ak'bar's time.

113. नरहरि सहाय, the bard *Nar'hari Sahāy*, entitled *Mahapātr'*, of *As'nī*, district *Fatih'pur*. Fl. 1550 A.D.

? Rāg. He attended the court of the emperor *Ak'bar*, and was endowed by him with the village of *As'nī*. According to a curious tradition, when *Shēr Shāh* (fl. 1540) defeated *Humāyūn* the latter fled to the west, leaving a Bēgam named *Chōlī* at *Dillī*, who was captured by the conqueror. Shortly afterwards, Shēr Shāh being pleased with some verses of Nar'hari, told him to ask a boon. The bard accordingly asked that Chōlī Bēgam might be given to him, which the king granted. Nar'hari carried off Chōlī to *Bāndhō* (*Rīwā̃*), where, soon after, she gave birth to *Ak'bar*. The details of this tradition are certainly incorrect, as Ak'bar was born at *Amar'kōṭ*, in *Mār'wār*. He seems, however, to have been befriended as a boy by the king of Bāndhō. Cf. No. 24. See *Rep. Arch. Sur. Ind.* xvii, 101; xxi, 109. One of Nar'harī's sons was the poet *Hari Nāth* (No. 114). Descendants of Nar'harī still survive in *Banāras* and in *Bētī*, district *Rāy Barēlī*, and are scattered about in other parts of India. The village of As'nī is no longer in possession of his family, and his original house has been washed away by the Ganges. The ruins of the latter are now sold as rubble, and have become the day-haunts of jackals and other impure animals. Although no complete work of this poet has survived, numerous detached verses by him are still quoted.

Ak'bar gave him the title of *Mahāpātr'*, saying that other bards were vessels of virtue (*gun kā pātr'*), but he was a great vessel (*mahāpātr'*).

He is possibly the same as a *Nar'harī Dās* mentioned in the preface to Rāg.

114. हरि नाथ कबि, the bard *Hari Nāth*, entitled *Mahāpātr'*, of *As'nī*, district *Fatih'pur*. Fl. 1587 A.D.

A celebrated poet, and son of *Nar'hari* (No. 113), the court poet of the emperor *Ak'bar*. He made a tour from court to court, receiving rich presents for his verses; thus king *Nējā*[1] *Rām*, the Baghēl of *Bāndhō* (*Rīwā̃*), gave him a lākh of rupees for a single *dōhā*, and *Mān Singh* (No. 109) of *Amēr* gave him two lākhs for two *dōhās*. On his way home he met a mendicant of the Nāgā sect, who recited a *dōhā* to him, at which he was so pleased that he gave the beggar all the presents he had collected, and returned home empty handed. Arrived there he passed the remainder of his life squandering his father's savings in a similar manner.

115. करनेस कबि बन्दीजन, the poet and bard *Kar'nēs*, or *Karan*. B. *1554* A.D.

He used to visit the emperor *Ak'bar's* court in company with the poet *Nar'harī* (No. 113). He wrote three important works—the *Karnābharan*, the *Sruti-bhūkhan*, and the *Bhūp-bhūkhan*.

[1] This king's name is not mentioned in the list given in vol. xxi of *Rep. Arch. Sur. Ind.*

116. **मान राय,** the bard *Mān Rāy*, of *As'nī*, district *Fatih'-pur*. B. *1523* A.D.

117. **जगन्दीस कबि,** the poet *Jag'dīs*. B. *1531* A.D.

118. **जोध कबि,** the poet *Jōdh*. B. *1533* A.D.

These three all attended the court of the emperor *Ak'bar*.

119. **गङ्गा परन्साद,** *Gaŋgā Par'sād*, the Brāhman. Commonly known as *Gaŋg Kabi*, or the poet *Gaŋg*. B. *1538*.

Sun. He was a Brāhman of *Ek'nāūr*, district *Iṭāwā̃*. He was a bard attached to the court of *Ak'bar*. He received many presents from *Bīr'bal*, *Khān'khānā*, and others. He is not mentioned in Mr. Blochmann's translation of the *Āīn-i-Akbarī*. He is mentioned by Captain Price as having written on rhetoric in 1555 (*Hindee and Hindoostanee Selections*, Pref., p. x). Cf. Garcin de Tassy, i, 182.

120. **जैत कबि,** the poet *Jait*. B. *1544* A.D.

He attended the court of the emperor *Ak'bar*. He is possibly the same as a *Jait Rām Kabi* mentioned by Sib Siŋgh, without date, as a quietistic (शान्ति रस) poet.

121. **अम्रित कबि,** the poet *Amrit*. B. *1545* A.D.

122. **जगन्नज,** *Jagannaj*. Fl. (?) 1575 A.D.

123. **जगामग,** *Jagāmag*. Fl. (?) 1575 A.D.

These three all attended the court of the emperor *Ak'bar*.

124. **लछ्न्मी नारायन,** *Lachh'mī Nārāyan*, of Mithilā. Fl. 1600 A.D.

125. **परन्सिद्ध कबि,** the poet *Par'siddh*, the elder. B. *1533*.

These two attended the court of *'Abdu'r Raḥīm Khān'khānā* (No. 108).

126. होल राय कबि, the poet and bard *Hōl Rāy*, of *Hōl'pur*, district *Bārābaŋkī*. Fl. 1583 A.D.

His patron was Rājā *Haribans Rāy*, Dīwān of the emperor *Ak'bar*, who gave the poet a tract of land, on which he founded the village of Hōl'pur. Once *Tul'sī Dās* (No. 128) passed through that village and gave Hōl Rāy his brass vessel or *lōṭā*, which the latter set up as a god and worshipped. It is there still, and is worshipped to this day. The village is still owned by Hōl Rāy's descendants. *Giri Dhar* (No. 483), *Nīl Kaṇṭh* (No. 132), *Lachhirām* (No. 723), and *Sant Bak's* (No. 724), were all natives of Hōl'pur.

127. मुकुन्द सिङ्ह हाड़ा, Rājā *Mukund Siŋgh*, the *Hāṛā*, of *Kōṭā*. B. *1578*.

The ally of *Shāh Jahān* (1628—1658). He was himself a poet besides being a patron of poets. See Tod ii, 514; Calc. ed. ii, 553.

CHAPTER VI.

TUL'SI DAS.

128. गोसाँइँ तुलसी दास, the holy master *Tul'sī Dās*. Fl. 1600 A.D.; D. 1624 A.D.

Rāg. We now come to the greatest star in the firmament of mediæval Indian poetry, *Tul'sī Dās*, the author of the well-known vernacular *Rāmāyan* (Rāg.), which competes in authority with the Sanskrit work of *Vālmīki*.

I much regret that the materials available are so scanty; and it is the more tantalising to me that I have received information of a very full account of his life, entitled *Gosāī Charitr'*, by *Bēnī Mādhab Dās*, of *Pas'kā*, who lived in the poet's companionship. I have never been able to obtain a copy of this work, though I have long searched for it, and I have been compelled to base my account principally on the enigmatic verses of the *Bhakt Mālā* aided by the glosses of *Priyā Dās* and others. The text and literal translation of these will be found in the introduction to Mr. Growse's translation of the Rāmāyan, from which I have freely drawn.

The importance of Tul'sī Dās in the history of India cannot be overrated. Putting the literary merits of his work out of the question, the fact of its universal acceptance by all classes, from *Bhāgal'pur* to the *Pañjāb* and from the *Himālaya* to the *Nar'madā*, is surely worthy of note. "The book is in every one's hands,[1] from the court to the cottage, and is read or heard and appreciated alike by every class of the Hindū community, whether high or low, rich or poor, young or old." It has been interwoven into the life, character, and speech of the Hindū population for more than three hundred years, and is not only loved and admired by them for its poetic beauty, but is reverenced by them as their scriptures. It is

[1] Mr. Growse (from whom this quotation is taken) states that the professional Sanskrit Paṇḍits profess to despise Tul'sī Dās's work as an unworthy concession to the illiterate masses, but this has not been my experience.

the Bible of a hundred millions of people, and is looked upon by them as as much inspired as the Bible is considered inspired by the English clergyman. Paṇḍits may talk of the *Vēdas* and of the *Upaniṣads*, and a few may even study them; others may say they pin their faith on the *Purāṇas*: but to the vast majority of the people of *Hindūstān*, learned and unlearned alike, their sole norm of conduct is the so-called *Tul'sī-krit Rāmāyan*. It is indeed fortunate for Hindūstān that this is so, for it has saved the country from the tantric obscenities of Shaivism. *Rāmānand* was the original saviour of Upper India from the fate which has befallen Bengal, but *Tul'sī Dās* was the great apostle who carried his doctrine east and west and made it an abiding faith.

The religion he preached was a simple and sublime one,—a perfect faith in the name of God. But what is most remarkable in it, in an age of immorality, when the bonds of Hindū society were loosened and the Mughal empire being consolidated, was its stern morality in every sense of the word. Tul'sī was the great preacher of one's duty towards one's neighbour. *Vālmīki* praised *Bharat's* sense of duty, *Lachhman's* brotherly affection, and *Sītā's* wifely devotion, but *Tul'sī* taught them as an example.

So, too, in an age of license no book can be purer in tone than his *Rāmāyan*. He himself justly exclaims,—"Here are no prurient and seductive stories, like snails, frogs, and scum on the pure water of *Rām's* legend, and therefore the lustful crow and the greedy crane, if they do come, are disappointed." Other Vaishnava writers, who inculcated the worship of *Krish'n*, too often debased their muse to harlotry to attract their hearers; but *Tul'sī Dās* had a nobler trust in his countrymen, and that trust has been amply rewarded.

Tul'sī Dās was a *Sar'bariyā* Brāhman. He was born early in the sixteenth century and died at a good old age in 1624 A.D. As the old rhyme says:—

Sambata sōraha sāṁ asī, Asī Gaṅga ke tīra,
Sāwana sukalā sattamī, Tulasī tajeu sarīra :

—on the 7th of the light half of *Çrāvaṇa*, in Sambat 1680, *Tul'sī* left his body at *Asī*, on the bank of the *Ganges*.

According to the *Bhakt Sindhu* and the *Brihad Rāmāyan Māhātmya* his father's name was *Ātmā Rām*, his mother's name was *Hulasī*, and he was born at *Hastināpur*; but according to other authorities he was born at *Hājīpur*, near *Chitrakuṭ*. The usual tradition is, however, that *Rāj'pur*, in the district of *Bāḍā*, on the banks of the *Jamunā*, has the honour of being his birthplace. As a child he lived at *Sūkar'khēt* (*vulgo Sōrō*),[1] where he was first imbued with devotion to Rām. According to *Priyā Dās* (see Nos. 51 and 319) his wife first persuaded him to exchange an earthly for a divine love, and, incited by her remonstrances, he left her and went to *Banāras,* where he spent the greater part of his life, visiting frequently *Ajodhyā, Mathurā, Brindāban, Kuruchhētr' Prayāg* (Allāhābād), *Purukhōttam'purī,* and other holy places. The only other fact in his life about which there is any reasonable certainty (beyond the dates of some of his works) is that he was appointed arbitrator in a land dispute between two men, *Ānand Rām* and *Kanhāy.* The deed of arbitration in his handwriting is still in existence, and is dated Sambat 1669, or eleven years before his death. A photograph, transliteration, and translation of it, are appended to this work. A few legends mentioned by *Priyā Dās,* and given in full by Mr. Growse in the introduction to his translation of the Rāmāyan, may be briefly noted here. A grateful ghost introduced him to Hanumān, through whom he obtained a vision of Rām and Lachhman. He recognised a murderer, who piously uttered the name of Rām, as a saved man, and when challenged to prove his statement he did so by making the guilty man's offering accepted by Çiva. Some thieves came to rob him, but his house was guarded by a mysterious watchman, who was no other than Rām himself, and, instead of stealing, the thieves became converted and pure of heart. He restored a Brāhman to life.[2] His fame reached *Dillī,* where *Shāh Jahān* (1628—1658; but the poet died in 1624) was emperor. The monarch called upon him to perform a miracle and to produce the person of Rām, which Tul'sī Dās refusing to do, the king threw him into confinement. He was, however, speedily compelled to release him, for myriads of monkeys having collected about the prison began to demolish it and the adjacent buildings. Shāh Jahān having set the poet at liberty desired him to solicit some favour as a reparation for the indignity he had suffered. Tul'sī Dās accordingly requested him to quit ancient *Dillī,* which was the abode of Rām; and in compliance with this request the emperor left it and founded the new city, thence named *Shāh-Jahān-ābād.* After this Tul'sī went to *Brindāban,* where he had an interview with *Nābhā Dās* (the author of the *Bhakt Mālā*). There he strenuously advocated the worship of Rām in preference

[1] Rām., Bā., Dōhā, 87.

[2] The following is nearly in Wilson's words.

to that of Krish'n, though the latter god appeared in person and assured him that there was no difference between the two. Out of this tissue of childish legends it is perhaps possible to extract a few threads of fact; but till we can find a copy of the *Gosāī̃ Charitr'* there does not appear to be much hope of our being able to do so.

His most famous work is the *Rām-Charit-Mānas,* 'the Lake of the Gests of Rām,' which he commenced to write in *Ajodhyā* on Tuesday, the 9th Chaitra, Sambat 1631 (A.D. 1574-75).[1] It is often incorrectly called the *Rāmāyan,* or the *Tul'sī-krit-Rāmāyan,* or (alluding to its metre) the *Chāūpāī Rāmāyan,* but, according to the forty-fourth *chāūpāī* of the *Bāl Kāṇḍ* of the poem, the above is its full and proper name. Two copies of this work are said to have existed in the poet's own handwriting. One of them, which was kept at *Rāj'pur,* has disappeared, all but the second book. The legend is that the whole copy which existed was stolen, and that the thief being pursued flung the manuscript into the river *Jamunā,* whence only the second book was rescued. I have photographs of ten pages of this copy, and the marks of water are evident. The other copy exists in *Malihābād* (so Sib Siṇgh ; Growse says in the temple of Sītā Rām at *Banāras*), of which only one leaf is missing. I am in possession of an accurate *literatim* copy of so much of the Rāj'pur manuscript as exists. I have also a printed copy of the poem carefully compared with, and corrected from, a manuscript in the possession of the Mahārāj of Banāras, which was written in Sambat 1704 (A.D. 1647), or only about twenty-four years after the author's death.

Little as the *Rām-Charit-Mānas* is known to European students, still less is known of the poet's other works. Those which I have seen and read are the following :—

(1) The *Gītābalī* (Rāg.).—This is the story of Rām told in the form of sonnets adapted for singing. There are several incorrect editions of it in print, some of which have commentaries of varying excellence.

(2) The *Kabittābalī* or *Kabitta Rāmāyan* (Rāg.).—It deals with the same subject, and is in the *Kabitta* metre.

(3) The *Dōhābalī* or *Dōhā Rāmāyan* (Rāg.).—As its name imports, it is in the *dōhā* metre. It is rather a moral work than an epic poem. I am not sure that it is not a collection of *dōhās* from his other works by a later hand. I have, at any rate, been able to identify many of them.

---

[1] Rām. Bā. ch. 42.

(4) The *Chhappai Rāmāyan*.—In the *chhappai* metre. I have only seen one incorrect and unintelligible manuscript of this work, from which an edition of the same character has been printed.

(5) *Sat Saī* (Rāg.).—A collection (*Sapta Çatikā*) of seven hundred emblematic *dōhās*.

(6) The *Pañch Ratan* (Rāg.), or five jewels.—A set of five short poems, usually grouped together. They are (*a*) the *Jānakī Maŋgal*, (*b*) the *Pārbatī Maŋgal*, (*c*) the *Bairāgya Sandīpinī*, (*d*) *Rām Lālā kar Nah'chhū*, (*e*) the *Bar'wai Rāmāyan* (Rāg.). The first two of these are songs celebrating the marriages of Sītā and Gaurī respectively; the third is a didactic treatise; the fourth is a song in honour of the *Nah'chhū* or ceremonial nail-paring of Rām at his wedding; and the fifth, a short history of Rām in the *Bar'wai* metre.

(7) The *Srī Rām Agyā*, also called the *Rām Sagunābalī*.—A collection of seven books of seven chapters, each of seven *dōhās* to each chapter. It is a collection of omens connected with the life of Rām. I suspect it is spurious, and partly made up of extracts from the poet's other works. I have met with one very inferior commentary upon it.

(8) The *Saŋkaṭ Mōchan*.—A short didactic work. I have only seen it in one vilely-printed edition.

(9) The *Binay Pattrikā* (Rāg.).—A collection of 279 hymns to Rām: much admired, and deservedly so. It has often been printed, and has a very fair commentary by *Sib Par'kās* (No. 643).

(10) The *Hanumān Bāhuk* (Rāg.).—A collection of sonnets in honour of *Hanumān*, who according to tradition gave him a vision of Rām and Lachhman.

In addition to these the *Sib Siŋgh Sarōj* mentions the following:—

(11) *Rām Salākā* (Rāg.).

(12) The *Kundaliyā Rāmāyan*.

(13) The *Kaṛ'kā Rāmāyan*.

(14) The *Rōlā Rāmāyan*.

(15) The *Jhūl'nā Rāmāyan*, none of which I have seen. The last four are named after the metres in which they are written.

(16) A *Krishnābalī* (Rāg.) in the Braj dialect is also printed and sold in the bazārs. It deals with the life of Krish'n, and I do not believe that it is by the *Tul'sī Dās* whom we are now considering.

Many of these have been printed, always most incorrectly, and some with commentaries. One of the most highly esteemed commentaries on the *Rām-Charit-Mānas* is that of *Rām Charan Dās*. The best on the

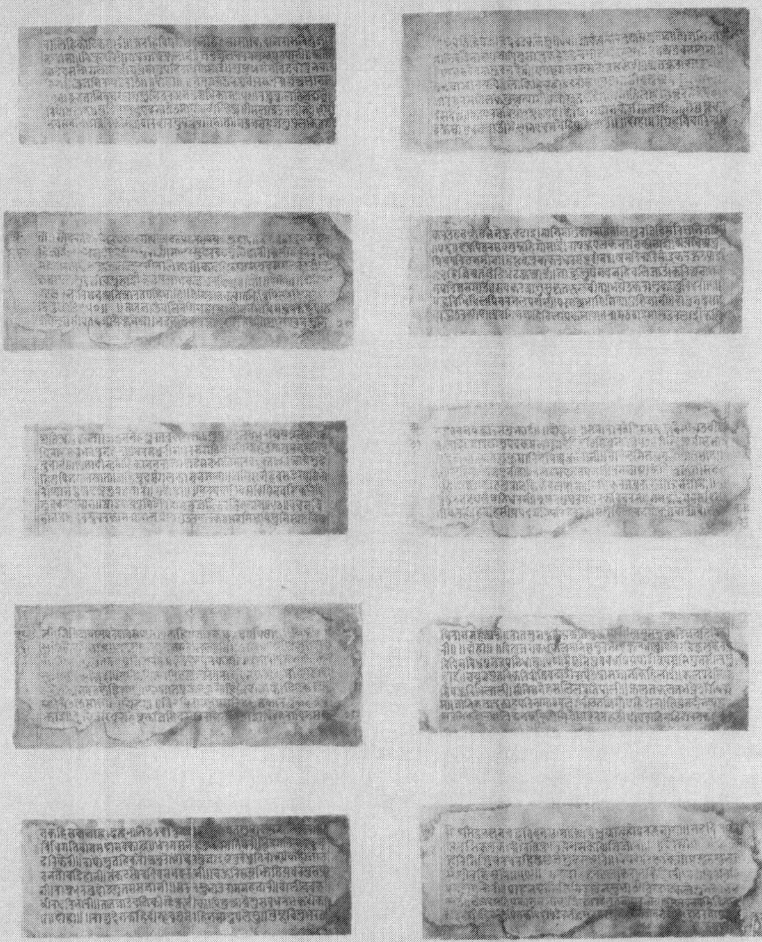

REDUCED FACSIMILE OF TEN PAGES OF THE RÁÑPUR RÁMAYAN.

Gītābalī, the *Kabittābalī*, and the *Sat Saī* are by *Bāij'nāth*. Rām Charan Dās's commentary has been printed by Nawal Kishōr, of Lakh'-naū, but is now out of print. The other commentaries can be bought in any Indian bazār. All the commentators have a great tendency to avoid difficulties, and to give to simple passages mystical meanings, which Tul'sī Dās never intended. They are unfortunately utterly wanting in the critical faculty. Though there are abundant materials for obtaining an absolutely accurate text of at least the Rām-Charit-Mānas, the commentators have never dreamed of referring to them, but have preferred trusting their inner consciousness. As an extreme example, I may mention one who drew up a scheme of the number of verses which each section of each canto *ought* to have, in a numerically decreasing order, after the pattern of the steps of a bathing *ghāṭ*, because the poem is called a lake (*mānas*). Nothing could be prettier than this idea; and so he hacked and hewed his unfortunate text to fit this Procrustean bed, and then published it with considerable success. It never occurred to him or his readers to see if this was what Tul'sī Dās had written; and if they had done so, the ludicrous nature of his theory would have been evident at the first glance.

Regarding Tul'sī Dās's style, he was a master of all varieties, from the simplest flowing narration to the most complex emblematic verses. He wrote always in the old Bais'wārī dialect, and, once the peculiarities of this are mastered, his *Rām-Charit-Mānas* is delightful and easy reading. In his *Gītābalī* and *Kabittābalī* he is more involved, but still readable with pleasure; in his *Dōhābalī* he is sententious; and in his *Sat Saī* as difficult and obscure as any admirer of the *Nalōdaya* could wish. The Sat Saī is a veritable *tour de force*, and I am glad that this, almost the oldest specimen[1] of a kind of writing which was brought to perfection fifty years later by *Bihārī Lāl* (No. 196) (the mine of commentators), is being edited with a commentary by Professor *Bihāri Lāl Chaūbē* in the *Bibliotheca Indica*.[2] The *Binay Pattrikā* is again in another style. It is a book of prayers, often of the most elevated description, but its difficulties are very unsatisfactorily elucidated by either of the two commentaries on it which I have seen.

---

[1] It was written (Sat. i. 21) in Sambat 1642, *i.e.* A.D. 1585. Bidyāpati's emblematic verses were written about A.D. 1400.

[2] Since this was written an edition of this work, with a commentary by Bāij'nāth, the editor of the Gītābalī and Kabittābalī, has been published in 1886 by Nawal Kishōr, of Lakh'naū.

Regarding his poetic powers I think it is difficult to speak too highly. His characters live and move with all the dignity of a heroic age. Das'rath, the man of noble resolves which fate had doomed to be unfruitful; Rām, of lofty and unbending rectitude, well contrasted with his loving but impetuous brother Lachhman; Sītā, the 'perfect woman nobly planned;' and Rāban, like Das'rath, predestined to failure, but fighting with all his demon force against his fate, almost like Satan in Milton's epic, the protagonist of half the poem,—all these are as vividly before my mind's eye as I write as any character in the whole range of English literature. Then what a tender devotion there is in Bharat's character, which by its sheer truth overcomes the false schemes of his mother Kaikēyī and her maid. His villains, too, are not one black picture. Each has his own character, and none is without his redeeming virtue.

For sustained and varied dramatic interest I suppose the *Rām-Charit-Mānas* is his best work; but there are fine passages in his other poems. What can be more charming than the description of Rām's babyhood and boyhood in the commencement of the *Gītābalī*, or the dainty touches of colour given to the conversation of the village women as they watch Rām, Lachhman, and Sītā treading their dreary way during their exile. Again, what mastery of words is there in the *Sundar Kāṇḍ* of the *Kabittābalī* throughout the description of the burning of Laṅkā. We can hear the crackling of the flames and the crash of the falling houses, the turmoil and confusion amongst the men, and the cries of the helpless women as they shriek for water.

Still even Tul'sī Dās was not able to rise altogether superior to the dense cloud which fashion had imposed upon Indian poetry. I must confess that his battle descriptions are often luridly repulsive, and sometimes overstep the border which separates the tragic from the ludicrous. To Native minds these are the finest passages which he has written; but I do not think that the cultivated European can ever find much pleasure in them. He was hampered, too, by the necessity of representing Rām as an incarnation of Vishnu, which leads him into what, although only meet adoration to the pious believer, sounds to us *Mlēchchhas* as too gross hyperbole.

The reasons for the excellence of this great poet's work are not far to seek. The most important of all was the great modesty of the man. The preface to the *Rām-Charit-Mānas* is one of the most remarkable portions of the book. *Kālidāsa* may begin his *Raghuvaṃça* with a comparison of himself to a dwarf, and of his powers over language to a skiff on the boundless ocean; but from under this modest statement there gleams a consciousness of his own superiority. His modesty is evidently a mock one, and the poet is really saying to himself all the time, 'I shall soon show my readers how learned I am, and what a command I have over all the nine *rasas*.' But (and this is another reason for his superiority) Tul'sī never wrote a line in which he did not himself believe heart and soul. He was full of his theme, the glory and love of his master; and so immeasurably above him did that glory and that love seem, that he was full of humility with regard to himself. As he expresses it :—'My intellect is beggarly, while my ambition is imperial. May good people all pardon my presumption and listen to my childish babbling, as a father and mother delight to hear the lisping prattle of their little one.' *Kālidāsa* took Rām as a peg on which to hang his graceful verses; but *Tul'sī Dās* wove wreaths of imperishable fragrance, and humbly laid them at the feet of the god whom he adored.[1] One other point I would urge, which has, I believe, escaped the notice of even Native students of our author. He is, perhaps, the only great Indian poet who took his similes direct from the book of Nature and not from his predecessors. He was so close an observer of concrete things, that many of his truest and simplest passages are unintelligible to his commentators, who were nothing but learned men, and who went through the beautiful world around them with eyes blinded by their books. Shakespeare, we know, spoke of the white reflection of the willow leaves in the water, and thus puzzled all his editors, who said in their wisdom that willow leaves were green. It was, I think, Charles Lamb who thought of going to the river and seeing if Shakespeare was right, and who thereby swept away a cloud of proposed emendations.[2] So, too, it has been reserved for Mr. Growse to point out that Tul'sī Dās knew far more about Nature than his commentators do.

It remains now to point out the necessity there is of printing a correct text of this poet's works. At present the printed bazār editions

[1] Bābū Jawāhir Mall, of Dāūd'nagar, in the district of Gayā, informs me that he knew an old man whose ancestor knew the poet, and that Tul'sī Dās told the ancestor that he had never written a line of poetry into which either the letter र *r* or the letter म *m* (the first and last letters of the word Rām) did not come. This (if found to be true) is a valuable test for deciding whether doubtful passages are genuine or not.

[2] The under surface, and therefore the reflection, of the willow-leaf is white.

available are very deficient. The best of them is that by Paṇḍit *Rām Jasan*; but he, like all the other editors, has printed only a modernised copy of the *textus receptus*. I have carefully compared the latter with the original text, and am in a position to state that anything more misleading can hardly be imagined. Tul'sī Dās wrote phonetically the words as they were pronounced at his time, and in an archaic dialect. In the printed books the dialect is altered to the standard of the modern Hindī, and the spelling improved (?) according to the rules of Pāṇini. Examples of the modernisation of the dialect are the following :—Tul'sī Dās uses the short *u* as the termination of the nominative singular, leaving the crude base in *a* for its legitimate purposes in composition, thus following the rules of the Apabhraṁça Prākṛit. Thus he wrote *kapi-kaṭaku*, an army of monkeys; *prabala-mōha-dalu*, a powerful band of delusions; and so on: but all the modern editions give *-kaṭaka* and *-dala*, according to the modern pronunciation. So also modern editors write *prasāda*, 'favour,' for the original *pasāu*; *bhujaŋginī*, 'snake,' for original *bhuaŋginī*; *yajñavalkya* for *jagabaliku*; *bandāū*, 'I revere,' for *bandaū*; *bhakti*, 'faith,' for *bhagati*, and so on. Examples can be gathered in almost every line. Instances of alteration of spelling are equally numerous. One example must suffice. Tul'sī Dās evidently pronounced the name of Rām's father as *Dasarathu*, for that is the way he wrote it; but modern editors write the Sanskrit *Daçaratha*, which is not even the way it is pronounced nowadays. But there are other and greater errors than these in the *textus receptus*. It abounds in *lacunæ*. Whole pages are sometimes omitted, and minor changes occur in every page. In short, opening the printed edition at random, I count no fewer than thirty-five variations from the original, some most important ones, in one page of twenty-three lines. I am glad, therefore, to be able to record that an enterprising publisher of Patna (Bābū *Rām Dīn Siŋgh*, of the Khaḍg Bilās Press, Bāŋkīpur) is now engaged in publishing a text of the Rām-Charit-Mānas founded on the old manuscripts I have already mentioned.

In the Addendum to this chapter I give samples of the true text of the Rām-Charit-Mānas, founded on the Banāras and Rāj'pur manuscripts, already alluded to, together with photographs of the originals. The footnotes show the readings of the *textus receptus*. I am indebted to the kindness of Rājā Siva Prasād, C.S.I., for these photographs.

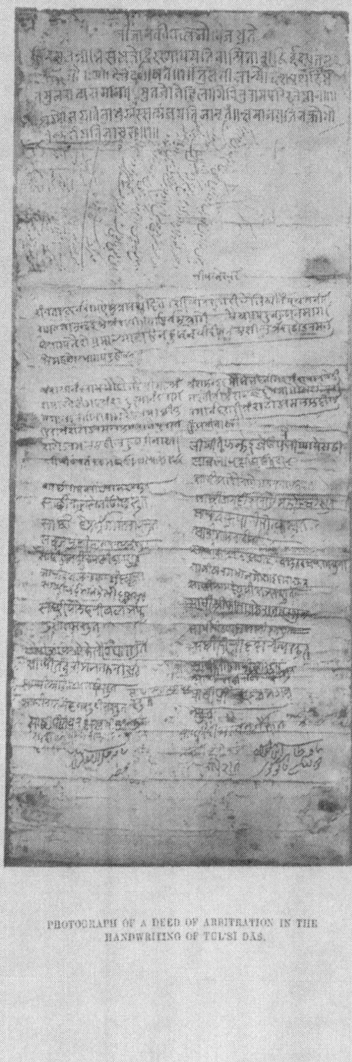

PHOTOGRAPH OF A DEED OF ARBITRATION IN THE HANDWRITING OF TUL'SI DĀS.

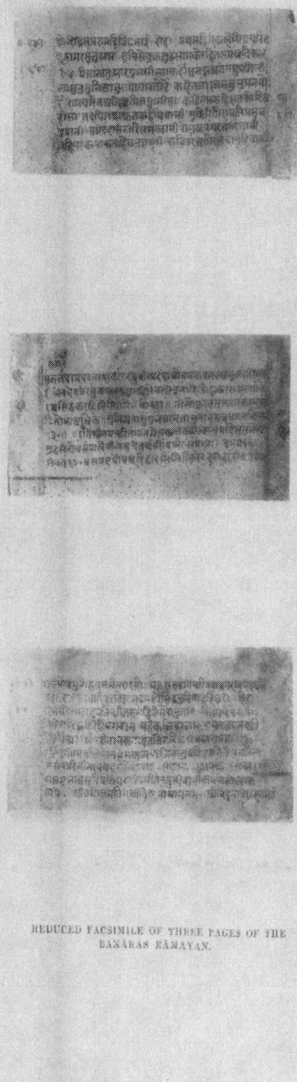

REDUCED FACSIMILE OF THREE PAGES OF THE BANĀRAS RĀMAYAN.

129. निपट निरञ्जन स्वामी, the master *Nipaṭ Nirañjan*. B. *1593* A.D.

Nir. According to Sib Siŋgh this master ranks as a holy man with *Tul'sī Dās*. Besides hundreds of short poems which have not been collected, he is the author of the *Sānt Sar'sī* and the *Nirañjan Saŋgrah*.

130. बेनी माधव दास, *Bēnī Mādhab Dās*, of *Pas'kā*, district *Gōṇḍā*. Fl. 1600 A.D.

He was a disciple of the holy master *Tul'sī Dās*, and was his constant companion. He wrote a biography of him entitled *Gosāī Charitr'* (quoted in this work as 'Gō.') and died in *1642* A.D.

131. निधि कबि, the poet *Nidhi*. Fl. 1600.

Go., (?) Rāg.

132. नील कण्ठ मिसर, *Nīl Kaṇṭh Misar*, of the *Dōāb*. Fl. 1600 A.D.

Go., Nir.

133. नीला धर कबि, the poet *Nīlā Dhar*. Fl. 1600 A.D.

Gō., Nir.

ADDENDA TO CHAPTER VI.

I.—THE TEXT OF TUL'SĪ DĀS.

In order to show how the text of Tul'sī Dās's works has been altered in the course of centuries, the following extracts from the Rāmāyan are given, exactly as taken from the oldest manuscripts in existence. In the footnotes are given the variations of the best printed editions. The manuscripts used are those referred to in Chapter VI, namely the Rāj'pur copy of the Ajodhyā Kāṇḍ, said to be in the poet's own handwriting, and the Banāras copy, made only twenty-four years after his death.

FROM THE *Bāl Kāṇḍ (Banāras MS.)*.

(The footnotes show the variations of the *textus receptus*.)

Chaūpāī.

Kō Shiwa[1] sama Rāmahi[2] priya bhāī ||.

Dōhā.

Prathamahi maī kahi Shiwa-charita
Būjhā maramu tumhāra | [3]
Suchi sēwaka tumha[4] Rāma kē
Rahita samasta bikāra || 104 ||[5]

Chaūpāī.

Maī[6] jānā tumhāra guna sīlā |
Kahaū sunahu[7] aba Raghu-pati-līlā ||
Sunu muni āju samāgama tōrē[8]
Kahi na jāi[9] jasa sukhu[10] mana mōrē ||[11]
Rāma-charita ati amita munīsā |
Kahi na sakahi[12] sata kōṭi ahīsā ||
Tadapi jathā shruta[13] kahaū bakhānī |
Sumiri Girā-pati Prabhu dhanu-pānī ||
Sārada dāru-nāri-sama, Swāmī |
Rāmu[14] sūtra-dhara antara-jāmī ||.
Jehi para kṛipā karahi janu[15] jānī |
Kabi-ura ajira nachāwahi[16] Bānī ||

FROM THE *Ajodhyā Kāṇḍ (Rāj'pur MS.)*.

Chaūpāī.

(Dēhī ku)chālihi kōṭi ka[17] gārī ||
Jarahī bikhama jara[18] lēhi usāsā |
Kawani[19] Rāma binu jīwana-āsā ||
Bipula[20] biyōga prajā akulānī |
Janu[21] jala-chara-gana sūkhata pānī ||
Ati bikhāda-basa lōga logāī[22] |
Gayē mātu pahī[23] Rāmu[24] gosāī[25] ||
Mukhu[26] prasanna chita chaū-guna chāū |
Miṭā sōchu[27] jani rākhai[28] rāū ||

Dōhā.

Nawa gayandu Raghu-bīra-manu[29]
Rāju[30] alāna samāna |
Chhūṭa jāni bana-gawanu[31] suni
Ura-anandu[32] adhikāna || 51[33] ||

---

[1] Siwa.
[2] Rāmahī.
[3] Prathama kahē maī Siwa-charita būjhā marama tumhāra |
[4] tuma.
[5] 112.
[6] maī.
[7] sunahū.
[8] tōrē.
[9] jāya.
[10] sukha.
[11] mōrē.
[12] sakahī.
[13] sruta.
[14] Rāma.
[15] karahī jana.
[16] nachāwahī. *One edition of text. rec. gives* anī *for* bānī.
[17] hu.
[18] jwara.
[19] kawana.
[20] Bikula.
[21] Jimi.
[22] lugāī.
[23] pahā.
[24] Rāma.
[25] gusāī.
[26] Mukha.
[27] ıhaī sōcha.
[28] rākhahī.
[29] gayanda Raghu-bansa-mani.
[30] Rāja.
[31] gawana.
[32] ānāda.
[33] 50.

Chaūpāī.

Raghu-kula-tilaka jōri doū[1] hāthā |
Mudita mātu-pada nāyeu[2] māthā ||
Dīnhi[3] asīsa lāī ura līnhē |
Bhūkhana basana nichhāwari kīnhē ||
Bāra bāra mukha chumbati[4] mātā |
Nayana nēha-jalu[5] pulakita gātā ||
Gōda rākhi puni hṛidaya lagāē[6] |
Shrawata[7] prēma-rasa payada suhāē[8] ||
Prēmu pramōdu[9] na kachhu kahi jāī |
Raŋka Dhanada-padawī janu pāī ||
Sādara sundara badanu[10] nihārī |
Bōlī madhura bachana mahatārī ||
'Kahahu, Tāta, jananī bali-hārī |
Kabahī lagana muda-maŋgala-kārī ||
Sukṛita-sīla-sukha-sīwa[11] suhāī |
Janama-lābha kaï awadhi[12] aghāī ||

Dōhā.

Jehi chāhata nara-nāri saba
Ati ārata ehi[13] bhā̃ti |
Jimi chātaka-chātaki trikhita[14]
Bṛiṣṭi sarada-ritu[15] swāti || 52[16] ||

Chaūpāī.

Tāta jāū bali bēgi nahāhū[17] |
Jō mana bhāwa madhura kachhu khāhū ||
Pitu samīpa taba jāyehu bhaïā |
Bhaï baḍi[18] bāra jāi bali maïā' ||
Mātu-bachana suni[19] ati anukūlā |
Janu sanēha-sura taru kē phūlā ||
Sukha-makaranda-bharē Shriya[20]-mūlā |
Nirakhi Rāma-manu bhawaru[21] na bhūlā ||
Dharama[22]-dhurīna dharama[23] gati jānī |
Kaheu mātu sana ati mṛidu bānī ||
'Pitā dīnha mohi kānana-rājū |
Jahā̃ saba bhā̃ti mōra baḍa[24] kājū ||
Āyesu dēhi[25] mudita mana mātā |
Jēhi[26] muda-maŋgala kānana jātā ||
Jani sanēha-basa ḍarapasi bhōrē[27] |
Ānā̃du amba[28] anugraha tōrē[29] ||

Dōhā.

Barakha[30] chāri-dasa bipina basi
Kari pitu-bachana-pramāna |
Āī[31] pāya puni dēkhihaū
Manu[32] jani karasi malāna' || 53[33] ||

Chaūpāī.

Bachana binīta madhura Raghubara kē |
Sara sama lagē mātu-ura kara kē ||
Sahami sūkhi suni sītali[34] bānī |
Jimi jawāsa pare[35] pāwasa-pānī ||
Kahi na jāï kachhu hṛidaya-bikhādū |
Manahū mṛigī suni[36] kēhari-nādū ||
Nayana sajala,[37] tana[38] thara thara kāpī[39] |
Mājahi khāï mīna janu māpī[40] ||

---

[1] dwaū.
[2] nāyaū.
[3] Dīnha.
[4] chūmati.
[5] jala.
[6] lagāī.
[7] Srawata.
[8] suhāī.
[9] Prēma-pramōda.
[10] badana.
[11] sīwa.
[12] Janma-lābha kahi (*or* lahi) awadha.
[13] ihi.
[14] chātaki-chātaka triṣita.
[15] ṛitu.
[16] 51.
[17] anhāhū.
[18] baṛi.
[19] Here ends leaf 28 of the MS.
[20] Shrī.
[21] Rāma-mana bhā̃wara.
[22] Dharma.
[23] dharma.
[24] baṛa.
[25] Āyasu dēhu.
[26] Jehi.
[27] bhōrē.
[28] Ānā̃da mātu.
[29] tōrē.
[30] Barkha.
[31] Āya.
[32] Mana.
[33] 52.
[34] sītala.
[35] para.
[36] janu sahame kari.
[37] Salila.
[38] tanu.
[39] kā̃pī.
[40] Mājā manahū mīna kahā bvānī.

Dhari dhīraju[1] suta-badanu[2] nihārī |
Gadagada[3]-bachana kahati mahatārī ||
Tāta pitahi tumha[4] prāna-piārē |
Dēkhi mudita nita charita tumhārē ||
Rāju[5] dēna kahū̃[6] subha dina sādhā |
Kaheu jāna bana kehi aparādhā ||
Tāta sunāwahu mōhi nidānū |
Kō dina-kara-kula bhayeu[7] kṛisānū' ||

Dōhā.

Nirakhi Rāma-rukha sachiwa-suta.
Kāranu[8] kaheu bujhāī |
Suni prasaṅgu[9] rahi mūka jimi[10]
Dasā barani nahi[11] jāī || 54[12] ||

Chāū̃pāī.

Rākhi na sakaī[13] na kahi saka jāhū |
Duhū̃ bhā̃ti ura dāruna dāhū ||
Likhata sudhā-kara, gā[14] likhi Rāhū |
Bidhi-gati bāma sadā saba kāhū ||
Dharama[15]-sanēha ubhaya mati ghērī |
Bhaī gati sā̃pa chhuchhundari kērī ||
Rākhā̃ū̃ sutahi karā̃ū̃[16] anurōdhū |
Dharamu[17] jāī aru bandhu-birōdhū ||
Kahā̃ū̃ jāna bana tā̃ū̃ baḍi[18] hānī |
Saṅkaṭa sōcha bibasa[19] bhaī rānī ||
Bahuri sumujhi tiya-dharamu[20] sayānī |
Rāmu Bharatu doū[21] suta-sama jānī ||

Sarala subhāū[22] Rāma-mahatārī |
Bōlī bachana dhīra dhari bhārī ||
'Tāta, jāū̃ bali, kīnhehu[23] nīkā |
Pitu-āyesu[24] saba dharama ka[25] ṭīkā ||

Dōhā.

Rāju[26] dēna kahi,[27] dīnha banu[28]
Mōhi na sō[29] dukha-lēsa |
Tumha[30] binu Bharatahi bhū-patihi
Prajahi prachaṇḍa kalēsa || 55[31] ||

Chāū̃pāī.

Jā̃ū̃[32] kēwala pitu-āyesu[33] tātā |
Tā̃ū̃ jani jāhu jāni baḍi mātā[34] ||
Jā̃ū̃[35] pitu-mātu kaheu[36] bana jānā |
Tā̃ū̃ kānana sata Awadha samānā ||
Pitu bana dēwa, mātu bana-dēwī |
Khaga mṛiga charana-sarōruha-sēwī ||
Antahu uchita nṛipahi bana-bāsū |
Baya bilōki hiya hōī[37] harāsū ||
Baḍa[38] bhāgī banu,[39] Awadha abhāgī |
Jō[40] Raghu-bansa-tilaka tumha[41] tyāgī ||
Jā̃ū̃[42] suta kahā̃ū̃ saṅga mohi lēhū |
Tumharē hṛidaya hōī sandēhū ||
Pūta[43] parama priya tumha[44] saba-hī kē |
Prāna prāna kē jīwana jī ke ||
Tē tumha[45] kahahu mātu bana jā̃ū̃ |
Mā̃ī[46] suni bachana bā̃ṭhi pachhitā̃ū̃ ||

[1] dhīraja.
[2] badana.
[3] Gadgada.
[4] tuma.
[5] Rāja.
[6] kahā̃.
[7] bhayā̃ū̃.
[8] kārana.
[9] prasaṅga.
[10] mūka-gati.
[11] nahī.
[12] 53.
[13] sakahī. Here ends leaf 29 of MS.
[14] likhi gā.
[15] Dharma.
[16] hōī.
[17] Dharma.
[18] baṛi.
[19] bikala.
[20] dharma.
[21] Rāma Bharsta dwā̃ū̃.
[22] subhāwa.
[23] kīnheū
[24] āyasu.
[25] dharma ke.
[26] Rāja.
[27] kahā̃.
[28] bana.
[29] muhi na sōcha.
[30] Tuma.
[31] 54.
[32] Jā̃ū̃.
[33] āyasu.
[34] jāī bali mātā
[35] Jā̃ū̃.
[36] kahā̃ī.
[37] hōta.
[38] Baṛa.
[39] bana.
[40] Jā̃ū̃.
[41] tuma.
[42] Jā̃ū̃.
[43] Putra.
[44] tuma.
[45] Tuma.
[46] Mā̃ī.

Dōhā.

Ehi[1] bichāri nahi[2] karaū haṭha.
Jhūṭha sanēhu baḍhāi[3] |
Māni mātu kara[4] nāta bali
Surati bisari jani jāi || 56[5] ||

Chaūpāī.

Dēwa pitara saba tumhahi gosāī[6] |
Rākhahū[7] palaka nayana kī nāī ||
Awadhi ambu, priya parijana mīnā |
Tumha[8] karunā-'kara dharama[9]-dhurīnā ||
Asa bichāri soī karahu upāī |
Saba-hi jiata jēhi[10] bhēṭahu āī ||
Jāhu sukhēna banahī bali jāū |
Kari anātha jana parijana gāū ||
Saba kara āju sukṛita phala bītā |
Bhayeu karālu kālu[11] biparītā' ||
Bahu-bidhi bilapi charana lapaṭānī |
Parama abhāgini āpuhi jānī ||
Dāruna dusaha dāhu[12] ura byāpā |
Barani na jāhī[13] bilāpa-kalāpā ||
Rāma uṭhāī mātu ura lāī[14] |
Kahi mṛidu bachana bahuri samujhāī[15] ||

Dōhā.

Samāchāra tehi samaya sun
Sīya uṭhī akulāī |
Jāi sāsu-pada-kamala-juga[16]
Bandi baiṭhi siru[17] nāī || 57[18] ||

Chaūpāī.

Dīnhi[19] asīsa sāsu mṛidu bānī |
Ati sukumāri dēkhi akulānī ||
Baiṭhi namita mukha sōchati Sītā |
Rūpa-rāsi pati-prēma-punītā ||
'Chalana chahata bana jīwana-nāthū[20] |
Kehi sukṛitī[21] sana hōihi sāthū[22] ||
Kī tanu-prāna, ki kēwala prānā |
Bidhi karatabu[23] kachhu jāi[24] na jānā' ||
Chāru charana-nakha lēkhati dharanī |
Nūpura mukhara madhura kabi baranī ||
Manahū prēma-basa binatī karahī |
'Hamahī Sīya-pada jani pariharahī' ||
Mañju bilōchana mōchati bārī |
Bōlī dēkhi[25] Rāma-mahatārī ||
'Tāta sunahu Siya ati sukumārī |
Sāsu sasura parijanahi piārī[26] ||

Dōhā.

Pitā Janaka bhūpāla-mani
Sasura bhānu-kula-bhānu |
Pati rawi-kula-kairawa-bipina
Bidhu guna-rūpa-nidhānu || 58[27] ||

Chaūpāī.

Maī puni putra-badhū priya pāī |
Rūpa-rāsi guna-sīla suhāī ||
Nayana-putari kari[28] prīti baḍhāī[29] |
Rākheū prāna Jānakihi lāī ||
Kalapa-bēli[30] jimi bahu bidhi lālī |
Sīchi sanēha-salila pratipālī ||
Phūlata phalata bhayeu[31] bidhi bāmā |
Jāni na jāi kāha parināmā ||
Palāga-pīṭha taji gōda hīḍōrā |
Siya na dīnha[32] pagu awani kaṭhōrā ||

1 Yaha.
2 nahī. Here ends leaf 30 of the MS.
3 sanēha baṛhaī.
4 kē.
5 55.
6 tumahi gusāī.
7 Rākhahu.
8 Tuma.
9 dharma.
10 jiyata jehi.
11 Bhayē karāla kāla.
12 dāha.
13 jāī.
14 lāwā.
15 bahuta samujhāwā.
16 paga-kamala-yuga.
17 sira.
18 56.
19 Dīnha.
20 nāthā.
21 Kawana sukṛita.
22 sāthā.
23 karataba.
24 jāta.
25 Here ends leaf 31 of MS
26 parijanahī pyārī
27 57.
28 iwa.
29 barhāī.
30 Kalpa-bōli.
31 bhayē.
32 dīna.

Jiana-mūri[1] jimi jogawata[2] rahaũ[3] |
Dīpa-bāti nahi[4] ṭārana kahaũ[5] ||
Soĩ[6] Siya chalana chahati bana sāthā |
Āyesu[7] kāha[8] hōi Raghu-nāthā ||
Chanda[9]-kirana-rasa-rasika chakōrī |
Rawi-rukha nayana sakaĩ kimi jōrī ||

Dōhā.

Kari kēhari nisi-chara charahī̃
Duṣṭa jantu bana bhūri |
Bikha-bāṭikā ki sōha suta
Subhaga sā̃jīwani[10] mūri || 59[11] ||

Chaũpāī.

Bana hita kōla kirāta-kisōrī |
Rachī Birañchi bikhaya-sukha[12]-bhōrī ||
Pāhana-kṛimi jimi kaṭhina subhāū |
Tinahi kalēsu[13] na kānana kāū ||
Kaĩ tāpasa-tiya kānana jōgū[14] |
Jinha[15] tapa-hētu tajā saba bhōgū ||
Siya bana basihi tāta kehi bhā̃tī[16] |
Chitra-likhita kapi dēkhi ḍerātī ||
Sura-sara-subhaga-banaja-bana-chārī |
Ḍābara-jōgu[17] ki hansa-kumārī'

Conclusion of the Kis'kindhā Kāṇḍ[18] *(Banāras MS.).*

(The two following extracts are given for the sake of the colophons.)

Chhand.[19]

(Jō sunata gāwata kahata sa)mujhata
parama pada nara pāwaī |
Raghu-bīra-pada-pāthōja madhu-kara
Dāsa Tulasī gāwaī ||

Dōhā.

Bhawa-bhēkha-ja-Raghu-nātha-jasu[20]
Sunahi jē nara aru nārı |
Tinha kara sakala manōratha
Siddha karahī Trisirā-'ri[21] ||

Sōraṭhā.

Nīlōtpala tana[22] syāma
Kāma kōṭi sōbhā adhika |
Sunia[23] tāsu guna-grāma
Jāsu nāma agha-khaga-badhika || 30[24]

Iti Çrī[25]-Rāma-charita-mānasē sakala-kali-kaluṣa-vidhvaṁsanē, Visuddha (*sic*)-santōṣa-sampādinī[26]-nāma chaturthas sōpānaḥ samāptaḥ || Çubham astu[27] || Sambat 1704 samaē, Pā̃kha-shūdi-dwārasi[28] likhitaṁ Raghutīvārī Kāsyāṁ ||

---

[1] Jīwana-mūri.
[2] jugawati.
[3] raheũ.
[4] nahī.
[5] kaheũ.
[6] Sō.
[7] Āyasu.
[8] kahā.
[9] Chandra.
[10] sajīwana.
[11] 58.
[12] rasa.
[13] Tinahī kalēsa.
[14] yōgū.
[15] Jina.
[16] bhā̃tī.
[17] yōga.
[18] These are the names of the *kaṇḍs* as given in the printed edition. Tulsī-Dās, it will be seen, gave other names.

[19] Passages in the Chhand metres are always in highly Sanskritized style, and hence are seldom altered in the printed texts.
[20] jasa.
[21] Tripurā-'ri.
[22] tanu.
[23] Suniya.
[24] *System of numbering different from that of the printed text, which here has* 2.
[25] In Sanskrit passages, I transliterate श by *Ç*; in Gaudian passages, by *Sh*.
[26] vimala-vaĩrāgya-sampādanō.
[27] Çubham astu | Siddhir astu.
[28] *A very interesting form. This date is of course omitted in the printed editions.*

Conclusion of the Laykā Kāṇḍ (Banāras MS.).

Chhand.

(Mati-manda Tulasī) Dāsa sō Prabhu mōha-basa bisarāïyō ||
Yaha Rāwanā-'ri-charitra pāwana Rāma-pada-rati-prada sadā |
Kāmā-''di-hara bigyāna-kara sura-siddha-muni gāwahī mudā ||

Dōhā.

Samara-bijaya Raghu-mani-charita[1]
Sunahī je sadā sujāna[2] |
Bijaya bibēka bibhūti nita
Tinhahī[3] dēhī Bhagawāna ||
Yaha Kali-kāla malā-''yatana
Mana kari dēkhu bichāra |
Shrī Raghu-nāyaka-nāmu[4] taji
Nahi kachhu āna adhāra[5] || 120[6] ||
Iti Çrī-Rāma-charita-mānasē sakala kali-kaluṣa-vidhvaṁsanē, Vimala-vijñāna-sampādinī[7]-nāma ṣaṣṭhas sōpānaḥ samāptaḥ[8] || Çubham astu ||· Samba 1704 samaē || Māgha-sūdi pratipad likhitaṁ Raghutivārī Kāsyāṁ (?) Lōlā-(r)ka samipē (*sic*) || Çrī-Rāmō jayati || Çrī-Viçva-nāthāya namaḥ || Çrī-Vindu-mādhavaē (? *sic*) namaḥ ||

II.—OTHER VERSIONS OF THE RĀMA LEGEND.

In addition to the various poems of Tul'sī Dās, a number of works have been written by later authors dealing with the same subject. The following are those with which I am acquainted :—

(1) A Rāmāyan was written by *Chintāmanī Tripāṭhī* (143).

(2) *Mān Dās* (172) wrote the *Rām Charitr'*, founded on the *Rāmāyaṇa* of *Vālmīki* and on the *Hanuman Nāṭaka*.

(3) *Bhag'want Rāy*, the *Khīchī* (333), wrote a Rāmāyan.

(4) *Sambhu Nāth* (357) wrote a Rāmāyan entitled *Rām Bilās*.

(5) *Gulāb Siŋgh* (486) wrote a Vedantic Rāmāyan (whatever that may mean).

(6) *Gaj'rāj Upādhyā* (585) wrote a Rāmāyan.

(7) *Sahaj Rām* (592) wrote a Rāmāyan, founded on the *Raghuvaṁça* and on the *Hanuman Nāṭaka*.

(8) *Saŋkar Tripāṭhī* (613) wrote a Rāmāyan in Kabitta metres.

(9) *Iswarī Par'sād Tripāṭhī* (*675*) wrote a translation of the *Rāmāyaṇa* of *Vālmīki*.

(10) *Chandr' Jhā* (*686*) wrote a Rāmāyan in the Maithilī dialect.

(11) *Jānakī Par'sād* (*689*) wrote a *Rām-nibās Rāmāyan*.

(12) *Samar Siŋgh* (*711*) wrote a *Rāmāyan*.

(13) *Pūran Chand Jūth* (*829a*) wrote the *Rām Rahasya Rāmāyan*.

The above list does not include the many works dealing with one or more detached episodes of the Rāma legend; nor does it include the countless Rāmāyans in prose and verse which have been issued of late years. Of these the best in language and style is the (14) *Rām Kathā* of the late Paṇḍit *Chhōṭū Rām Tiwārī* (No. 705).

[1] Samara-bijaya Raghubīra kē.
[2] Charita je sunahī sujāna.
[3] Tinahī.
[4] -nātha-nāma.
[5] Nāhi na na.
[6] 118.
[7] vimala-jñāna-sampādanō.
[8] *Printed editions omit all after this.*

CHAPTER VII.

THE ARS POETICA. [1580—1692 A.D.]

The end of the sixteenth century and the whole of the seventeenth century, a period corresponding closely with the supremacy of the Mughal empire, presents a remarkable array of poetic talent. Within this period the most prominent figures not already dealt with are *Kēsab Dās, Chintāmani Tripaṭhī,* and *Bihārī Lāl.* Kēsab and Chintāmani are the most salient examples of a school founded by the first of these authors which devoted itself to the technical development of the art of poetry; and this group will alone be considered in the present chapter. The next chapter will deal with the remaining poets of the seventeenth century.

134. केसब दास सनाढ्य मिसर, *Kēsab Dās Sanāḍhya Misar,* of *Bundēl'khanḍ.* Fl. 1580 A.D.

Nir., Sun., Sat., Rāg. His original home was in *Ṭeh'rī,* but he visited king *Madhukar Shāh,* of *Uṛ'chhā,* and received much honour from him. Subsequently king *Indar'jīt* (No. 136), Madhukar's son, endowed him with twenty-one villages, whereupon he and his family finally settled in Uṛ'chhā. He was the first poet to describe in the vernacular (in his *Kabi-priyā* (Rāg.), a work which subsequent writers have frequently imitated), the ten constituents (अङ्ग) of a poem. His first important work was the *Bigyān Gītā,* which he wrote under the name of *Madhukar Shāh.* Then he wrote the *Kabi-priyā* for *Par'bīn Rāī Pāturī* (No. 137). This was followed by the *Rām-chandrikā* (Rāg.) under the name of king *Indar'jīt.* He also wrote the learned *Rasik-priyā* (Rāg.) on composition (साहित्य) and the *Rām-alaṃkrit-mañjarī* on prosody.

Commentaries on the *Kabi-priyā* were written by (1) *Sar'dār* (571), (2) *Nārāyan Rāy* (572), (3) *Phāl'kā Rāw* (678), (4) *Hari* (761); on the *Rām-chandrikā* by (1) *Jānakī Par'sād* (577), (2) *Dhanī Rām* (578); and on the *Rasik-priyā* by (1) *Sūrati Misar* (326), (2) *Ya'qūb Khān* (394), (3) *Īsuf Khān* (421), (4) *Sar'dār* (571), (5) *Hari Jan* (575).

When the emperor *Ak'bar* fined king Indar'jīt ten million rupees for disobedience and revolt because *Par'bīn Rāī Pāturī* did not appear in his (Ak'bar's) court, *Kēsab Dās* had a secret audience with Rājā *Bīr'bal* (No. 106), the emperor's minister, and recited the well-known lines ending दियो करतारो दुहूँ करतारो (given in *Sib Siŋgh Sarōj*, pp. 31, 32). Rājā Bīr'bal was much pleased with them and got the fine remitted, but Par'bīn Rāï Pāturī had nevertheless to appear in court.

135. बलिभद्र सनाढ्य मिसर, *Balibhadr' Sanāḍhya Misar*, of *Uṛ'chhā*, in *Bundēl'khāṇḍ*. Fl. 1580 A.D.

He was brother of *Kēsab Dās*. His *Nakh'sikh* (see note to No. 87) is admitted by all poets to be a standard work. He also wrote a commentary on the *Bhāgavata Purāṇa*. His Nakh'sikh has a commentary by *Par'tāp Sāhi* (No. 149), and another by an anonymous poet of *Uniyārā* (No. 660).

136. इन्दरजीत सिङ्घ, Rājā *Indar'jīt Siŋgh*, the Bundēlā of *Uṛ'chhā*, in *Bundēl'khaṇḍ*. Fl. 1580 A.D.

Rāg. As a poet he wrote under the name of *Dhīraj Narind*. *Kēsab Dās Sanāḍhyā Misar* (No. 134) the poet, and *Par'bīn Rāi Pāturī* (No. 137) the poetess, attended his court. See these names for the account of an adventure he had with the emperor *Ak'bar*.

137. परबीन राइ पातुरी, *Par'bīn Rāī Pāturī*, the courtezan of *Uṛ'chhā*, in *Bundēl'khaṇḍ*. Fl. 1580 A.D.

Kēsab Dās (No. 134) composed his *Kabi-priyā* in honour of this courtezan, and in its dedication highly honoured her. She was authoress of numerous short poems which have a great reputation. She attended the court of king *Indar'jīt* (No. 136), and the emperor *Ak'bar*, hearing of her fame, summoned her to him. *Indar'jīt* refused to allow her to go, and thereupon *Ak'bar* fined him ten million rupees as a rebel. Kēsab Dās repaired to Ak'bar's court, and interceding through *Bīr'bal* (No. 106) got the fine remitted. Par'bīn had, however, to appear before Ak'bar, and after giving a sample of her learning was allowed to depart. The whole interview is poetically described by Sib Siŋgh, p. 448.

138. **बाल क्रिशन्न त्रिपाठी,** *Bāl Krish'n Tripāṭhī.* Fl. 1600 A.D.

He was son of *Balibhadr',* nephew of *Kēsab Dās,* and brother of *Kāsī Nāth.* He was the author of a good prosody entitled *Ras-chandrikā.*

There is another poet of the name *Bāl Krish'n,* of whom I know no particulars.

139. **कासी नाथ कबि,** the poet *Kāsī Nāth.* Fl. 1600 A.D.

A graceful poet. He was son of *Balibhadr',* nephew of *Kēsab Dās,* and brother of *Bāl Krish'n Tripāṭhī.*

140. **देव दत्त॰,** *Dēb Datt' alias Dēb Kabi,* the Brāhman of *Samānēgāw,* district *Māin'purī.* B. *1604* A.D.

According to Native opinion he was the greatest poet of his time, and indeed one of the great poets of India. He is said to have written no less than seventy different works. The following are those which are best known:—(1) *Prēm Taraŋg,* (2) *Bhāw-bilās,* (3) *Ras-bilās,* (4) *Rasānand-laharī,* (5) *Sujān-binōd,* (6) *Kābya-rasāyan* [a treatise on prosody (*piŋgal*) and rhetoric (*alaŋkār*)], (7) *Ashṭa-jām* (Rāg.) (printed), (8) *Dēb-māyā Prapañch* (a play), (9) *Prēm-dīpikā,* (10) *Sumil-binōd,* (11) *Rādhikā-bilās.* Garcin de Tassy (i, 157), quoting from Ward, (ii, 480), calls him *Dēb Rāj,* and says that he is author of a *Nakh'sikh* (see note to No. 87), which is probably one of the above-mentioned works.

141. **हरी राम,** *Harī Rām.* B. *1623* A.D.

The author of a *Nakh'sikh* (see note to No. 87). Possibly the same as a *Harī Rām Kabi,* the author of a *Piŋgal* (Rāg.), or treatise on prosody, mentioned by Sib Siŋgh as B. (? Fl.) *1651* A.D.

142. **सुन्दर दास कबि,** the poet *Sundar Dās,* a Brāhman of *Gwāliyar.* Fl. 1631 A.D.

Nir., Sun. He attended the court of the emperor *Shāh Jahān.* He was first given the title of *Kabi Rāy,* and afterwards of *Mahā Kabi Rāy.* His principal work is on composition, and is entitled *Sundar Sriŋgār,* a work on lovers. He was also author of a Braj Bhākhā translation of the *Siŋghāsan Battīsī* (Rāg.), the origin of *Lallū Jī Lāl's*

Hindustānī version, and of a philosophical work entitled *Gyān Samudra*. Garcin de Tassy (i, 482) suggests that he may also have been the author of a work entitled *Sundar Bidyā*.

143. चिन्तामनि त्रिपाठी, *Chintāmani Tripāṭhī*, of *Ṭik'māpur*, district *Kānh'pur*. Fl. 1650 A.D.

Nir., Sat. He is counted as one of the great masters of vernacular composition (साहित्य). The legend in the Dōāb is that his father used continually to visit a shrine of Dēvī and worship her. The shrine is still shown at a distance of a mile from Ṭik'māpur. One day the goddess, being pleased at his devotion, appeared to him, and showing him four skulls promised that they should all be born as sons to him. As a matter of fact so it turned out, and he obtained four sons, viz. (1) *Chintāmani*, (2) *Bhūkhan*, (3) *Mati Rām*, and (4) *Jaṭā Saŋkar alias Nīl Kaṇṭh*. Of these, the last obtained the blessing of a saint and became a poet. The other three studied Sanskrit and became so learned that it is said that their fame will remain to the end of the world. From Mati Rām were descended *Sītal* and *Bihārī Lāl*, who were alive in 1844 A.D., and *Rām Dīn*. *Chintāmani* attended for a long time the court of *Bhōmalā Makarand Shāh*, of the solar race at *Nāg'pur*. Under his name he composed an important treatise on prosody entitled *Chhand-bichār*. He also wrote the (2) *Kābya-bibēk*, (3) *Kabi-kul Kalpa-taru*, (4) *Kābya-par'kās*, and (5) a *Rāmāyan*. The last is an excellent work in Kabitta and other metres. Amongst his patrons were *Rudr' Sāhi*, the *Sulaŋkī*, the emperor *Shāh Jahān* (1628—1658), and *Jain Dīn Aḥ'mad* (No. 144). He often wrote under the *nom de guerre* of *Mani Lāl*. He is possibly the same as another *Chintāmani*, also mentioned by Sib Siŋgh.

144. जैन दीन अहम्मद, *Jāin Dīn Aḥ'mad*. B. *1679* (?) A.D.

He was a poet himself, and also a great patron of poets. Amongst his *protegés* may be mentioned *Chintāmani Tripāṭhī* (No. 143), of *Ṭik'māpur*.

145. भूखन त्रिपाठी, *Bhūkhan Tripāṭhī*, of *Ṭik'māpur*, district *Kānh'pur*. Fl. 1660 A.D.

Nir., Haj., Rāg. He was brother of *Chintāmani Tripāṭhī* (No. 143), and excelled in the tragic, heroic, and terrible styles. At first he attended for six months the court of king *Chhattr' Sāl* (No. 197), of *Par'nā* (*Pannā*). Thence he went to *Sib Rāj,* the *Sulaṅkī,* of *Sitārā,* where he was much honoured and received many times enormous presents for his works. On one occasion he got as much as five elephants and twenty-five thousand rupees for a single poem. His poems in honour of Sib Rāj are the most famous of their class. Having exploited this monarch he returned home, and on his way passed through Par'nā. Chhattr' Sāl, feeling himself quite unable to reward the poet as Sib Rāj had done, instead of giving him money, helped with his own shoulder to carry him in his palankeen on his way. This occurrence is the origin of some of the poet's most famous verses. After resting at home Bhūkhan set out on a tour through Rāj'putānā, proclaiming the glory of Sib Rāj. He finally found himself at *Kumāō,* and recited a verse in honour of the king of the place. The king imagined that Bhūkhan had come to look for a reward, and that all the story of his having been enriched by Sib Rāj was pure invention: so he offered him a handsome present of elephants, horses, and money. To this Bhūkhan replied:—"I hunger[1] not for this. I came only to learn if Sib Rāj's fame had penetrated here or not."

His principal works are (1) *Sib Rāj Bhūkhan,* (2) *Bhūkhan Hajārā,* (3) *Bhūkhan Ullās,* and (4) *Dūkhan Ullās.* Seventy short pieces by him in all styles are included in the Hajārā of Kālidās Tribēdī.

146. मति राम त्रिपाठी, *Mati Rām Tripāṭhī,* of *Tik'mā-pur,* district *Kānh'pur.* Fl. cir. 1650—1682 A.D.

Nir., Rāg., Sun., Sat. He was brother of *Chintāmani Tripāṭhī* (No. 143). He led a wandering life, going from one royal court to another.

His best works are (1) *Lalit Lalām,* a work on rhetoric, which he wrote in the name of Rāw *Bhāw Siṅgh,* of *Būndī* (1658—1682; cf. Tod, ii, 489; Calc. ed ii, 527); (2) *Chhand Sār,* a treatise on prosody, in the name of *Fatih Sāhi,* the Bundēlā of *Srinagar;* and (3) *Ras Rāj* (Rāg.), a treatise on lovers. See Garcin de Tassy, i, 332.

147. सम्भु नाथ सिङ्ह, Rājā *Sambhu Nāth Siṅgh Sulaṅkī alias Sambhu Kabi, alias Nāth Kabi, alias Nrip Sambhu,* of *Sitārā.* Fl. cir. 1650.

[1] This (इस की अब भूख नहीं) is a pun on the poet's name भूखन।

Sun., Sat. Not only a patron of poets, but author of an admired work. It is in the erotic style, and is called *Kābya Nirālī*. It is considered the best work on lovers extant. He was a great friend of *Matī Rām Tripāṭhī* (No. 146).

148. नील कण्ठ त्रिपाठी, *Nīl Kaṇṭh Tripāṭhī*, *alias* *Jaṭā Saŋkar*, of *Ṭik'mpāur*, district *Kānh'pur*. Fl. cir. 1650 A.D.

Nir., Sat. A brother of *Chintāmanī Tripāṭhī* (No. 143). No complete works by him are known to be extant.

149. परताप साहि, the bard *Par'tāp Sāhī*,[1] of *Bundēl'khaṇḍ*. Fl. 1633 (?) A.D.

He was son of the poet *Rat'nēs* (No. 199), and attended the court of king *Chhattr' Sāl* (No. 197), of *Par'nā* (*Pannā*). He wrote a work on vernacular composition (भाखा साहित्य) entitled *Kābya Bilās*. At the suggestion of *Bikram Sāhī* he wrote a commentary to the *Bhākhā Bhūkhan* and to the *Nakh'sikh* (see note to No. 87) of *Balibhadr'* (No. 135). Another work of his is entitled the *Bigyārthakāumudī*. I do not know the work here entitled Bhākhā Bhūkhan. The only work of that name with which I am acquainted was written by *Jas'want Siŋgh* (No. 377) at the end of the eighteenth century, and has been frequently commentated on. Who the Bikram Sāhī referred to above is I do not know. He cannot be the well-known *Bikram Sāhī* of *Char'khārī* (No. 514) if the account given above, which is that given in the *Sib Siŋgh Sarōj*, is correct. Bikram of Char'khārī flourished in 1804 A.D. If he is the man referred to, then the poet cannot have attended the court of Chhattr' Sāl (fl. 1650), and the Bhākhā Bhūkhan referred to was probably that by Jas'want Siŋgh. The matter being doubtful, I place Par'tāp provisionally here.

150. सीपति कबि, the poet *Srīpati*, of *Par'yāg'pur*, district *Bahirāīch*. B. *1643* A.D.

---

[1] This word *Sāhī* or *Shāhī* is the same as *Shāh*, but is an older form, preserving in its final *ī* a trace of the ending *ya* in the Zend *kshāyathiya*, which has disappeared in the modern Persian *Shāh*. See *Zoroastrian Deities on Indo-Scythic Coins*, by A. Stein, reprinted from *The Oriental and Babylonian Record*, August 1887, p. 9.

Sūd., Sun. He is counted as one of the masters of vernacular composition. His most famous works are (1) the *Kābya Kalpa-drum,* (2) *Kābya Sarōj,* (3) *Srīpati Sarōj.*

151. सरस्वती कवीन्द्र, *Saraswatī,* the poet-laureate, a Brāhman of *Banāras.* Fl. 1650 A.D.

He was learned in Sanskrit composition (साहित्य), and at the instance of the emperor *Shāh Jahān* (1628—1658) he took to writing poems in the vernacular. His principal work of this nature was the *Kabīndra-kalpa-latā,* in which there are many poems in praise of prince *Dārā Shukōh* and the *Bēgam Sāhib.*

152. सिब नाथ कबि, the poet *Sib Nāth,* of *Bundēl'khaṇḍ.* Fl. 1660 A.D.

He attended the court of Rājā *Jagat Siṅgh* Bundēlā, the son of *Chhattr' Sāl* (No. 197), of *Par'nā* (*Pannā*), and was the author of a work on poetry entitled *Ras Rañjan.* The above is Sib Siṅgh's account; but, according to Tod, Chhattr' Sāl, the Bundēlā, had no son named Jagat. See Tod's *Rājāsthān,* ii, 491; Calc. ed. ii, 527. Hunter's *Gazetteer,* s.v. Jaitpur, mentions a Jagatrāj, son of Chhattr' Sāl. The *Rep. Arch. Sur. Ind.* xvii, 106, gives some verses by a poet named *Sib* (or *Shiu*) *Patī,* who lived about the same time.

153. तुलसी कबि, the poet *Tul'sī,* the son of *Jadu Rāy.* Fl. 1655.

He was only a mediocre poet himself, but he compiled in 1655 A.D. an excellent anthology, entitled the *Kabi-mālā.* It includes poems by seventy-five different poets, dating from Sambat 1500 (A.D. 1443) down to Sambat 1700 (A.D. 1643).

154. मण्डन कबि, the poet *Maṇḍan,* of *Jait'pur,* in *Bundēl'khaṇḍ.* B. *1659.*

Nir., Sun. He attended the court of king *Maṅgad Siṅgh.* He wrote three works on composition (साहित्य), entitled (1) *Ras Ratnābalī,* (2) *Ras Bilās,* and (3) *Nain Pachāsā.*

155. रतन कबि, the poet *Ratan.* B. *1681* A.D.

He attended the court of *Sabhā Sāhi,* (cf. No. 346), Rājā of *Par'nā* (*Pannā*), and translated the *Rasa Mañjarī* into the vernacular. Probably the same as the poet *Ratan,* of *Srīnagar,* in *Bundēl'khaṇḍ,* who attended the court of Rājā *Fat'ḥ Sāhi,* the Bundēlā of *Srīnagar.* Under this king's name he composed two works on vernacular composition, entitled *Phatēshāh Bhūkhan* and *Phatē Par'kās* respectively. Mr. Whish, Deputy Comissioner of *Hamīr'pur,* informs me that Fat'ḥ Sāhi was a descendant of *Chhattr' Sāl* (No. 197), but never came to the throne.

156. मुरली धर कबि, the poet *Mur'lī Dhar.* B. (? Fl.) *1683* A.D.

Haj., Sun. Probably the same as a *Mur'lī Kabi* in Rāg., and as a *Mur'lī Dhar Kabi* mentioned by Sib Siŋgh (without date) as joint author with *Srī Dhar* (No. 157) of a work on prosody entitled *Kabi Binōd.*

157. स्री धर कबि, the poet *Srī Dhar.* Fl. (?) *1683* A.D. Sun. Joint author with *Mur'lī Dhar* (No. 156) of a prosody entitled *Kabi Binōd.*

158. बारन कबि, the poet *Bāran,* of *Bhūpāl.* B. *1683* A.D.

He attended the court of *Shujāu'l Shāh Nawāb,* of *Rāj'gaṛh.* He wrote a highly esteemed work on composition (साहित्य) entitled *Rasik Bilās.*

159. कालिदास त्रिबेदी, *Kālidās Tribēdī,* of *Ban'pūrā,* in the *Dōāb.* Fl. cir. 1700 A.D.

Nir., Sat. He was an excellent and famous poet of the *Dōāb.* At first he remained for many years in attendance on the emperor *Āuraŋg'zēb* in *Gōkul'kuṇḍā* and other places in the Deccan. Thereafter he lived with king *Jōgājīt Siŋgh* Raghubansī, of *Jambū,* and under his name composed a fine work entitled the *Badhū-binōd.* His best known work is an anthology entitled the *Kālidās Hajārā* (quoted in this work as 'Haj.'), in which he has included a thousand poems by two hundred and twelve poets dating from A.D. 1423 down to A.D. 1718. Sib Singh states that he has derived great assistance from this work in writing his *Sarōj* (which indeed appears to be the fact). He adds that he has in his library a splendid work by the same author entitled *Jañjīrāband*.

His son was *Uday Nāth Kabīndr'* (No. 334), and his grandson the poet *Dūlah* (No. 358), both celebrated authors.

160. **सुख देव मिसर,** *Sukh Dēb Misar,* the Kabirāj or poet-laureate, of *Kampilā*. Fl. cir. 1700 A.D.

Nir., Sat., Sun. He is counted as one of the masters of vernacular composition. He attended the court of Rājā *Rāj Singh,* son of Rājā *Arjun Singh,* of *Gāur,* and obtained from him the title of Kabirāj or poet-laureate. There he wrote a treatise on prosody entitled *Brit Bichār,* which is considered to be the best of all works of its kind. Thence he went to the court of Rājā *Himmat Singh,* of *Amēṭhī,* where he wrote another prosody entitled *Chhand Bichār*. Thence he repaired to Nawāb *Fāẓil 'Alī Khān,* minister of *Āurang'zēb,* where he wrote a famous work on vernacular composition (साहित्य) entitled *Phājil Alī Par'kās* (attributed by Garcin de Tassy, i, 479, but with hesitation, to one *Sukdēb,* quoting from Ward, *A View, etc.,* ii, 481). He was also author of the *Adhyātma Par'kās* and the *Das'rath Rāy*. His most famous pupil was *Jāi Dēb* (No. 161), of *Kampilā*. Cf. No. 661.

161. **जै देव कबि,** the poet *Jāi Dēb,* of *Kampilā*. Fl. cir. 1700 A.D.

He attended the court of Nawāb *Fāẓil 'Alī Khān,* and was a pupil of *Sukh Dēb Misar* (No. 160), of *Kampilā*.

162. **नाथ,** *Nāth*. Fl. cir. 1700 A.D.

? Sun. He attended the court of *Fāẓil 'Alī Khān*. He is possibly the same as a *Nāth* Kabi who attended the court of *Bhag'want Rāy, Khīchī* (No. 333), who died 1760. (Cf. Nos. 68, 147, 440, 632, and 850.)

CHAPTER VIII.

OTHER SUCCESSORS OF TUL'SI DAS. [1600—1700 A.D.]

Part I.—Religious Poets.

[Arranged as far as possible in order of date.]

163. **दादू,** *Dādū,* the cotton-carder, of *Narāin,* in *Āj'mēr.* Fl. 1600 A.D.

The founder of the Dādū Panthī sect. He was born at *Ahmadābād,* but in his twelfth year removed to *Sāmbhar.* He finally settled at *Narāin,* a place about four kōs from Sāmbhar, where he received his inspiration. His principal works are the *Dādū kī Bānī* and the *Dādū Panthī Granth.* The latter has been translated by Lieut. G. R. Siddons in the J. A. S. B., vi, pp. 480 and 750. See Wilson, *Religious Sects of the Hindūs,* i, 103, and Garcin de Tassy. One of his disciples was *Sundar,* the author of the *Sundar Saṅkhyā.* The Bānī extends to 20,000 lines. Dādū's life by *Jan Gōpāl* runs to 3,000 lines. Fifty-two disciples spread his doctrines throughout *Rāj'putānā* and *Āj'mēr,* each of them leaving a large collection of religious verse. Thus, the poems and hymnology of *Garīb Dās* are said to amount to 32,000 lines; *Jāīsā* is stated to have composed 1,24,000 lines; *Par'yāg Dās,* 48,000 lines; *Rajab Jī,* 72,000; *Bakh'nā Jī,* 20,000 lines; *Saṅkar Dās,* 4,400; Bābā *Ban'wārī Dās,* 12,000 lines; *Sundar Dās,* 1,20,000 lines; and *Mādhō Dās,* 68,000 lines. See *Memorandum on Bhāshā Literature* by John Traill, of Jāīpur: 1884.

164. **सुन्दर दास कबि,** the poet *Sundar Dās,* of *Mēwār.* Fl. cir. 1620 A.D.

He was a disciple of *Dādū* (No. 163) and wrote a quietistic work entitled *Sundar Sāṅkhyā.*

165. **सेनापति कबि,** the poet *Sēnāpati,* of *Brindāban,* in *Braj.* B. *1623* A.D.

Haj., Sūd. He was a devotee at *Brindāban*, and was the author of a standard work entitled *Kābya Kalpadrum*.

166. स्री धर कवि, the poet *Srī Dhar*, of *Rāj'putānā*. B. *1623* A.D.

Sūd (?). The author of a work dealing with Durgā, entitled *Bhawānī Chhand*.

167. प्रान नाथ, *Prān Nāth*, the Chhattrī of *Par'nā* (*Pannā*), in *Bundēl'khanḍ*. Fl. 1650.

The founder of the *Prān'nāthī* sect, an attempt at uniting the Hindū and Musalmān religions. He attended the court of *Chhattr' Sāl* (fl. 1650), of *Par'nā* (*Pannā*) (No. 197). See Growse, J. A. S. B., xlviii, p. 171, where a specimen of one of his works (the *Qiyāmat Nāmā*) is given and translated. Mr. Growse is wrong in putting him at the beginning of the eighteenth century, for Chhattr' Sāl died in 1658. Prān Nāth was the author of fourteen works, of which a list is given by Mr. Growse, l.c. The language is peculiar, the grammatical structure being purely Hindī while the vocabulary is mainly supplied from Persian and Arabic.

168. बीर भान, *Bīr Bhān*, of *Brijhasīr*. Fl. 1658 A.D.

The founder of the sect of Sādhs, the doctrines of which he taught in consequence of a miraculous communication received from one *Uday Dās*, According to others he was a disciple of one *Jōgī Dās*. The doctrines taught by his superhuman instructor were communicated in the form of Sabds and Sākhīs, detached Hindī verses like those of *Kabīr*. They are collected into manuals and read at the religious meetings of the Sādhs. See Wilson, *Religious Sects of the Hindūs*, i, 354, and Garcin de Tassy, i, 125.

169. गोबिन्द सिङ्ह, Srī Guru *Gōbind Singh*. B. 1666 A.D.

The celebrated founder of the militant Sīkh religion. He was a Panjābī[1] of the Sōḍī Khattrī caste, and was born in *Anand'pur*, in

[1] I am indebted for most of this information to Rāy Jay Krish'n, of Paṭ'nā, who is a trustee of the Sikh temple there.

Paṭ'nā City, on the seventh of the light half of Pūs, Sambat 1723 (1666 A.D.). His father was Guru *Tēg Bahādur,* who was summoned by *Āurang'zēb* to Delhī and there compelled to embrace Muhammadanism. Tēg Bahādur died in 1675 A.D. (fifth of light half of Ag'han, Sam. 1732). Some say that he committed suicide, others that he was murdered by Āurangzēb. When that monarch began to oppress the Hindūs, Gōbind Siŋgh felt himself to be commissioned by god to appear in this world in human form to destroy tyrants. In the summer of 1697 A.D. (first of light half of Chaīt, Sam. 1754), he commenced a severe penance, and offered sacrifices to the goddess Kālī on the hill of *Naīnā Dēbī,* in the district of Hushiār'pur, in the Panjāb. After a year's penance, on the ninth of light half of Chaīt, Sam. 1755 (A.D. 1698), the goddess appeared to him and commanded him to ask a boon. He exclaimed,—"Goddess, grant me the boon that I may always be engaged in good works, and that when I go forth to fight the enemy I may always be victorious and never terrified." The goddess disappeared, saying "Be it so."

After he had convinced his disciples of the truth of his mission, he made a collection of works containing not only poems by himself, but also selections from the works and prophecies of other authors. It is called the *Granth Sāhib* (see No. 22), and is in four parts, all in verse:—

(1) The *Sunīti Par'kās,* a treatise on morals.

(2) The *Sarb Lōh Par'kās,* a commentary on *Nānak's* (No. 22) writings.

(3) The *Prēm Sumārg,* dealing with the Sīkh religion. It contains a section entitled the *Bachitra Nāṭak,* which is a short account of Gōbind's life and mission.

(4) The *Buddh Sāgar,* consisting of hymns and invocations.

Gōbind Siŋgh wrote well in Braj Bhākhā, Panjābī, and Persian, and was altogether a famous poet.

Cf. Garcin de Tassy, i, 191. According to Wilson, *Religious Sects of the Hindūs,* i, 274, the chief work of the sect is known as the *Das Pādshāh kā granth.*

170. **खुमान,** the bard *Khumān,* of *Char'khārī,* in *Bundēl'khaṇḍ.* B. *1683* A.D.

He was born blind and was quite uneducated. It happened that a holy man came to his house, and after staying there four months was escorted out of Char'khārī by many respectable and learned men of the place. When they had gone a little way the others returned, but Khumān stayed by him, in spite of the saint advising him to go home. Khumān's argument was, "Why should I return to my home? I am blind, ignorant, and of no use in the house. As the proverb says, I am like the washerman's donkey, who belongs neither to the house nor to the washing place."[1] Pleased at this the saint wrote the *mantra* of Saraswatī on his tongue, and told him first to compose a poem in honour of his (the saint's) gourd pot. Khumān immediately composed twenty-five verses in its honour, and after worshipping the saint's feet returned home. There he began to compose epics in Sanskrit and in the vernacular.

Once he was attending the court of Rājā *Sendhiā* (Scindia), of *Gwāliyar,* who commanded him to spend the whole night in writing a work in Sanskrit. Khumān agreed to do this, and in one night composed seven hundred çlōkas.

He is considered to have been truly an inspired poet. His best known works are the *Lachhman Satak* and the *Hanuman Nakh'sikh.*[2]

He is possibly the same as a poet named *Khumān Kabi* (date unknown), who metrically translated a section of the *Amara Kōça* (Rāg.) into the vernacular.

Part II.—Other Poets.

[These are grouped as far as possible according to their patrons or the states to which they were attached.]

171. नजीर, *Najīr (Naẓīr),* of *Āg'rā.* Fl. before 1600 A.D.

Rāg. A poet of considerable fame, first prominently introduced to European readers by Mr. Fallon in the preface to his Hindūstānī Dictionary. Mr. Fallon says that he is the only poet whose verses have made their way to the people, and that there is scarcely an indifferent line in all that he has written. To these very wide statements I am quite unable to subscribe. His writings (quoted as *Naẓīr kī Shāir* in Rāg.) certainly are popular among certain classes, but they have nothing like the general acceptance of the works of poets like *Tul'sī Dās, Sūr Dās, Malik Muḥammad Jāyasī,* and other giants

---

[1] *I.e.,* he is always going backwards and forwards between them.

[2] See note to No. 87.

of the period. Neither can I agree with Mr. Fallon's estimate of the literary value of his works, which, although couched in popular language, are so filthily indecent as to be unreadable by any person of European training and taste.

172. मान दास कबि, the poet *Mān Dās*, of *Braj*. B. *1623* A.D.

Rāg. A favourite poet. His principal work was a vernacular poem entitled *Rām Charitr'*, founded on the *Rāmāyaṇa* of *Vālmīki* and on the *Hanuman Nāṭaka*.

173. ठाकुर कबि, the poet *Ṭhākur* the elder. Fl. 1643 A.D.

Haj., Sun. According to one account he was a bard of the village *As'nī*, district *Fatih'pur*, and lived about the time of *Muḥammad Shāh* (1719—1748.). Others say he was a Kāyasth of *Bundēl'khaṇḍ*. There is a legend in Bundēl'khaṇḍ that one time the Bundēlās were assembled at *Chhattr'pur* in order to murder *Himmatī Bahādur* (No. 378), the Gosāĩ, and that Ṭhākur sent them a poem commencing कहिबे सुनिब को कछू न हियाँ,[1] on receipt of which they dispersed. Himmatī Bahādur rewarded the poet for this service with a present of money. But Himmatī Bahādur flourished in 1800, while this poem is included in the Hajārā of Kālidās Tribēdī, No. (159), which was completed in or about the year 1708. It is probable, therefore, that there were two poets of this name, who have been confounded. Moreover, Sib Siŋgh states that he has in his possession hundreds of excellent short poems by a *Ṭhākur Kabi* who was alive in Sambat 1700 (A.D. 1643), and hence the present poet's date is fixed as above.

174. बेदाङ्ग राय, *Bēdāŋg Rāy*. Fl. cir. 1650.

Author of the *Pār'sī Par'kās*, a work describing the manner of counting the months, etc., by Hindūs and Musalmāns, which was compiled under orders of *Shāh Jahān*. See Garcin de Tassy, i, 519.

175. कासी राम कबि, the poet *Kāsī Rām*. B. *1658* A.D.

[1] The whole poem in given in the *Sib Siŋgh Sarōj*, p. 124.

He attended the court of *Nizāmat Khān,* Subēdār of *Āuraṅg'zēb* (1658—1707). His poems are said to be graceful.

176. **इन्दरजीत त्रिपाठी,** *Indar'jīt Tripāṭhī,* of *Ban'pūrā,* in the *Dōāb*. B. *1682* A.D.

A servant of *Āuraṅg'zēb* (1658—1707).

177. **ईस्वर कवि,** the poet *Īswar.* B. *1673* A.D.

He attended the court of *Āuraṅg'zēb* (1658—1707). His poems are said to be full of taste.

178. **सामन्त कवि,** the poet *Sāmant.* B. *1681.*

Haj. He attended the court of *Āuraṅg'zēb* (1658—1707).

179. **अबदुल जलील,** *'Abdu'l Jalīl,* of *Bil'grām,* district *Har'dōī.* B. *1682* A.D.

He originally wrote in Arabic and Persian, and was an attendant at the court of the emperor *Āuraṅg'zēb* (1658—1707). He subsequently studied vernacular poetry under *Haribans Misar* (No. 209), of *Bil'grām,* and wrote some good vernacular verses.

180. **क्रिशन कवि,** the poet *Krish'n.* B. *1683* A.D.

He attended the court of the emperor *Āuraṅg'zēb* (1658—1707). Possibly the same as *Krish'n Kabi,* of *Jāipur* (No. 327).

181. **आलम कवि,** the poet *'Ālam.* B. *1700* A.D.

Nir., Sun. He was originally a Sanāḍhya Brāhman, but falling in love with a Muhammadan woman, a dyer by trade, he turned Musalmān, and was for a long time in the service of prince *Mu'azzam Shāh,* son of the emperor *Āuraṅg'zēb* (1658—1707) and afterwards the emperor *Bahādūr Shāh* (1707—1712). His poems are said to be very beautiful.

182. **अबदुल रहिमान,** *'Abdu'r Rahimān,* of *Dillī.* B. *1681* A.D.

He attended the court of *Mu'azzam Shāh,* afterwards the emperor *Bahādūr Shāh* (1707—1712), and wrote an ingenious work entitled *Jamak-Satak,* or a century of puns.

183. परस्साद कबि, the poet *Par'sād.* B. *1623* A.D.

He attended the court of the king of *Udaipur* (*Mēwār*), and is said by Sib Singh to be a well-known poet.

184. जगत सिङ्ह, Rānā *Jagat Singh,* of *Mēwār.* Fl. 1628—1654 A.D.

One of the most famous of the kings of Mēwār, and founder and rebuilder of *Udaipur.* A bard, name unknown, wrote the *Jagat Bilās,* a chronicle of his times (Tod's *Rājāsthān,* i, xiv; Calc. ed. i, xiii). He reigned during the above years (Tod. i, 372; Calc. ed. i, 394).

185. राज सिङ्ह, Rānā *Rāj Singh,* of *Udaipur* in *Mēwār.* Reigned 1654—1681 A.D.

The celebrated opponent of *Āurang'zēb.* (See Tod's *Rājāsthān,* i, 374; Calc. ed i, 396.) A poet, name unknown, wrote a chronicle of his name, entitled the *Rāj Par'kās* (Tod, i, xiv; Calc. ed. i, xiii).

186. मान कबीस्वर, the poet-laureate and bard *Mān,* of *Rāj'putānā.* Fl. 1660 A.D.

At the suggestion of Rānā *Rāj Singh,* of *Mēwār* (No. 185), he wrote the *Rāj Dēb Bilās,* which deals with the fights between *Āurang'zēb* and *Rāj Singh.* Cf. Tod, i, 214, 374, and ff., and 391; Calc. ed. i, 231, 396, and ff., and 414.

187. सदासिब कबि, the poet and bard *Sadāsib.* Fl. 1660 A.D.

He lived at the court of Rānā *Rāj Singh,* of *Mewār* (No. 185), the enemy of *Āurang'zēb,* and wrote his patron's life under the title of *Rāj Ratnākar.* Cf. Tod, i, 214, 374, and ff; Calc. ed. i, 231, 396, and ff.

188. जै सिङ्ह, Rānā *Jai Singh,* of *Udaipur* in *Mēwār.* Reigned 1681—1700 A.D.

He was son of Rānā *Rāj Siŋgh* (No. 185), and was a patron of poets. He had written a work, entitled the *Jāī Dēb Bilās,* which is a series of lives of the kings whom he had conquered. Cf. Tod, i, xiv, 214, and 391-94; Calc. ed. i, xiii, 231, and 414-418.

189. रन छोर कबि, the poet *Ran Chhōr.* Fl. 1680 A.D.

His date is doubtful. He was author of the *Rāj Pattanā,* a bardic chronicle of Mēwār. Cf. Tod, i, 286; ii, 59; Calc. ed. i, 305; ii, 65.

190. लीला धर कबि, the poet *Līlā Dhar.* Fl. 1620 A.D.

He attended the court of Mahārāj *Gaj Siŋgh* (1620—1638), of *Jōdh'pur,* in *Mār'wār.* Cf. Tod, ii, 41; Calc. ed ii, 46.

191. अमर सिङ्ग, *Amar Siŋgh,* of *Jōdh'pur,* in *Mār'wār.* Fl. 1634 A.D.

The grandson of Mahārāj *Sūr Siŋgh,* who in one day distributed 6,00,000 rupees amongst six 'lords of verse' (see Tod, ii, 39; Calc. ed. ii, 43), and son of *Gaj Siŋgh* (see No. 190), who was a great patron of poets. Amar Siŋgh was praised by the poet *Ban'wārī Lāl.* He was exiled in A.D. 1634 by his father, and repaired to the court of the emperor *Shāh Jahān,* whom he subsequently attempted to murder in open court in revenge for a slight. He was cut down after killing a number of courtiers. Cf. Tod, ii, 45; Calc. ed. ii, 49. He should be distinguished from Amar Siŋgh of Mewār (fl. 1600 A.D., cf. Tod, i, 346; Calc. ed. i, 371), who collected the works of the poet *Chand* (No. 6). Cf. Tod, i, xiii; Calc. ed. i, xii.

192. बन॰वारी लाल कबि, the poet *Ban'wārī Lāl.* Fl. 1634.

Haj. A panegyrist at the court of Prince *Amar Siŋgh* (No. 191), of *Jōdh'pur.*

193. रघु नाथ राय कबि, the poet *Raghu Nāth Rāy.* Fl. 1634.

Sun. He attended the court of Prince *Amar Siŋgh* (No. 191), of *Jōdh'pur.* Cf. Tod, ii, 44; Calc. ed. ii, 49.

194. सूजा *Sūjā (Shujā').* Fl. 1681.

A bard at the court of *Jas'want Siŋgh* (1638—1681), of *Mār'wār.* Cf. Tod, ii, 59; Calc. ed. ii, 62.

195. अजीत सिङ्ह, Mahārāj *Ajīt Siŋgh,* the Raṭhāūr, of *Jōdh'pur,* in *Mār'wār.* Lived 1681—1724 A.D.

This king got written a work entitled the *Rāj Rūpakākhyāt.* This contains a history of events from A.D. 469, when *Nayana Pāla* conquered *Kanāūj* and killed *Ajaya Pāla,* its king, to the time of king *Jāī Chand.* In a second part the history is carried on to the death of Mahārāj *Jas'want Siŋgh* in A.D. 1681; and again, in a third part, is related the history from the commencement of the solar race to the year 1734 A.D. Cf. Tod, ii, 2, 4, 58, and ff., 91*n*, and 107*n*; Calc. ed. ii, 2, 4, 64, and ff., 99*n*, and 117*n*.

196. बिहारी लाल चौबे, *Bihārī Lāl Chāūbē,* of *Braj.* Fl. 1650 A.D.

Sat., Nir., Rāg. One of the most celebrated authors of India, his fame resting on his *Sat Saī* (Rāg.), or collection of seven hundred dōhās, for each line of which he received a reward of a gold *ashrafī* from king *Jāī Siŋgh.* The elegance, poetic flavour, and ingenuity of expression in this difficult work, are considered to have been unapproached by any other poet. He has been imitated by numerous other poets, but the only one who has achieved any considerable excellence in this peculiar style is *Tul'sī Dās* (No. 128), who preceded him by writing a Sat Saī (treating of Rām, as Bihārī Lāl's treated of Krish'n) in the year 1585 A.D. Other good Sat Saīs are those of *Bikram* and *Chandan.* Bihārī's poem has been dealt with by innumerable commentators. Its difficulty and ingenuity are so great that it is called a veritable *akṣara-kāmadhēnu.* The best commentary is that by *Sūrati Misar* (No. 326), Agar'wālā. The verses were arranged in the order in which they now stand for the use of prince *A'ẓam Shāh,* and hence this edition is called the Āzim Shāhī recension. It has been translated into elegant Sanskrit verse by Paṇḍit *Hari Praçāda,* under the auspices of *Chēt Siŋgh,* Rājā of Banāras. Little is known about this great poet's life. His patron was a Rājā Jāī Siŋgh Kachh'wāhā, of *Amēr.* In 1600 A.D. Rājā *Mān Siŋgh* reigned at Amēr, and between him and the year 1819 there were three Jāī Siŋghs. The most probable patron of Bihārī Lāl was *Jāī Siŋgh Mirzā*, the grandson of *Jagat Siŋgh*, brother of Mān Siŋgh, and this would fix Bihārī Lāl as flourishing in the first half of the seventeenth century, or as a successor of Tul'sī Dās. (See Tod's *Rājasthān* ii, 364; Calc. ed. ii, 392.) Garcin de Tassy (i, 123) makes him contemporary with *Kabīr* (about 1400 A.D.), and states that the English call him the Thompson of India. He also, however, states that he lived in the sixteenth century, which is nearer the truth. Amongst those who have commentated on the Sat Saī may be mentioned *Chandr'* (No. 213), *Gōpāl Saran* (No. 215), *Sūrati Misar* (No. 326), *Krish'n* (No. 327), *Kāran* (No. 346), *Anwar Khān* (No. 397), *Zū'lfaqār* (No. 409), *Yūsuf Khān* (No. 421), *Raghu Nāth* (No. 559), *Lāl* (No. 561), *Sar'dār* (No. 571), *Lallū Jī Lāl* (No. 629), *Gaŋgā Dhar* (No. 811), *Rām Bakhsh* (No. 907).

197. छत्त्र॰ साल, *Chhattr' Sāl*, Rājā of *Par'nā* (*Pannā*), in *Bundēl'khaṇḍ*. Fl. 1650 A.D.

He was a great and famous patron of learning. He ordered *Lāl Kabi* to write the *Chhattra Par'kās* (Rāg.), in which is contained the whole history of the Bundēlās, from the beginning down to his time. See No. 202. He was killed in 1658 A.D. Cf. Tod, ii, 481; Calc. ed. ii, 526.

198. निवाज, *Niwāj* (*Nawāz*), the Brāhman, of the *Dōāb*. Fl. 1650 A.D.

Sun. He attended the court of Rājā *Chhattr' Sāl* (No. 197), the Bundēlā of *Par'nā*. Under orders from *A'ẓam Shāh* he translated the *Çakuntalā* into the vernacular.

The similarity of names has led to his being confounded with Niwāj (No. 448), the Muhammadan weaver, so that there is a general false impression that this poet turned a Musalmān.

199. रतन॰नेस कबि, the poet *Rat'nēs*. Fl. ? 1620 A.D.

He was father of the bard *Par'tāp Sāhi* (No. 149). He was author of many admired erotic verses.

200. पुरुखोत्तम कबि, the poet and bard *Purukhōttam*, of *Bundēl'khaṇḍ*. Fl. 1650 A.D.

Rāg.

201. विजयाभिनन्दन, *Bijayābhinandan*, of *Bundēl'khaṇḍ*. Fl. 1650 A.D.

These two attended the court of Rājā *Chhattr' Sāl* (No. 197), the Bundēlā of *Par'nā* (*Paṇnā*).

202. लाल कबि, the poet *Lāl*. Fl. 1658 A.D.

He attended the court of Rājā *Chhattr' Sāl* (No. 197), the Bundēlā. He was present at the battle of *Ḍhōl'pur* between *Dārā Shukōh* and *Āuraṅg'zēb*, in which *Chhattr' Sāl* was killed (1658). He wrote a treatise on lovers (see note to No. 87), entitled *Bishnu Bilās*; but he is most famous for the *Chhattra Par'kās* (Rāg.), or History of Chhattr', in Hindī or Braj Bhākhā verse. Garcin de Tassy (i, 304) gives the following account of this work, which I have not myself seen :—'It deals with the wars and order of succession of the ancient Rājās of *Bundēl'khaṇḍ*, and with the valour of the warrior nation of the Bundēlās. It contains minute details of the life of Chhattr' Sāl and of his father, Rājā *Champati Rāy*.[1] * * * Capt. Pogson has given a translation of Lāl's work, under the title of "A History of the Bundēlās," and Major Price has given the text of that portion of the work which refers to Chhattr' Sāl under the title of the "Chhatra Prokash, or Biographical Account of Chhatra Sāl." '

203. हरि केस कबि, the poet *Hari Kēs*, of *Jahāngīrābād Sehuḍā*, in *Bundēl'khaṇḍ*. Fl. 1650 A.D.

Sun.

204. हरि चन्द, the bard *Hari Chand*, of *Char'khārī*, in *Bundēl'khaṇḍ*. Fl. 1650.

205. पञ्चम कबि, the bard *Pañcham* the elder, of *Bundēl'-khaṇḍ*. Fl. 1650 A.D.

These three attended the court of Rājā *Chhattr' Sāl* (No. 197), the Bundēlā.

---

[1] According to Tod, Chhattr' Sāl's father's name was *Gōpī Nāth*.—*G.A.G.*

206. गम्भीर राय, *Gambhīr Rāy,* of *Nūr'pur.* Fl. 1650.

The bard who celebrated the rebellion of *Jagat Siŋgh,* of *Maū,* against *Shāh Jahān* (1628—1658). Text and translation of portion by Mr. Beames in J. A. S. B., vol. xliv (1875), p. 201. Interesting and important.

207. राव रतन, *Rāw Ratan,* the Raṭhāūr. Fl. 1650 A.D.

He was great grandson of Rājā *Uday Siŋgh,* of *Rat'lām.* In his honour an anonymous bard wrote a famous history entitled *Rāy'sā Rāw Ratan.* Cf. Tod, ii, 49 ; Calc. ed. ii, 55.

208. गोपाल कबि, the poet *Gōpāl* the elder. B. *1658* A.D.

He attended the court of *Mitrajīt Siŋgh.*

209. हरिबन्स मिसर, *Haribans Misar,* of *Bil'grām,* district *Har'dōī.* Fl. 1662.

According to a copy of the Padmāwat in his handwriting, he attended the court of Rājā *Hanumant Siŋgh,* of *Amēṭhī.* He is a well-known poet, and was vernacular teacher of *'Abdu'l Jalīl* (No. 179), of *Bil'grām.*

210. सबल सिङ्घ चौहान, *Sabal Siŋgh,* the Chāūhān. B. *1670* A.D.

The author of a condensed metrical translation of 24,000 verses of the *Mahābhārata.* There are various traditions as to who he was. Some say he was Rājā of *Chand'gaṛh,* others that he was Rājā of *Sabal'gaṛh.* Sib Siŋgh considers that he was a zamindār of some village in district *Iṭāwā̃.* He is possibly the same as another *Sabal Siŋgh Kabi* mentioned also by Sib Siŋgh as author of two works on composition (साहित्य)—(1) *Khaṭ Ritu* (Rāg.), (2) *Bhākhā Ritūpasaŋghār.*

211. स्री गोबिन्द कबि, the poet *Srī Gōbind.* B. (? Fl. Cf. No. 145) *1673* A.D.

He attended the court of *Sib Rāj,* the *Sulaŋkī,* of *Sitārā.*

212. देवी दास कबि, the poet *Dēbī Dās*, of *Bundēl'khaṇḍ*. Fl. 1685 A.D.

In the above year he was already a prolific author, and went to the court of king *Ratan Pāl Siŋgh*, of *Karāulī*, where he remained till his death. He wrote under that king's name a moral work entitled *Prēm Ratnākar*, which is said to be of rare excellence.

213. चन्द्र॰ कबि, the poet *Chandr'* the younger. B. *1692* A.D.

He attended the court of *Bandan Bābū*, of *Bhūpāl*, brother to *Sul'ṭān Paṭhān*, Nawāb of *Rāj'gaṛh*. He wrote a commentary on the *Sat Saī* of *Bihārī* (No. 196) in the *Kuṇḍaliyā* metre under the name of Sul'ṭān Paṭhān.

There is another mediocre poet of the same name, about whom Sib Siŋgh gives no particulars.

214. मुहम्मद खान, Sul'ṭān Nawāb *Muḥammad Khān alias Sul'ṭān Paṭhān*, of *Rāj'gaṛh*, in *Bhūpāl*. B. *1704* A.D.

He was a patron of poets, and the poet *Chandr'* the younger (No. 213) wrote in his name a commentary to the *Sat Saī* of *Bihārī* (No. 196) in the *Kuṇḍaliyā* metre.

215. गोपाल सरन, Rājā *Gōpāl Saran*. B. *1691* A.D.

His principal work is a commentary on the *Sat Saī* of *Bihārī* (No. 196), entitled *Prabandh Ghaṭ'nā*.

216. मोती राम कबि, the poet *Mōtī Rām*. B. *1683* A.D.

Haj. Author of the Braj version of the novel *Mādhōnal*, translated into Hindustānī by *Lallū Jī Lāl* (No. 629) and *Maẓ'har 'Alī Khān Wilā*. See Garcin de Tassy, i, 351, for further particulars.

217. घाघ, *Ghāgh*, of *Kanāuj*, in the *Dōāb*. B. *1696* A.D.

He was an agricultural poet, whose aphorisms have a wide authority all over Northern India. A number of them are inserted in *Bihār Peasant Life*. Poets in the same style, but of a more local (Eastern) reputation, were *Bhaḍḍar* and *Ḍāk*.

ADDENDA TO CHAPTER VIII.

218. जग नन्द कवि, the poet *Jag Nand,* of *Brindāban.* B. *1601* A.D.

Haj.

219. जोयसी कवि, the poet *Jōyasī.* B. *1601* A.D.

Haj.

220. खड़ग सेन, *Khaṛag Sēn,* the Kāyasth, of *Gwāliyar.* B. *1603* A.D.

He wrote two esteemed works, entitled *Dān-Līlā* and *Dīp-Mālikā Charitr'.*

221. गोकुल बिहारी, *Gōkul Bihārī.* B. *1603* A.D.

222. परम्मेस कवि, the poet *Par'mēs* the elder. B. *1611* A.D.

Haj., Sun. (? cf. No. 616).

223. गोबिन्द अटल कवि, the poet *Gōbind Aṭal.* B. *1613.*

Haj.

224. अहम्मद कवि, the poet *Ah'mad.* B. *1613* A.D.

He was a Sufi by religion, and sympathised with the Vēdānta system of belief (so Sib Siṅgh; but judging from his writings, he appears to have been rather a Vaishṇava). His verses in the *dōhā* and *sōr'ṭhā* metres are said to be very voluptuous.

225. गोप नाथ कवि, the poet *Gōp Nāth.* B. *1613* A.D.

226. बिहारि दास कवि, the poet *Bihārī Dās,* of *Braj.* B. *1613.*

Rāg.

227. ब्रिन्दाबन दास, *Brindāban Dās,* of *Braj.* B. *1613* A.D.

Rāg.

I have collected in Mithilā songs (apparently belonging to the Kabīr Panthī sect), by a Brindāban. I do not know if he is the same poet as he who is quoted in Rāg.

228. कला निधि कवि, the poet *Kalā Nidhi* the elder. B. *1615* A.D.

229. अभिमन्यु कवि, the poet *Abhimanya.* B. *1623* A.D.

His poems are said to deal expertly with the passion of love.

230. घासी राम कवि, the poet *Ghāsī Rām.* B. *1623* A.D.

Haj. A poem by him is given in *Rep. Arch. Sur. Ind.* xvii, 107.

231. तत्त्व बेता कवि, the poet *Tattwa Bētā.* B. *1623* A.D.

Haj.

232. ब्रज पति कवि, the poet *Braj Patī.* B. *1623* A.D.

Rāg.

233. राजा राम कवि, the poet *Rājā Rām.* B. *1623* A.D.

Haj. Cf. No. 396.

234. सदानन्द कवि, the poet *Sadānand.* B. *1623* A.D.

Haj., Dig.

235. सन्त दास, *Sant Dās,* of *Braj.* Fl. *1623* A.D.

Rāg. However all the poems given under his name are identical with others by *Sūr Dās* (No. 37).

236. सेख कवि, the poet, *Sēkh.* B. *1623.* A.D.

Haj., Sūd.

237. हीरा मनि कवि, the poet *Hīrā Manī.* B. *1623* A.D.

Haj.

238. जदु नाथ कवि, the poet *Jadu Nāth.* B. *1624* A.D.

Māl.

239. बल्लभ रसिक कबि, the poet *Ballabh Rasik*. B. *1624* A.D.

Haj., Rāg. He is possibly the same as a *Ballabh Kabi* mentioned by Sib Siṇgh as the author of much admired *dōhās*.

240. भीखम कबि, the poet *Bhīkham*. B. *1624* A.D.

Haj. He is possibly the same as a poet of the same name also in Haj., whom Sib Siṇgh dates as B. *1651* A.D. He is also possibly the same as a *Bhīkham Ḍās* in Rāg.

241. मधु सूदन कबि, the poet *Madhu Sūdan*. B. *1624* A.D.

Haj.

242. ब्यास जी कबि, the poet *Byās Jī*. B. *1628* A.D.

Rāg. The author of many celebrated *dōhās* on morals. Many of them are included in Haj.

243. मलूक दास, *Malūk Dās*, a Brāhman of *Kaṛā Mānik'pur*. B. *1628* A.D.

Rāg.

244. गोबरन्धन कबि, the poet *Gōbar'dhan*. B. *1631* A.D.

245. भगन्वती दास *Bhag'watī Dās*. B. *1631* A.D.

A Brāhman who composed a work entitled *Nām'kētōpākhyān*.

246. घन राय कबि, the poet *Ghan Rāy*. B. *1633* A.D.

247. बेनी कबि, the poet *Bēnī* the elder, of *As'nī*, district *Fatih'pur*. B. *1633* A.D.

? Sun. The author of a treatise on lovers. (See note to No. 87.)

248. सकल कबि, the poet *Sakal*. B. *1633* A.D.

Haj.

249. हरि जन कबि, the poet *Hari Jan*. B. *1633* A.D.

Haj.

250. अनन्त कबि, the poet *Anant*. B. *1635* A.D.

Sun. A poem by him, entitled the *Anantānand*, deals with the subject of lovers. (See note to No. 87.)

251. परन्बीन कबिराय, *Parbīn*, the poet-laureate. B. *1635* A.D.

Haj. The author of quietistic (शान्ति रस) poems on morals (नीति).

252. राम जी कबि, the poet *Rām Jī*. B. *1635* A.D.

Haj.

253. मदन मोहन, *Madan Mōhan*. B. *1635* A.D.

Rāg.

254. निधान कबि, the poet *Nidhān* the elder. B. *1641* A.D.

Haj.

255. ससि सेखर कबि, the poet *Sasi Sēkhar*. B. *1642* A.D.

Haj.

256. भू धर कबि, the poet *Bhū Dhar*, of *Banāras*. B. *1643* A.D.

Haj.

257. चतुर सिङ्घ राना, king *Chatur Siṇgh*. B. *1644* A.D.

He wrote poems in a simple style.

258. पति राम कबि, the poet *Pati Rām*. B. *1644* A.D.

Haj.

259. पहन्लाद कबि, the poet *Pah'lād*. B. *1644* A.D.

Haj.

260. ब्रज लाल कबि, the poet *Braj Lāl*. B. *1645* A.D.

Haj.

261. देब दत्त, *Dēb Datt'*, the Brāhman of *Kus'maṛā* (?), district *Kanāuj*. B. *1646* A.D.

No particulars. Possibly the same as a *Dēb Datt' Kabi* mentioned by Sib Singh as born *1648* A.D., and as another *Dēb Datt'* mentioned by the same as B. (? fl.) *1695* A.D. and author of a work entitled *Jōg-Tattwa*.

262. सिरोमनि कबि, the poet *Sirōmanī*. B *1646*.

Haj. Cf. No. 267.

263. बल देब कबि, the poet *Bal Dēb* the elder. B. *1647* A.D.

Haj., Sun.

264. जग जीवन कबि, the poet *Jag Jiban*. B. *1648* A.D.

Haj.

265. तोख कबि, the poet *Tōkh*. B. *1648* A.D.

Māl., Haj., Sun.

266. मुकुन्द कबि, the poet *Mukund* the elder. B. *1648*.

Haj.

267. रसिक सिरोमनि कबि, the poet *Rasik Sirōmanī*. B. *1648* A.D.

Haj. Cf. No. 262.

268. रूप नारायन कबि, the poet *Rūp Narāyan*. B. *1648* A.D.

Haj. Possibly the same as a *Rūp Kabi* mentioned by Sib Singh without particulars.

269. स्याम लाल कबि, the poet *Syām Lāl*. B. *1648* A.D.

Sūd. (?) Possibly the same as a *Syām Kabi* in Haj. Cf. No. 341.

270. हर जू कबि, the poet *Har Jū*. B. *1648* A.D.

Haj.

271. तेग पानि कबि, the poet *Tēg Pānī*. B. *1651* A.D.

Haj.

272. बजीदा कबि, the poet *Bajīdā*. Fl. *1651* A.D.

Haj.

273. भरम्मी कबि, the poet *Bhar'mī*. B. *1651* A.D.

Haj.

274. भिङ्ग कबि, the poet *Bhriṅg*. B. *1651* A.D.

Haj.

275. सही राम कबि, the poet *Sahī Rām*. B. *1651* A.D.

Haj.

276. हुसेन कबि, the poet *Ḥusēn*. B. *1651* A.D.

Haj.

277. अच्छर अनन्य कबि, the poet *Achchhar Ananya*. B. *1653* A.D.

Has written quietistic (शान्ति रस) poems.

278. कमञ्च कबि, the poet *Kamañch*, of *Rāj'putānā*. Fl. before *1653* A.D.

Sib Singh states that he has met some poems by him in a Mār'wārī anthology dated Sambat 1710 (A.D. 1653).

279. रघु नाथ, *Raghu Nāth* the elder. B. *1653* A.D.

Haj.

280. उदय नाथ बन्दीजन, *Uday Nāth*, the bard of *Banāras*. B. *1654* A.D.

281. अमर दास कबि, the poet *Amar Dās*. B. *1655* A.D.

Sib Singh describes him as having written some commonplace verses, and adds that he has neither seen nor heard of any complete work of his.

282. कुलपति मिसर, *Kul'pati Misar*. B. *1657* A.D.

Haj., Rāg.

283. ग्वाल, *Gwāl* the elder. B. *1658* A.D.

Haj.

284. मोहन कबि, the poet *Mōhan*. B. *1658* A.D.

Haj., Rāg. Cf. No. 329.

285. रस राम कबि, the poet *Ras Rām*. Fl. *1658* A.D.

Haj. An erotic poet.

286. बनमाली दास गोसाँईं, the master *Ban'mālī Dās*. B. *1659* A.D.

He was learned in Arabic, Persian, and Sanskrit. His Vedantic dōhās are much admired.

287. अनाथ दास कवि, the poet *Anath Dās*. B. *1659* A.D.

The author of poems in the quietistic style (शान्ति रस), and also of a complete work entitled the *Bichār Mālā*.

288. जनार्दन कवि, the poet *Janārdan*. B. *1661* A.D.

An erotic writer.

289. बलि जू कवि, the poet *Bali Jū*. Fl. *1665* A.D.

Haj.

290. बुध राम कवि, the poet *Budh Rām*. Fl. *1665* A.D.

Haj.

291. कल्यान कवि, the poet *Kalyān*. B. *1669* A.D.

Haj., Rāg.

292. बिद्या नाथ कवि, the poet *Bidyā Nāth* of the *Dōāb*. B. *1673* A.D.

293. लाल बिहारी कवि, the poet *Lāl Bihārī*. B. *1673* A.D.

294. मीर रुस्तम कवि, the poet *Mīr Rustam*. B. *1678* A.D.

Haj.

295. मीरी माधव कवि, the poet *Mīrī Mādhab*. B. *1678* A.D.

Haj.

296. मुहम्मद कवि, the poet *Muhammad*. B. *1678* A.D.

Haj.

297. गोपाल दास, *Gōpāl Dās*, of Braj. B. *1679* A.D.

Rāg.

298. बिहारी कवि, the poet *Bihārī*. B. *1681* A.D.

Haj.

299. आसिफ खाँ कवि, the poet *Āsiph (Āṣaf) Khān*. B. *1681* A.D.

300. केसव राय बाबू, *Kēsab Rāy Bābū*, of *Bundēl'khaṇḍ*. B. *1682* A.D.

Sat. He has written an excellent work on lovers. (See note to No. 87.)

301. कनक कवि, the poet *Kanak*. B. *1683* A.D.

An erotic poet.

302. मनःसुख कवि, the poet *Man'sukh*. B. *1683* A.D.

Haj.

303. मिसर कवि, the poet *Misar*. B. *1683* A.D.

Haj.

304. रबि दत्त कवि, the poet *Rabi Datt' alias* Bābū *Sabitā Datt'*. B. *1685* A.D.

Sat.

305. गोबिन्द जी कवि, the poet *Gōbind Jī*. B. *1693* A.D.

Haj.

306. देबी बन्दीजन, the bard *Dēbī*. B. *1693* A.D.

He wrote a *Sūr Sāgar* in the comic style.

307. देबी राम कवि, the poet *Dēbī Rām*. B. *1693* A.D.

A commonplace quietistic (शान्ति रस) poet.

308. कुन्दन कवि, the poet *Kundan*, of *Bundēl'khaṇḍ*. Fl. *1695* A.D.

Haj. He has written a good treatise on lovers. (See note to No. 87.)

309. स्याम सरन कवि, the poet *Syām Saran*. B. *1696* A.D.

The author of a work entitled *Swarōday* (Rāg.).

310. गोध कवि, the poet *Gōdh*. B. *1698* A.D.

311. छेम कवि, the poet *Chhēm*. B. *1698* A.D.

No particulars. He is possibly the same as a *Chhēm Karan*, of the *Dōāb* mentioned by Sib Siṇgh. Cf. Nos. 87 and 103.

312. छैल कवि, the poet *Chhāil.* B. *1698* A.D.

Haj.

313. जुगुल कवि, the poet *Jugul.* B. *1698* A.D.

Rāg. He is said to have written some very ingenious verses. He is possibly the same as a *Jugul Dās* Kabi mentioned by Sib Singh without date.

314. द्विज चन्द्र कवि, the poet *Dwij Chandr'.* B. *1698* A.D.

315. ब्रज दास, *Braj Dās* the elder. B. *1698* A.D.

Haj., ? Rāg.

316. स्याम दास कवि, the poet *Syām Dās.* B. *1698* A.D.

Rāg.

317. कारे बेग फकीर, *Karē Bēg,* the mendicant. B. *1699* A.D.

Haj.

318. सन्त कबि, the poet *Sant.* B. *1702* A.D.

An erotic poet.

CHAPTER IX.

THE EIGHTEENTH CENTURY.

Introductory note.

THE period embraced in the present chapter includes two series of events of capital importance in the history of India,—the decline and fall of the Mughal empire and the supremacy and fall of the Marāṭhā power. *Bahādur Shāh* succeeded to the throne of *Āuraŋg'zēb* in 1707, and *Shāh 'Ālam* was rescued from the hands of the Marāṭhās by Lord Lake in 1803. He died in 1806, his son *Ak'bar* II succeeding only to the nominal dignity of emperor. On the other hand *Bālājī Vishwanāth*, the first *pēshwā*, rose to power with the accession of *Sāhu* to the Marāṭhā throne in 1707, and the last *pēshwā* was overthrown in the second Marāṭhā war in 1803-4.

Such times were favourable neither to the founding of new religions nor to the cultivation of the arts. A few religious reformers, it is true, sprung up, but their efforts, though crowned with a certain temporary success, have had none of the abiding effect on Hindūstān which was left by *Rāmānand* and *Ballabhāchār'j*. Rāj'putānā, the home of the bards, was no longer a nation united against the Mughals, but was torn by intestine strife. As one of these bards himself exclaimed at a feast given by the two princes, 'Jōdh'pur and Ambēr can dethrone the enthroned; but the latter slew his son, and the former murdered his father.' In the scramble for the *curée* no relationship, no tie of friendship, was allowed to interfere. The same haste to seize upon the plunder of the decaying empire attacked the greatest and best of the kings of Rājāsthān. Even *Jāī Siŋgh*, of *Jāīpur*, the royal historian and astronomer, one of the most learned scientific men that India has ever produced, did not disdain to wrest the sovereignty of *Būndī* from his own sister's husband. Such actions the bards could not approve, and so they remained silent. Only two bardic chronicles appear to have been written in the eighteenth century, and of these, one, the *Bijāī Bilās*, records the fratricidal warfare between *Bijāī* and *Rām Siŋgh* of *Jōdh'pur*.

In other branches of literature no name of the first class appears. Some of the great writers on the *ars poetica* of the seventeenth century left pupils, who carried on their style with some success, but the century now under consideration shone most as an age of commentators. Nearly all the great poets of the preceding period found their best annotators and explainers in the eighteenth century. Perhaps this, too, was a natural sequence. Kēsab Dās and his followers laid down and fixed for ever the canons of Indian poetic criticism, and the next generation adopted these lines and applied them to already existing acknowledged poetic masterpieces.

Part I.—Religious Poets.

[Arranged as far as possible in order of date.]

319. प्रिया दास, the master *Priyā Dās*, of *Brindāban*, in the *Dōāb*. Fl. 1712 A.D.

In the above year he wrote his well-known gloss on the *Bhakt Mālā* of *Nābhā Dās* (see No. 51). He is possibly the same as the author of a *Bhāgavat* in the dialect of *Bundēl'khaṇḍ* mentioned by Ward (*View of the History of the Hindūs*, vol. ii, p. 481). See Garcin de Tassy, i, 405.

320. गङ्गा पति, *Gaṅgā Pati*. Fl. 1719 A.D.

Author of a work entitled *Bigyān Bilās*, written in Sambat 1775. It is a treatise on the different philosophical doctrines of the Hindūs, and recommends the Vedantic system and a mystic life. It is written in the form of a dialogue between a preceptor and his disciple. There is a copy of the work in the Mack. Coll. See Garcin de Tassy, i, 182.

321. सिब नारायन, *Sib Nārāyan*, the Rāj'pūt of the Nēri-vāna tribe, of *Chandāwan*, near *Ghāzīpur*. Fl. cir. 1735 A.D.

The founder of the sect of *Sib Nārāīnīs*. He flourished in the reign of *Muḥammad Shāh* (1719—1748). He was a voluminous writer in the inculcation of his doctrines, and eleven books in Hindī verse are ascribed to him. These are entitled (1) *Laō* or *Law Granth*, (2) *Sānt Bilās*, (3) *Bhajan Granth*, (4) *Sānt Sundar*, (5) *Guru Nyās*, (6) *Sāntāchārī*, (7) *Sāntōpadēs*, (8) *Sabdābalī*, (9) *Sānt Par'wān*, (10) *Sānt Mahimā*, (11) *Sānt Sāgar*. There is also a twelfth, the seal of the whole, but it has not yet been divulged, remaining in the exclusive possession of the head of the sect. Cf. Wilson, *Religious Sects of the Hindūs*, i, 359, quoted by Garcin de Tassy, i, 475.

322. **लाल जी,** *Lāl Jī,* the Kayasth of *Kādhalā,* district *Muzaffar'nagar.* Fl. 1751 A.D.

In the above year he wrote a commentary to the *Bhākt Mālā* (see No. 51) entitled *Bhakt Urbasī.*

323. **जग जीवन दास,** *Jag Jīban Dās,* the Chandēlā of *Koṭ'wā,* district *Bārābaŋkī.* Fl. 1761 A.D.

He was founder of the *Satya Nāmī* sect, and also wrote poems in the vernacular. Amongst his successors and disciples may be mentioned *Jalālī Dās, Dūlam Dās,* and *Dēbī Dās* (No. 487), all of whom were poets. He and they excelled in the quietistic style. Amongst his works may be mentioned the *Gyān Par'kās,* the *Mahā-par'lāī,* and the *Pratham Granth.* See Wilson, *Religious Sects of the Hindūs,* p. 357; Garcin de Tassy, i, 256.

324. **दुल्हा राम,** *Dulhā Rām.* Fl. 1776 A.D.

He became a *Rām Sanēhī* in 1776, and died in 1824. He was third spiritual teacher of the sect. He left about 10,000 *Sabads* and 4,000 *Sākhīs.* See Garcin de Tassy, i, 161.

Part II.—Other Poets.

[Arranged as far as possible according to their patrons, or the states to which they were attached.]

325. **जै सिङ्ह सवाई,** Rājā *Jāī Siŋgh Sawāī,* the *Kachh'wāhā,* of *Amēr.* Reigned 1699—1743 A.D.

He was not only a patron of poets, but wrote his own autobiography, entitled *Jāī Siŋgh Kalpadrum,* which is a valuable historical work. He was one of the most remarkable men of his time. See Tod's *Rājāsthān,* ii, 356-68 (Calc. ed. 393—407).

326. **सूरति मिसर,** *Sūrati Misar,* of *Āg'rā.* Fl. 1720 A.D.

Sūd. The author of an esteemed commentary on the *Sat Saī* of *Bihārī Lal* (No. 196), also of a work entitled *Saras Ras* (Rāg.), a *Nakh'sikh* (see note to No. 87), a commentary to the *Rasik Priyā* (see No. 134), and a work on rhetoric entitled *Alaŋkār Mālā.* During the reign of *Muḥammad Shāh* (1719—1748) he translated the *Baītāl Pachīsī* (Rāg.) into Braj Bhākhā under orders of *Jāī Siŋgh Sawāī* (No. 325, 1699—1743) from the Sanskrit *Vētāla Pañchaviṁçatikā* of *Çiva Dāsa.* The Braj Bhākhā version is the foundation of the well-known Hindūstānī version of *Lallū Jī Lāl* (see No. 629). See Garcin de Tassy, i, 306, 484, and also preface to the last-named work.

327. क्रिश्न कबि, the poet *Krish'n,* of *Jāīpur.* Fl. 1720 A.D.

He was a pupil of the poet *Bihārī Lāl* (No. 196), and entered the service of Rājā *Jāī Siŋgh* (No. 325) *Sawāī.* He wrote a poetical commentary on *Bihārī Lāl's Sat Saī* together with a supplementary gloss. Cf. No. 180.

328. क्रिपा राम कबि, the poet *Kripā Rām,* of *Jāīpur.* Fl. 1720 A.D.

He was one of the astronomers of Rājā *Jāī Siŋgh Sawāī* (No. 325). He wrote an astronomical work in the vernacular called *Samay-bōdh* (? *Samay-ōgh*).

329. मोहन कबि, the poet *Mōhan.* Fl. 1720 A.D.

He attended the court of Rājā *Jāī Siŋgh Sawāī* (No. 325). Cf. No. 284.

330. बुद्ध राव, *Buddh Rāw,* the *Hāṛā.* Fl. 1710—1740 A.D.

He was rājā of *Būndī,* and was married to the sister of *Jāī Siŋgh Sawāī,* of *Āmēr* (No. 325). *Bahādur Shāh* (1707—1712), the emperor, owed him in great measure his throne in the contest with his brother *'Ālam.* Buddh also saved him in the rebellion of *Sayyad Bar'hānā* in 1724 and restored him to power. For his signal services in the contest for the emperor's throne he was granted the title of Rāw Rājā. He was conquered and deposed about 1740 by his brother-in-law Jāī Siŋgh. He was himself a poet and a patron of poets. See Tod, ii, 482 and ff. (Calc. ed. ii, 528 and ff.).

331. **भोज मिसर कबि,** the poet *Bhōj Misar* the elder. Fl. 1720 A.D.

He attended the court of *Buddh Rāw* (No. 330), and was the author of a work entitled *Misar Siŋgār.*

332. **गुर दत्त॰ सिङ्घ॰,** Rajā *Gur Datt' Siŋgh alias Bhūpati Kabi,* of *Amēṭhī,* in *Āudh.* Fl. cir. 1720 A.D.

Sat., Sun. He was not only a poet himself, but was a great patron of poets. In Sun. he is called *Chhitipāl.* Garcin de Tassy, i, 121, mentions a *Bhūpati* or *Bhū Dēo,* but a Kāyasth by caste, the author of a work in Hindī verse entitled *Srī Bhāgawat.* Cf. No. 604.

333. **भग॰वन्त राय खीँची,** *Bhag'want Rāy* the *Khīchī,* of *Asōthar,* district *Fatih'pur.* Fl. 1750 A.D.

? Sun. He was son of one *Arārū,* founder of the *Asōthar* family. He maintained his independence for several years, and successfully opposed the emperor's troops, but finally, in 1760, was killed by treachery, and was succeeded by his son *Rūp Rāy.* See Growse, *Supplement to the Fatih'pur Gazetteer*, pp. 5, 8, where 1860 is a misprint for 1760. He was author of a *Rāmāyan,* and ancestor of *Kām'tā Par'sād* (No. 644). He is possibly the same as *Bhag'want Kabi* and as a *Bhag'wān Kabi,* both mentioned by Sib Siŋgh ; and as a *Bhag'-want Kabi* quoted in Sun.

334. **उदय नाथ त्रिबेदी कबीन्द्र॰,** *Uday Nāth Tribēdī,* the poet-laureate, of *Ban'pūrā,* in the *Dōāb.* Fl. cir. 1720 A.D.

Sat. He was son of *Kālidās Tribēdi* (No. 159), the author of the *Hajārā,* and was as famous a poet as his parent. At first he attended the court of king *Himmat Siŋgh,* of *Amēṭhī* (cf. No. 160), and usually signed his poems as by *Uday Nāth.* Subsequently the king gave him the title of *Kabīndr'* or poet-laureate, and thereafter he signed himself Kabīndr'. He got the title as a reward for writing a work entitled *Ras-chandrōday,* or *Rati-binōd* or *Chandrōday,* or *Ras-chandrikā.* It deals with vernacular composition (भाखा साहित्य), and was written

Sambat 1804 (A.D. 1747). Subsequently he stayed a short time with king *Gur Datt' Siŋgh* (No. 332), of *Amēṭhī,* with *Bhāg'want Rāy* (No. 333), *Khīchī,* of *Asōthaṛ* (d. 1760), with *Gaj Siŋgh,* Rājā of *Āj'mēr,*[1] and with king *Buddh Rāw, Hāṛā,* of *Būndī* (1710—1740) (No. 330). By all these was he highly honoured.

It may be mentioned that there was another *Kabīndr' Tribēdī,* of *Bētī,* in the district of *Rāy Barēlī,* who also was a poet of repute.

335. सुख देब कबि, the poet *Sukh Dēb,* of the *Dōāb.* Fl. cir. 1750 A.D.

He is possibly the same as the *Sukh Dēb Misar,* of *Dāulat'pur* (No. 356), or as the other poet of the same name of Kampilā (No. 160). He attended the court of *Bhag'want Rāy, Khīchī* (No. 333) (d. 1760), of *Asōthar,* in *Fatih'pur.*

336. भू धर कबि, the poet *Bhū Dhar,* of *Asōthar,* district *Fatih'pur.* Fl. cir. 1750 A.D.

He attended the court of *Bhag'want Rāy, Khīchī* (No. 333) (d. 1760), of *Asōthar,* in *Fatih'pur.*

337. मल्ल कबि, the poet *Mall.* Fl. cir. 1750 A.D.

He attended the court of *Bhag'want Rāy, Khīchī* (No. 333) (d. 1760), of *Asōthar,* in *Fatih'pur.*

338. सम्भु नाथ मिसर कबि, the poet *Sambhu Nāth Misar,* of *Asōthar,* district *Fatih'pur.* Fl. cir. 1750 A.D.

Sat. He attended the court of *Bhag'want Rāy, Khīchī* (No. 333) (d. 1760), of *Asōthar,* in *Fatih'pur.* He was author of (1) *Ras Kallōl,* (2) *Ras Taraŋginī,* (3) *Alaŋkār Dīpak.* He was preceptor of the poet *Sib Ar'sēlā* (No. 339), and of many other poets.

339. सिब अरसेला कबि, the poet and bard *Sib Ar'sēlā,* of *Deutahā̃,* district *Gōṛā.* Fl. cir. 1770 A.D.

---

[1] I can find no mention of this Rājā in Tod.

He was a pupil of *Sambhu Nāth Misar* (No. 338), of *Asōthar,* in *Fatih'pur,* and became teacher of *Jagat Siŋgh Bisēn* (No. 340). He wrote a work on vernacular composition (साहित्य) entitled *Rasik Bilās.* He also wrote (2) *Alaŋkār Bhūkhan ;* (3) a prosody.

340. जगत सिङ्ह *Jagat Siŋgh, the Bisēn.* Fl. cir. 1770 A.D.

He belonged to the family of the Rājā of *Gōḍā* and *Bhin'gā.* He was ta'alluq'dār of *Deutahā̃,* in which village resided the bard *Sib Arsēlā* (No. 339). He became a pupil of his in the art of poetry, and wrote a treatise on prosody named *Chhand Sriŋgār.* He also wrote a treatise on rhetoric (अलङ्कार) entitled *Sāhitya Sudhā-nidhi.* Cf. No. 605.

341. स्याम लाल कबि, the poet *Syām Lāl,* of *Jahānābād.* Fl. cir. 1750 A.D.

Sūd. (?) He attended the court of *Bhag'want Rāy, Khīchī* (No. 333) (d. 1760), of *Asōthar,* in *Fatih'pur.* Cf. No. 269.

342. निवाज, *Niwāj (Nawāz),* the Brāhman of *Bundēl'khaṇḍ.* Fl. cir. 1750.

He attended the court of *Bhag'want Rāy Khīchī* (d. 1760), of *Asōthar,* in *Fatih'pur.* Possibly the same as No. 448.

343. सारङ्ग कबि, the poet *Sāraŋg,* of *Asōthar,* district *Fatih'pur.* Fl. cir. 1750 A.D.

He attended the court of *Bhawānī Siŋgh, Khīchī,* nephew of *Bhag'want Rāy, Khīchī* (No. 333) (d. 1760), of *Asōthar,* in *Fatih'pur.*

344. भिखारी दास, *Bhikhārī Dās,* the Kāyasth, of *Ar'wal,* in *Bundēl'khaṇḍ.* B. *1723.*

He is counted as one of the masters of vernacular composition. Amongst his works may be mentioned (1) a treatise on prosody entitled *Chhandōrnab,* (2) *Ras-sārāns,* (3) *Kābya-nir'nay,* (4) *Sriŋgār-nir'nay,* (5) *Bāg Bahār,* (6) *Prēm-ratnākar.* In No. 3 a number of poets are mentioned. It is quoted in this work as 'Nir.'

345. गिरि धर कबिराय, the poet-laureate *Giri Dhar*, of the *Dōāb*. B. *1713*.

Rāg. He was the famous author of verses on morals and occasional pieces in the *Kuṇḍaliyā* metre. He is considered the greatest master of this metre. See Kellogg's *Hindī Grammar, Prosody*, p. 25. Possibly the same as No. 483.

346. करन भट्ट, the bard *Karan*, of *Par'nā* (*Pannā*), in *Bundēl'khaṇḍ*. B. *1737*.

He composed under the patronage of Rājās *Sabhā Siŋgh* (cf. No. 155) and *Hir'dāī Sāhi*, the Bundēlās of *Par'nā* (*Pannā*), a commentary on the *Sat Saī* of *Bihārī* (No. 196) entitled the *Sāhitya Chandrikā*. He was skilled at impromptu versification, and at completing unfinished verses given to him suddenly as a test of skill, and this gained him many gifts and honours. The date given is taken from Sib Siŋgh, but I can find no trace of any king of Par'ṇā called Sabhā Siŋgh. The *Report of the Arch. Sur. Ind.* xxi, 112, mentions a Hir'dāī Sāhi of Pannā who succeeded his father Chattr' Sāl in A.D. (? Sambat) 1718. Cf. No. 504.

347. आनन्द घन कबि, the poet *Ānand Ghan*, of *Dillī*. Fl. 1720 ; D. 1739 A.D. 504.

Rāg., Sun. Sib Siŋgh states that his poems are as brilliant as the sun. He has never seen any complete work of his, but has as many as five hundred short pieces by him. According to the *Sāhitya Bhūkhan* of *Mahādēo Par'sād* he was a Kāyasth by caste, and was *Muḥammad Shāh's* (1719—1748) Munshī. Before his death he retired to *Brindāban*, and was killed in the capture of *Mathurā* by *Nādir Shāh*. His best known work is the *Sujān Sāgar*. He is possibly the same as another *Ānand Kabi* mentioned by Sib Siŋgh as born in 1654 A.D., and the author of a work on sexual intercourse entitled *Kōk Sār* (Rag.). He sometimes signed himself *Ghan Ānand*.

348. जुगुल किशोर भट्ट, *Jugul Kishōr Bhaṭṭ*, of *Kāithal*, district *Kar'nāl*, in the *Pañjāb*. Fl. 1740 A.D.

He was a prominent figure among the attendants at the court of the emperor *Muḥammad Shāh* (1719—1748). In Sambat 1803 (A.D.

1746) he wrote a first-rate work on rhetoric (अलङ्कार) entitled the *Alaŋkār-nidhi*, in which he has described ninety-six *alaŋkāras* with examples. He states in this work that there were four principal poets attending his own court, named, respectively, *Rudr' Mani Misar* (No. 352), *Sukh Lāl* (No. 354), *Sant Jīb* (No. 353), and *Gumān Jī Misar* (No. 349). A number of detached poems by him are included in a compilation entitled the *Kishōr Saŋgrah*. He is possibly the same as a *Jugul Kishōr Kabi* mentioned by Sib Siŋgh (without date) as an erotic writer.

349. गुमान जी मिसर, *Gumān Jī Misar*, of *Sā̃ṛī*, district *Har'dōī*. Fl. 1740 A.D.

He was skilled in composition and in Sanskrit. He attended the court of the emperor *Muḥammad Shāh* (1719—1748) of Dillī, under the protection of *Jugul Kishōr Bhaṭṭ* (No. 348). Subsequently he attended the court of *'Alī Ak'bar Khān Muḥammadī*, who was himself an excellent poet, and who had in his service *Nidhān* (No. 350), *Prēm Nāth* (No. 351), and other great poets. Gumān Jī wrote the *Kalā Nidhi*, which is an excellent line-for-line commentary in various metres on the *Naiṣadha* of *Çrī Harṣa*. He also wrote a special commentary named *Salil*[1] on the *Pañchanalīya*, which is the name of a difficult portion of the *Naiṣadha*. He is possibly the same as another *Gumān Kabi* mentioned by Sib Siŋgh as born in 1731, and author of a work entitled *Krish'n Chandrikā*.

350. निधान, *Nidhān*, the Brāhman. Fl. 1751 A.D.

He attended the court of *'Alī Ak'bar Khān Muḥammadī*, where he had great repute. He wrote a highly poetical *Sālihōtr'* or treatise on veterinary surgery in the vernacular. He was a fellow courtier of *Gumān Jī Misar* (No. 349) and *Prēm Nāth* (No. 351).

351. प्रेम नाथ, *Prēm Nāth* the Brāhman of *Kaluā*, district *Khērī*, in *Āudh*. Fl. 1770 A.D.

Sun. He attended the court of *'Alī Ak'bar Khān Muḥammadī*, and translated the *Brahmōttarakhaṇḍa* into the vernacular. He was a

[1] Or Sib Siŋgh, from whom this is taken, may mean that he made the Pañchanalīya as clear as water.

fellow courtier with *Gumān Jī Misar* (No. 349) and *Nidhān* (No. 350). He is possibly the same as a *Prēm Kabi* quoted by Sib Siŋgh.

352. **रुद्र मनि मिसर,** *Rudr' Mani Misar,* the Brāhman. Fl. 1740 A.D.

He attended the court of *Jugul Kishōr Bhaṭṭ* (No. 348) at *Dillī.*

353. **सन्त जीब कबि,** the poet *Sant Jīb.* Fl. 1740 A.D. He attended the court of *Jugul Kishōr Bhaṭṭ* (No. 348).

354. **सुख लाल कबि,** the poet *Sukh Lāl.* Fl. 1740 A.D. Sūd. He attended the court of *Jugul Kishōr Bhaṭṭ* (No. 348).

355. **हरि नाथ,** *Hari Nāth,* of *Guj'rāt,* afterwards of *Banāras.* B. *1769* A.D.

The author of a treatise on rhetoric entitled *Alaŋkār Dar'pan.* He is possibly the same as a Hari Nāth mentioned by Garcin de Tassy (i, 218) as author of the *Pōthī Shāh Muhammad Shāhī* or History of *Muḥammad Shāh* (1719—1748), of which a manuscript is preserved in the British Museum, No. 6651E, Additional Manuscripts.

356. **सुख देब मिसर कबि,** the poet *Sukh Dēb Misar,* of *Dāulat'pur,* district *Rāy Barēlī.* Fl. 1740 A.D.

He attended the court of Rāw *Mar'dan Siŋgh Bāīs,* of *Dāuṛiyā Khērā,* in *Āudh,* and wrote in his name a treatise on lovers (see note to No. 87) entitled *Rasār'nab* (Rāg.). The bard *Sambhu Nāth* (No. 357) was his pupil. See Garcin de Tassy, i, 479. Cf. No. 335.

357. **सम्भु नाथ कबि,** the poet and bard *Sambhu Nāth.* Fl. 1750 A.D.

He was pupil of *Sukh Dēb Misar* (No. 356), of *Dāulat'pur,* and was author of a *Rāmāyan* entitled *Rām Bilās.* Cf. No. 366.

358. दूलह त्रिबेदी, *Dūlah Tribēdī,* of *Ban'pūrā,* in the *Dōāb.* Fl. 1746 A.D.

Sat. He was son of *Uday Nāth Tribēdī* (No. 334), and grandson of *Kālidās Tribēdī* (No. 159), the celebrated compiler of the *Hajārā.* He wrote a work of great authority on vernacular composition (भाखा साहित्य) entitled *Kabi-kul Kaṇṭhābharan.*

359. बल देव कवि, the poet *Bal Dēb,* of *Baghēl'khaṇḍ.* Fl. 1746 A.D.

He attended the court of king *Bikram Shāh,* the Baghēl of *Dewarā-nagar.*[1] In the above year, at the suggestion of this prince, he compiled an anthology entitled *Sat-kabi-girā Bilās* (quoted in this work as 'Sat.') which contains poems by seventeen different authors, viz.—

(1) *Kēsab Dās* (No. 134).
(2) *Chintāmaṇi* (No. 143).
(3) *Mati Ram* (No. 146).
(4) *Sambhu Nāth, Sulaŋkī* (No. 147).
(5) *Nīl Kaṇṭh* (No. 148).
(6) *Kālidās Tribēdī* (No. 159).
(7) *Sukh Dēb Misar,* of *Kampilā* (No. 160).
(8) *Bihārī Lāl* (No. 196).
(9) *Kēsab Rāy* (No. 300).
(10) *Rabi Datt'* (No. 304).
(11) *Gur Datt' Siŋgh,* of *Amēṭhī* (No. 332).
(12) *Uday Nāth Tribēdī* (No. 334).
(13) *Sambhu Nāth Misar* (No. 338).
(14) *Dūlah* (No. 358).
(15) *Himmati Bahādur* (No. 377).[2]
(16) *Biswa Nāth Atāī* (No. 410).
(17) *Mukund Lāl* (No. 560).

He also wrote poetry himself.

---

[1] This must be a different person from the well-known *Bikram Sāhi* (No. 514), of *Char'khārī,* who was born 1785 A.D. Curiously enough a *Bal Dēb* also attended his court.

[2] Himmati Bahādur flourished in 1800 A.D., but he must have been an old man then.

360. मनबोध झा, *Man'bōdh Jhā alias Bhōlan Jhā,* of *Jam'sam,* district *Dar'bhaŋgā.* Fl. 1750 A.D.

One of the most celebrated poets of Mithilā. Little is known about him beyond the facts that he married the daughter of one *Bhikhārī Jhā,* and that his only child, a daughter, was ancestress of the present Mahārāj of Dar'bhaŋgā. He composed a version of the *Harivaṁça* in the Maithilī dialect, entitled *Haribans.* Only ten *adhyāyas* have come down to us, but these enjoy great popularity. See J. A. S. B., 1882, p 129, and 1884, Sp. No.

361. केसव, *Kēsab.* Fl. 1775 A.D.

A Maithil poet, who attended the court of Rājā *Par'tāp Siŋgh,* who was himself a poet, under the *alias* of *Mōd Nāṛāyan* (No. 362). See J. A. S. B., vol. liii, p. 89.

362. मोद नारायन, *Mōd Nārāyan alias* Rājā *Par'tāp Siŋgh.* Fl. c. 1775 A.D.

A king of *Mithilā,* who was a poet. He was son of *Narēndra Siŋgh,* of *Dar'bhaŋgā* the victor of *Kanar'pī Ghāṭ* (see *Lāl Jhā,* No. 363), and was the fifth in ascent before the present Mahārāj. See J. A. S. B., vol. liii, p. 82. The poet *Kēsab* attended his court (No. 361).

363. लाल झा, *Lāl Jhā* or *Kabi Lāl,* of *Māg'rāunī,* district *Dar'bhaŋgā.* Fl. 1780 A.D.

One of the most famous poets of *Mithilā.* The author of the poem entitled *Kanar'pī Ghāṭ Lāṛāī.* See J. A. S. B., vol. liv, p. 16.

His patron was *Narēndra Siŋgh,* who gave him the village of *Kanāil* as a reward for the poem. This village is now owned by his descendants.

364. तीरथ राज, *Tīrath Rāj,* the Brāhman, of *Bais'wārā.* B. *1743* A.D.

He attended the court of Rājā *Achal Siŋgh Bāis,* of *Dāuṛiyā Khērā,* in *Āudh,* and at his command he translated in the year 1750 A.D. the *Samara Sāra* into the vernacular.

365. दया निधि कबि, the poet *Dayā Nidhi*, of *Bais'wārā*. B. *1754*.

He wrote a treatise entitled *Sālihōtr'*, dealing with veterinary surgery, at the instance of Rājā *Achal Siŋgh Bāis*, of *Dāūṛiyā Khērā*, in *Āudh*. Cf. No. 787.

366. सम्भु नाथ कबि त्रिपाठी, the poet *Sambhu Nāt Tripāṭhī*. Fl. 1752 A.D.

Rāg. He is possibly the same as *Sambhu Nāth* (No. 357), author of the *Rām Bilās*. He attended the court of Rājā *Achal Siŋgh Bāis*, of *Dāūṛiyā Khērā*, in *Āudh*. Under the name of Rāw *Raghu Nāth Siŋgh* he wrote in the above year a vernacular translation of the Sanskrit *Vētāla Pañchaviṁçatikā* of *Çiva Dāsa* under the title of *Bāitāl Pachīsī* (Rāg.). He also translated the astrological *Muhūrta Chintāmaṇi* into the vernacular in various metres.

367. सूदन कबि, the poet *Sūdan*. B. *1753* A.D.

He attended the court of *Sujān Siŋgh*, son of *Badan Siŋgh*. In one poem ten verses mentioned by Sib Siŋgh containing the names of several poets are praised by him. Nine of these verses have been lost, and Sib Siŋgh is only able to give the last, which (quoted in this work as 'Sūd') contains the following names :— *Sanēhī, Sabal Siŋgh, Sar'b Sukh, Sib Dās, Sib Rām, Sukh Lal, Sunām* (?), *Sumērū, Sūraj, Suratī, Sēnāpati, Sēkh, Sōm Nāth, Syām Lāl, Srī Dhar, Srī Pati, Hari, Hari Dās, Hari Bans, Harī Har, Hīras* (?), *Hit Rām, Husēn*.

368. रङ्ग लाल कबि, the poet *Raŋg Lāl*. B. cir. 1750.

He attended the court of *Sujān Siŋgh*, the son of *Badan Siŋgh*.

369. ब्रज बासी दास, *Braj Bāsī Dās*, of *Brindāban*, the *Dōāb*. Fl. 1770 A.D.

Rāg., Sun., ? Sriŋg. Sib Siŋgh says he was born *1753* A.D. He wrote in the year 1770 A.D. a work entitled *Braj Bilās* (Rāg.), descriptive of Krish'n's life during his residence at Brindāban. (See Wilson, *Religious Sects of the Hindūs*, p. 132, and Garcin de Tassy, i, 131.) He is possibly the same as another *Braj Bāsī Dās alias Dās Braj Bāsī* mentioned (without date) by Sib Siŋgh as having translated the play *Prabōdha Chandrōdaya* into the vernacular (Rāg.).

370. करन कबि बन्दीजन, the poet and bard *Karan,* of *Jōdh'pur* in *Mār'wār.* Fl. cir. 1730 A.D.

A poet of the Raṭhāūr Mahārājs. He wrote a work entitled the *Sūrya Par'kās* under the patronage of Mahārāj *Abhay Siŋgh* (1724—1750), the Raṭhāūr, son of *Ajīt Siŋgh* (No. 195). It is 7,500 çlōkas in length, and gives a history of the time from Mahārāj *Jas'want Siŋgh* (1638—1681) down to *Abhay Siŋgh* (1731 A.D.). Cf. Tod, i, xiv; ii, 4, 91, 107; Calc. ed. i, xiii; ii, 4, 99, 117. Tod gives an anecdote and quotation from this poet in ii, 120; Calc. ed. ii, 131.

371. बिजै सिङ्ह, *Bijāī Siŋgh,* Mahārāj of *Jōdh'pur,* in *Mār'wār.* Reigned 1753—1784 A.D.

He was an author himself, and got written the *Bijāī Bilās,* a historical work of 1,00,000 couplets, narrating the war between Bijāī Siŋgh and his cousin *Rām Siŋgh,* the son of *Abhay Siŋgh.* It was in consequence of this war that the Marāṭhās entered the state of Mār'wār. Sib Siŋgh wrongly states he was king of *Udāīpur,* in Mēwār. See Tod's *Rājāsthān,* i, xiv; ii, 4, 121 (Calc. ed. i, xiii; ii, 4; 134 and ff.).

372. मान कबि, the poet *Mān,* Brāhman, of *Bais'wārā.* Fl. 1761 A.D.

He wrote in the above year a vernacular translation of the *Kṛiṣṇa Khaṇḍa* entitled *Krish'n Kallōl.* The commencement of this work contains an important genealogy from *Çālivāhana* to *Champati Rāy* (? the father of *Chhattr' Sāl,* No. 197).

373. छेम करन कबि, the poet *Chhēm Karan,* the Brāhman of *Dhanāūlī,* district *Bārābaŋkī.* B. *1771* A.D.

He was author of (1) *Rām Ratnākar,* (2) *Rāmāspad* (?), (3) *Gurū Kathā,* (4) *Āhnik,* (5) *Rām-Gīt Mālā,* (6) *Krish'n-Charitāmrit,* (7) *Pad Bilās,* (8) *Raghu-rāj Ghanāchharī,* (9) *Britt-Bhāskar,* and other excellent works. He died in 1861, at the age of ninety.

374. चन्दन राय कवि, the poet and bard *Chandan Rāy*, of *Nāhil (? Māhil) Puwāwā̃*, district *Shāh-Jahān-pur*. Fl. 1773 A.D.

He attended the court of Rājā *Kēsarī Siŋgh*, of *Gāūr*. Under his name he wrote the *Kēsarī Par'kās*. Amongst his other works may be mentioned an important poem entitled the *Sriŋgār-sār*, the *Kallōl Taraŋginī* (dated 1789 A.D.), the *Kābyābharan*, the *Chandan Sat Saī*, and the *Pathikbōdh*. All these are highly esteemed. He had twelve pupils, all of whom became successful poets. The most celebrated was the poet *Man Bhāwan* (No. 375). A descendant of his was *Mak'rand Rāy* (No. 610).

375. मन भावन, *Man Bhāwan*, a Brāhman, of *Mūṛiyā*, district *Shāh-Jahān-pur*. Fl. 1780.

Rāg. He was the most successful of the twelve pupils of *Chandan Rāy* (No. 374). His best work is the *Sriŋgār Ratnābalī*.

376. रतन कुँअर, Bībī *Ratan Kũar*, of *Banāras*. B. cir. 1777 A.D.

Authoress of an account of devotees of Krish'n, entitled *Prēm Ratna*. She was grandmother of Rājā *Shiva Prasād*, C.S.I. (No. 699). This gentleman writes to me as follows concerning her:—'My grandmother, Bībī Ratan Kũar, died some 45 years ago' (written in 1887), 'when I was only 19 years old, attending the court of Colonel Sutherland, the Governor-General's Agent at Āj'mēr, as Wakīl of the late Mahārāj of Bharat'pur. Her age was between 60 and 70 when she left this world, but I regret I cannot give you exact dates. Besides the Prēm Ratna, she composed many *padas*. I have a manuscript book, called *Pad kī Pōthī*, in which she has written here and there with her own hands her *padas*. She was a good musician, and wrote a beautiful hand. She was well versed in Sanskrit, and knew a little Persian too. She knew medicines, and the best part of the little knowledge I may be credited with, I acquired from her.'

377. जसवन्त सिङ्ह, *Jas'want Siŋgh*, the Bhagēlā, of *Rājātir'wā*, in *Kanāuj*. Fl. 1797 A.D.

He was learned in Sanskrit and Persian. He compiled from other works on composition (साहित्य) a work on lovers (see note to No. 87) entitled *Sriŋgār Sirōmani*. He also wrote a famous treatise on rhetoric (अलङ्कार), founded on the Sanskrit *Chandralōka,* entitled *Bhākhā Bhūkhan* (Rāg.), and a treatise on veterinary surgery entitled *Sālihōtr'* (Rāg.). All these are excellent works. He died in 1814 A.D. The Bhākhā Bhūkhan has had numerous commentators, amongst whom the following may be mentioned:—*Par'tāp Sāhi* (?) (No. 149), *Nārāyan Rāy* (No. 572), *Giri Dhar Banār'sī* (No. 580), *Dal'pati Rāy* (No. 635), *Bansī Dhar* (No. 636), an anonymous poet of *Uniyārā* (No. 660), *Hari* (No. 761). It has been printed at Banāras in Sambat 1943 (1886) by Ambikā Charaṇ Chaṭṭōpadhyāya. A Bombay edition identifies the author with *Jas'want Siŋgh* (1638—1681) of *Mār'wār,* but this is very doubtful. See No. 149 and No. 149 Add.

378. हिम्मति बहादुर, Gosāī̃ Nawāb *Himmati Bahādur.* Fl. 1800 A.D.

Sat. His court was attended by many poets, including *Ṭhākur* (who saved his life; see No. 173) and *Rām Saran. Askand Giri* (No. 527) was descended from him.

He was a military guru or soldier-saint, who commanded a large force of *gosāī̃s* or religious devotees in the army of Sendhiyā. He instigated 'Alī Bahādur to attempt the conquest of Bundēl'khaṇḍ, but ultimately went over to the English during the second Marāṭhā war (1803—1806). He must have been an old man then, as poems by him are quoted in Sat., which was written in 1746.

379. राम सरन कबि, the poet *Rām Saran,* of *Hamīr'pur,* district *Iṭāwā̃.* Fl. 1800 A.D.

380. राम सिङ्घ कबि, the poet *Rām Siŋgh,* of *Bundēl'khaṇḍ.* Fl. 1800 A.D.

These two attended the court of *Himmati Bahādur.*

ADDENDA TO CHAPTER IX.

381. आदिल कबि, the poet *'Ādil.* B. *1703* A.D.

Sib Siŋgh has seen detached pieces by him, but no complete work.

382. ब्रज चन्द कबि, the poet *Braj Chand.* B. *1703* A.D.

383. भौन कबि, the poet *Bhāūn* the elder, of *Bundēl'khaṇḍ* B. *1703* A.D.

An erotic poet.

384. महब्बूब कबि, the poet *Mah'būb (Mahbūb).* B. *1705* A.D.

385. किशोर सूर कबि, the poet *Kishōr Sūr*. B. *1704* A.D.

Sriŋg., Sun. He has written many poems in the *chhappai* metre.

386. मदन किशोर कबि, the poet *Madan Kishōr*. Fl. 1710 A.D.

He attended the court of *Bahādur Shāh* (1707—1712). Cf. No. 50.

387. दया राम कबि त्रिपाठी, the poet *Dayā Rām Tripāṭhī*. B *1712*.

A quietistic (शान्ति रस) poet. Possibly the same as a *Dayā Rām* mentioned by Sib Siŋgh (without date) as author of a lexicographical work entitled *Anēkārth*.

388. पण्डरीक कबि, the poet *Paṇḍurīk*. B. *1712*.

389. गडु कबि, the poet *Gaḍu*, of *Rāj'putānā*. B. *1713*.

The emblematic (कूट) and occasional verses by him in the *chhappai* metre are famous.

390. नन्द लाल, *Nand Lāl*. B. *1717* A.D.

391. लाल मुकुन्द कबि, the poet *Lāl Mukund*. B. *1717*.

An erotic poet. Possibly the same as *Mukund Lāl* (No. 560).

392. इन्दु कबि, the poet *Indu*. B. *1719* A.D.

A commonplace poet.

393. ब्रज राज कबि, the poet *Braj Rāj*, of *Bundēl'khaṇḍ*. B. *1718* A.D.

394. याक़ूब खाँ कबि, the poet *Yakūb Khān* (*Ya'qūb*). B. *1718* A.D.

He wrote a commentary to the *Rasik-priyā* (see No. 134).

395. बीरन्बल, *Bīr'bal alias Bīr'bar*, a Kāyasth of *Dillī*. Fl. 1722 A.D.

The author of a work on composition (साहित्य) entitled *Krish'n Chandrikā*, written in the above year.

396. राजा राम कबि, the poet *Rājā Rām*. B. *1721* A.D.

An erotic poet. Cf. No. 233.

397. अनन्वर खाँ कबि, the poet *An'war Khān*. B. *1723* A.D.

He wrote a commentary on the *Sat Saī* of *Bihārī* (No. 196), and a work called the *An'war Chandrikā*, or possibly this last is the title of the commentary.

398. गुलाल सिंह, *Gulāl Siŋgh*. B. *1723*.

399. बेचू कबि, the poet *Bēchū*. B. 1723.

400. ब्रज नाथ कबि, the poet *Braj Nāth*. B. *1723* A.D.

The author of an admired work entitled *Rāg Mālā* (Rāg.). Cf. No. 904.

401. मधु नाथ कबि, the poet *Braj Nāth*. B. *1723* A.D.

402. मनोहर कबि, the poet *Manōhar*. B. *1723*.

403. महा कबि, the poet *Mahā* (? the great poet). Fl. *1723* A.D.

Sun.

404. रस राज कबि, the poet *Ras Rāj*. B. *1723* A.D.

The author of a good *Nakh'sikh* (see note to No. 87).

405. रसिक बिहारी, *Rasik Bihārī*. B. *1723* A.D.

Rāg.

406. रुद्र॰ मनि, *Rudr' Manī*, the Chauhān. B. *1723*.

407. दल सिंह, Rājā *Dal Siŋgh*, of *Bundēl'khaṇḍ*. B. *1724* A.D.

The author of a work entitled *Prēm Payōnidhi*, dealing with the loves and sports of Rādhā and Krish'n.

408. प्रान नाथ, *Prān Nāth*, of *Kōṭā*. B. *1724*.

He attended the court of the Rājā of *Kōṭā*.

409. **खुलन्फेकार कबि,** the poet *Jul'phekār (Zū'lfaqār).* B. *1725* A.D.

He wrote a good commentary on the *Sat Saī* of *Bihārī* (No. 196).

410. **कमल नयन कबि,** the poet *Kamal Nayan,* of *Bundēl'khaṇḍ.* B. *1727* A.D.

He was a prolific erotic writer, but no complete work of his is known. His poems are said to possess merit.

411. **बिस्सु नाथ अताई,** *Biswa Nāth Atāī,* of *Bundēl'khaṇḍ.* B. *1727.*

Sat.

412. **मञ्चित कबि,** the poet *Mañchit.* B. *1728.*

413. **बिहारी कबि,** the poet *Bihārī,* of *Bundēl'khaṇḍ.* B. *1729* A.D.

414. **नरिन्द कबि,** the poet *Narind.* B. *1731* A.D.

415. **रस रूप कबि,** the poet *Ras Rūp.* B. *1731* A.D.

416. **सिब राम कबि,** the poet *Sib Rām.* B. *1731* A.D.

Sūd. An erotic writer.

417. **सिब सिङ्घ,** *Sib Siŋgh.* B. *1731* A.D.

418. **अनन्य कबि,** the poet *Ananya.* B. *1733* A.D.

Many poems of his, dealing with the Vēdānta religion and morals, are extant. He also wrote didactic (चेतावन) poems and *vers d'occasion.* He is possibly the same as another *Ananya Kabi* mentioned by Sib Siŋgh as of date unknown, and the author of poems in honour of Durgā.

419. **तारा पति कबि,** the poet *Tārā Pati.* B. *1733* A.D.

Sriŋg. A writer of a *Nakh'sikh* (see note to No. 87). He is possibly the same as a *Tārā Kabi* mentioned by Sib Siŋgh as B. (? Fl.) *1779* A.D.

420. **रघु राय कबि,** the poet and bard *Raghu Rāy,* of *Bundēl'khaṇḍ.* B. *1733.*

His best known work is the *Jamunā Satak.* He is possibly the same as a *Raghu Rāy Kabi* mentioned by Sib Siŋgh as B. (? Fl.) 1773 A.D.

421. **ईसुफ खाँ कबि,** the poet *Īsuph (Yūsuf) Khān.* B. *1734* A.D.

He wrote commentaries to the *Sat Saī* of *Bihārī* (No. 196) and to the *Rasik-priyā,* of *Kēsab Dās* (No. 134).

422. **धन सिङ्घ कबि,** the poet and bard *Dhan Siŋgh,* of *Maurāwā,* district *Unāo.* B. *1734* A.D.

423. **प्रेम सखी,** *Prēm Sakhī.* B. *1734* A.D.

424. **सरब्ब सुख लाल,** *Sar'b Sukh Lāl.* B. *1734.*

Sūd.

425. **रबि नाथ कबि,** the poet *Rabi Nāth,* of *Bundēl'khaṇḍ.* B. *1734* A.D.

An erotic poet.

426. **नब खान कबि,** the poet *Nab Khān,* of *Bundēl'khaṇḍ.* B. *1735.*

427. **जग देब कबि,** the poet *Jag Dēb.* B. 1735 A.D.

428. **रस लाल कबि,** the poet *Ras Lāl,* of *Bundēl'khaṇḍ.* B. *1736* A.D.

An erotic poet.

429. **हरी हर कबि,** the poet *Harī Har.* B. *1737* A.D.

Sūd.

430. **ईस कबि,** the poet *Īs.* B. *1739* A.D.

His erotic and his quietistic poems are said to be very charming.

431. **सिब कबि,** the poet and bard *Sib,* of *Bil'grām,* district *Har'dōī.* B. *1739.*

Sun. The author of a work in the erotic style entitled *Ras Nidhi.*

432. **तोख निधि,** *Tōkh Nidhī,* a Brāhman, of *Kampilā Nagar.* B. *1741* A.D.

The author of three works—(1) *Sudhā Nidhi,* (2) *Byaŋgya Satak,* (3) a *Nakh'sikh* (see note to No. 87).

433. **प्रेमीयमन,** *Prēmīyaman,* the Musalmān of *Dillī.* B. *1741* A.D.

Rāg. He wrote an excellent lexicographical work in two parts entitled *Anēkārth* (Rāg.) and *Nām Mālā* (Rāg.) respectively.

434. **ठाकुर कवि,** the poet *Ṭhākur.* Fl. *1743* A.D.

See the poet Ṭhākur, who fl. *1643* A.D. (No. 173).

435. **मीर अहम्मद,** *Mīr Ah'mad,* of *Bil'grām,* district *Har'dōī.* B. *1743* A.D.

436. **अनूप दास कवि,** the poet *Anūp Dās.* B. *1744* A.D.

Several poems in the *kabitta* and *dōhā* metres, and songs in the quietistic style (शान्ति रस), are extant.

437. **कुमार मनि भट्ट,** the bard *Kumār Manī,* of *Gōkul,* in *Braj.* B. *1746* A.D.

A skilled poet, who wrote an esteemed work on composition (साहित्य) entitled *Rasik-rasāl.*

438. **जीवन कवि,** the poet *Jīban.* B. *1746* A.D.

He attended the court of *Muḥammad 'Alī.*

439. **तालिब अली,** *Tālib 'Alī alias Ras Nāyak,* of *Bil'grām,* district *Har'dōī.* B. (? Fl.) *1746* A.D.

An erotic poet. Possibly the same as a *Tālib 'Alī* mentioned by Sib Siŋgh as B. *1711* A.D.

440. **नाथ,** *Nāth.* B. *1746* A.D.

? Sun. He attended the court of one *Mānik Chand,* whose son appears to have been named *Īchhan.* Cf. No. 162.

441. **पद्मेस कवि,** the poet *Padmēs.* B. *1746* A.D.

442. **पूखी कवि,** the poet *Pūkhī,* a Brāhman of *Māīn'purī,* in the *Dōāb.* B. *1746* A.D.

Sriŋg.

443. **ब्राह्मन नाथ,** *Brāhman Nāth,* of *Bhōg Sāṛī,* district *Har'dōī.* B. (? Fl.) *1746* A.D.

Mentioned by Sib Siŋgh in connection with *Sōm Nāth* (No. 447).

444. **राम परसाद,** the bard *Rām Par'sād,* of *Bil'grām,* district *Har'dōī.* B. (? Fl.) *1746* A.D.

Rāg. Cf. No. 639.

445. **राम भट्ट,** *Rām Bhaṭṭ,* of *Purukhābād.* B. *1746* A.D.

He attended the court of Nawāb *Qiyām Khān,* and was the author of (1) *Sriŋgār Sāurabh,* (2) *Bar'wāī Nāyikā Bhēd.* (See note to No. 87.)

446. **सुखानन्द कवि,** the poet and bard *Sukhānand,* of *Chachēṛī.* B. *1746* A.D.

447. **सोम नाथ,** *Sōm Nāth,* of *Bhōg Sāṛī,* district *Har'dōī.* B. (? Fl. *1746* A.D.

Sūd. Mentioned by Sib Siŋgh in connection with *Brāhman Nāth* (No. 443).

448. **निवाज कवि,** the poet *Niwāj* (*Nawāz*), a Muhammadan weaver of *Bil'grām,* district *Hardōī.* B. *1747.*

An erotic poet. Possibly the same as No. 342. To be distinguished from No. 198.

449. बोधा कबि, the poet *Bōdhā*. B. *1747* A.D.

Sring., Sun. Cf. No. 500.

450. मदन किशोर कबि, the poet *Madan Kishōr*. Fl. *1750* A.D. Cf. No. 386.

451. लाल गिरि धर, *Lāl Giri Dhar*, of *Bais'wārā*. B. *1750* A.D.

The author of a learned treatise on lovers (see note to No. 87). Perhaps the same as Giri Dhar (No. 345).

452. कला निधि कबि, the poet *Kalā Nidhi* the younger. B. *1750* A.D.

His *Nakh'sikh* (see note to No. 87) is said to be good.

453. सखी सुख, *Sakhī Sukh*, a Brāhman of *Nar'war*, in *Bundēl'khaṇḍ*. B. *1750* A.D.

He was father of *Kabīndr'* (No. 496), and wrote himself.

454. नारायन, the bard *Nārāyan*, of *Kākūpur*, district *Kānh'pur*. B. *1752* A.D.

The author of a metrical history of the *Chandēlā* kings of *Sib'rāj'pur*.

455. किङ्कर गोबिन्द, *Kiṅkar Gōbind*, of *Bundēl'khaṇḍ*. B. *1753* A.D.

His poems in the quietistic style (शान्ति रस) are said to be excellent.

456. क्रिशन लाल कबि, the poet *Krish'n Lāl*. B. *1757* A.D.

Sring. He has written some admired love songs.

457. मकरन्द कबि, the poet *Mak'rand*. B. *1757*.

Sring., Sun. An erotic poet.

458. उदेस भाट, *Udēs*, the bard, of *Bundēl'khaṇḍ*. B. *1758* A.D.

A writer of occasional verses.

459. जै देव कबि, the poet *Jai Dēb*. B. *1758* A.D.

460. निहाल, *Nihāl*, a Brāhman of *Nigōhā*, district *Lakh'naū*. B. *1763* A.D.

461. धीर कबि, the poet *Dhīr*. Fl. 1765 A.D.

Sring. He attended the court of the emperor *Shāh 'Ālam* (1761—1806).

462. रस धाम कबि, the poet *Ras Dhām*. B. *1768* A.D.

The author of a work entitled *Alaṅkār Chandrikā*.

463. सिरताज कबि, the poet *Sir'tāj*, of *Bar'dhānā*. B. *1768*.

464. काली राम कबि, the poet *Kālī Rām*, of *Bundēl'khaṇḍ*. B. *1769*.

His poems are said to be good.

465. जसोदानन्द कबि, the poet *Jasōdānand*. B. *1771* A.D.

He wrote a treatise on lovers (see note to No. 87) entitled the *Bar'wāī Nāyikā Bhēd*. It is in the *Bar'wāī* metre. It is dated *Sambat* 1822 (1765 A.D.), if I read the passage (बिबिकरिब्रह्म) correctly. In this case *Sambat 1828* (*1771* A.D.), which Sib Singh gives as the date of the poet's birth, is wrong.

466. लच्छू कबि, the poet *Lachchhū*. B. *1771* A.D.

467. बाजेस कबि, the poet *Bājēs*, of *Bundēl'khaṇḍ*. B. *1774*.

A poet who wrote in praise of *Anūp Giri*.

468. भञ्जन कबि, the poet *Bhañjan*. B. *1774* A.D.

Sring.

469. लाला पाठक कबि, the poet *Lālā Pāṭhak*, of *Rukum'nagar*. B. *1774* A.D.

The author of a *Sālihōtr'* (Rāg.) or treatise on veterinary surgery.

470. लतीफ कवि, the poet *Latīph* (*Laṭīf*). B. *1777*.

An erotic poet.

471. सम्मन कवि, the poet *Samman*, a Brāhman of *Malāwā*, district *Har'dōī*. B. *1777*.

The author of admired *dōhās* on morals.

472. सन्तन कवि, the poet *Santan*, the Brāhman of *Bindukī*, district *Fatih'pur*. B. *1777* A.D.

Sriŋg.

473. सन्तन कवि, the poet *Santan*, a Brāhman of *Jāj'maū*, district *Unāo*. B. *1777*.

474. सिङ्घ कवि, the poet *Siŋgh*. B. *1778*.

Sriŋg. He is probably identical with some other poet whose name ends in Siŋgh.

475. कवि दत्त, *Kabi Datt'*. B. *1779* A.D.

Sriŋg., Dig. He is probably the same as *Dēb Datt'* (No. 508).

476. मधु सूदन दास, *Madhu Sūdan Dās*, the Māthur Brāhman of *Ishṭakāpurī*. B. *1782* A.D.

He translated the *Rāmāçvamēdha* into the vernacular.

477. मनि राम कवि मिसर, the poet *Mani Rām Misar*, of *Kanāuj*. B. *1782*.

Sriŋg. He has written one of the best works on prosody, the *Chhand Chhappanī*.

478. राम दास कवि, the poet *Rām Dās*. B. *1782* A.D.

479. सिब लाल दूबे, *Sib Lāl Dūbē*, of *Dāūṛiyā Khērā*, district *Unāū*. B. *1782* A.D.

The author of several works, amongst them may be mentioned a *Nakh'sikh* (see note to No. 87), *Khaṭ Ritu* (Rāg.) (a treatise on the six seasons), verses on morals, and comic verses.

480. सङ्गम कवि, the poet *Saŋgam*. B. *1783* A.D.

Sriŋg. He attended the court of one *Siŋgh Rāj*.

481. गङ्गा पति कवि, the poet *Gaŋgā Patī*. B. *1787* A.D.

Said to be a tasteful poet.

482. सागर कवि, the poet *Sāgar*, a Brāhman. B. *1786*.

The author of an erotic work entitled *Bāmā Man Rañjan*. He attended the court of *Ṭikāit Rāy*. See No. 484.

483. गिरि धर कवि, the poet and bard *Giri Dhar*, of *Hōl'pur*, district *Bārābaŋkī*. B. (? Fl.) *1787* A.D.

Possibly the same as No. 345. See No. 484.

484. बेनी कवि, the poet and bard *Bēnī* the younger, of *Bētī*, district *Rāy Barēlī*. B. (? Fl.) *1877* A.D.

These three attended the court of *Ṭikāit Rāy*, Dīwan of Nawāb *Āṣafu'd-dāūla* (Fl. 1775—1797), of *Lakhnaū*. *Bēnī* (? Sun.) died at an old age in or about *1835* A.D.

485. जवाहिर कवि, the poet and bard *Jawāhir*, of *Bil'grām*, district *Har'dōī*. B. *1788* A.D.

He wrote a book entitled the *Jawāhir Ratnākar*.

486. गुलाब सिङ्घ, *Gulāb Siŋgh*, the Pañjābī. B. *1789*. A.D.

He wrote several Vēdānta works, such as a *Rāmāyan*, the play *Chandra Prabōdh*, *Mōchh Panth*, *Bhāwar Sāwar*, etc.

487. देबी दास, *Dēbī Dās*. Fl. cir. 1790 A.D.

A quietistic poet, a pupil of *Jag Jīban Dās* (No. 323).

488. बालम दास कबि, the poet *Bālam Dās*. Fl. 1793.

He wrote in the above year a treatise on geomancy (रमल) entitled *Ramal Bhākhā*. It is an authority on the subject.

489. श्री लाल, *Srī Lāl*, the Guj'rātī, of *Bāḍēr*, in *Rāj'putānā*. B. *1793* A.D.

The author of a *Bhākhā Chandrōday* and other works.

490. प्रान नाथ कबि, the poet *Prān Nāth*, a Brāhman of *Bais'wārā*. Fl. 1793 A.D.

He wrote in the above year an *itihāsa* entitled *Chakābyūh*.

491. कान्ह कबि, the poet *Kānh* the elder. B. *1795*. A.D.

The author of a work on lovers. (See note to No. 87.)

492. गुन देब, *Gun Dēb*, of *Bundēl'khaṇḍ*. B. *1795* A.D.

Said to have written some good poetry.

493. गोपाल लाल कबि, the poet *Gōpāl Lāl*. B. *1795* A.D.

Said to have written some good quietistic (शान्ति रस) poems.

494. उमेद कबि, the poet *Umēd*. B. *1796* A.D.

His *Nakh'sikh* (see note to No. 87) is much admired. He appears to have lived in some village in the *Dōāb* or near *Shāh-Jahān-pur*.

495. ऊधो कबि, the poet *Ūdhō*. B. *1796* A.D.

Sriṅg., ? Rāg. Cf. No. 79.

496. कबीन्द्र, *Kabīndr'*, a Brāhman of *Nar'war*, in *Bundēl'khaṇḍ*, B. *1797* A.D.

He was son of *Sakhī Sukh* (No. 453), and was author of a work entitled the *Ras-dīp*.

497. इच्छा राम अबस्थी, *Ichchhā Rām Abasthī*, of *Pacharuā*, district *Bārābaṅkī*. Fl. 1798 A.D.

A very pious poet, who wrote in the above year a treatise on the Vēdānta philosophy named the *Brahm Bilās*.

498. साधर कबि, the poet *Sādhar*. B. *1798* A.D.

499. सुकबि कबि, the poet *Sukabi*. B. *1798*.

An erotic poet.

500. बोध कबि, the poet *Bōdh*. B. *1798* A.D. Cf. No. 449.

501. नरोत्तम, *Narōttam*, of *Bundēl'khaṇḍ*. B. *1799* A.D.

CHAPTER X.

HINDŪSTĀN UNDER THE COMPANY. [1800—1857.]

THE years commencing with the downfall of the Marāṭhā power and ending with the Mutiny form another convenient period in dealing with the literary history of Hindūstān. It was the period of renascence, of the practical introduction of the printing-press into Northern India, and of the foundation of the modern school which now shows such commendable activity. It was, moreover, the period of the birth of that wonderful hybrid language known to Europeans as Hindī, and invented by them. In 1803, under Gilchrist's tuition, *Lallū Jī Lāl* wrote the Prēm Sāgar in the mixed Ūrdū language of Akbar's camp-followers and of the market where men of all nations congregated, with this peculiarity, that he used only nouns and particles of Indian, instead of those of Arabic or Persian, origin. The result was practically a newly-invented speech; for though the grammar was the same as that of the prototype, the vocabulary was almost entirely changed. This new language, called by Europeans Hindī, has been adopted all over Hindūstān as the *lingua franca* of Hindūs, for a want existed which it fulfilled. It has become the recognised medium of literary prose throughout Northern India, but as it was nowhere a vernacular it has never been successfully used for poetry. The greatest geniuses have tried, and it has been found wanting at their hands. Northern India therefore at the present day presents the following unique state of literature,—its poetry everywhere written in local vernacular dialects, especially in Braj, in Bais'wārī, and in Bihārī, and its prose in one uniform artificial dialect, the mother tongue of no native-born Indian, forced into acceptance by the prestige of its inventors, by the fact that the first books written in it were of a highly popular character, and because it found a sphere in which it was eminently useful.

The star of literature during the half-century under notice shone brightest in *Bundēl'khaṇḍ* and *Baghēl'khaṇḍ*, at *Banāras*, and in *Āudh*, but it shone with marked differences in the quality of its light. In *Bundēl'khaṇḍ* and *Baghēl'khaṇḍ* the poets were the legitimate continuators of the traditions of the eighteenth century. *Pannā*, the capital of the heroic *Chhattr' Sāl, Char'khārī* made famous under milder auspices by *Bikram Sāhi,* and *Rīwā̃,* illustrious for its art-patrons from the days of *Nējā Rām* to those of *Biswanāth Siŋgh,* each formed a centre from which issued well-known standard works on the art of poetry. The writers, of whom perhaps *Padmākar* was the most famous, were those on whom the mantles of *Kēsab Dās* and *Chintāmani Tripāṭhī* fell. They were the last survivors of the learned writing for the learned. Bundēl'khaṇḍ remained during the whole half-century a country of semi-independent chiefs warring amongst themselves, with whom the printing-press found little favour.

Far different was the case of *Banāras.* The end of the eighteenth century saw that city a British possession; and with the *pax Britannica* came the introduction of printed books. This had its natural effect. The limitless multiplication of copies by the art of printing gave a new audience to the learned,—an audience that had hitherto been satisfied with the rough Doric of the folk-epic, and which in the earlier days of India's chivalry had been successfully addressed by Rāj'pūt bards. What an opportunity for making or marring a nation's character! And here again the pure and noble figure of *Tul'sī Dās* stands forward as the saviour of his fellow-countrymen. Hindūstān, happily in this differing from Baŋgāl,[1] had that figure to go back to as an example. His popularity gave its tone to the demand, and with characteristic acuteness the Banāras Paṇḍits fostered the supply. In 1829 was completed and printed for the Mahārāj of Banāras *Gōkul Nāth's* great translation of the companion epic to the *Rāmāyaṇa,* the *Mahābhārata.* This alone was sufficient to make our present period noteworthy, but it is only one early instance of the many valuable works issuing from the Holy City. Other authors, of a younger generation, of whom one of the greatest is happily still alive, endowed with a wider and more catholic mental vision, no longer bounded by the horizon of Paurānik cosmology, came to the front, and the benefit done to the intellect of Hindūstān by such men as Rājā *Siva Prasād* and *Harishchandr'* cannot easily be calculated.

The Taʿalūqdārs of *Āudh* also worthily upheld their reputations as encouragers of poetry. Although eclipsed by Banāras in this respect (for is not the Sundarī Tilak deservedly the most popular work of its

[1] It is needless to say that I am not referring to the great revival of Baŋgālī literature inaugurated by *Īshwar Chandra* (*Bidyāsāgar*) in later years, but to the insipid indecencies of *Bharat Chandra* and his imitators, which up to then were so popular.

kind in existence?), Āudh may boast of having produced an excellent anthology in the *Bidwan-Mōd-Taraŋginī*. These anthologies, of which *Kālidās's Hajārā*, written at the end of the seventeenth century, is the earliest important example, appeared in considerable numbers during the first half of the nineteenth century, and did much to extend the knowledge of sound vernacular literature of the preceding generations. As already said, one of the most popular, as it was one of the best, was the *Sundarī Tilak*; but the most important of all, both in bulk and in contents, was the *Rāg-Sagarōdbhab Rāg-Kalpadrum*, published in 1843.

For convenience of classification I divide this chapter into four parts, referring to Bundēl'khaṇḍ and Baghēl'khaṇḍ, to Banāras, to Āudh, and to other places respectively. As a rule, only those poets who were born or who flourished between 1800 and 1857 are given, but in a few instances, in order to complete groups, poets who belonged to an earlier period have been kept back for inclusion in this period, or history has been anticipated by including a few of a later date.

Part I.—Bundel'khand and Baghel'khand.

502. मोहन भट्ट, *Mōhan Bhaṭṭ*, of *Bāndā*. Fl. cir. 1800 A.D.

He is a well-known poet. He attended first the court of the Bundēlā Mahārāj *Hindūpati*, of *Par'nā* (*Pannā*), and subsequently those of *Par'tāp Siŋgh Sawāī* (1778—1803) and *Jagat Siŋgh Sawāī* of *Jāipur* (1803—1818) (Tod's *Rājasthān*, ii, 375; Calc. ed., ii, 414). His son was the celebrated *Padmākar* (No. 506), whose grandson was *Gadā Dhar* (No. 512). He also praises one *Sujān Siŋgh*; cf. Nos. 367, 368. Regarding Hindūpati, see No. 503.

503. रूप साहि, *Rūp Sāhi*, a Kāyasth of *Bāg'mahal*, near *Par'nā* (*Pannā*), in *Bundēl'khaṇḍ*. Fl. cir. 1800 A.D.

He attended the court of the Bundēlā Mahārāj *Hindūpati* (cf. No. 502) of *Par'nā* (*Pannā*). He was author of a work entitled *Rūp Bilās* (written, 1756 A.D.), in which he states that *Chhattr' Sāl's* (No. 197) son was *Hir'dāi Siŋgh* or *Hir'dēs* (cf. No. 346), whose son was *Sabhā Siŋgh* (cf. Nos. 155 and 346), whose son was *Hindūpati* (cf. No. 502).

504. **करन ब्राह्मन,** *Karan*, the Brāhman of *Bundēl'khaṇḍ*. Fl. cir. 1800 A.D.

He attended the court of the Bundēlā Māhārāj *Hindūpati* (cf. No. 502) of *Par'nā* (*Pannā*), and composed two important works—the *Ras Kallōl* and the *Sāhitya Ras*.

505. **हर देव कवि,** the poet *Har Dēb*. Fl. 1800 A.D.

He attended the court of *Raghu Nāth Rāw*, of *Nāg'pur* (1816—1818).

506. **पद्माकर भट्ट,** *Padmākar Bhaṭṭ*, of *Bāndā*. Fl. 1815 A.D.

Rāg., Sun., Sriṇg. He was son of *Mōhan Bhaṭṭ*, of Bandā (No. 502). Padmākar at first attended the court of *Raghu Nāth Rāw*, of *Nāg'pur*, commonly known as the *Appā Sāhib* (reigned 1816—1818), where he received great rewards for his poetry. Subsequently he went to *Jāipur*, where he compiled, in the name of *Jagat Siṇgh Sawāī* (1803—1818), a work entitled *Jagad Binōd* (Rāg.). Being richly rewarded for this, he devoted the rest of his life to the worship of the Ganges, and wrote a work entitled *Gaṇgā Laharī*. Amongst his grandsons may be mentioned *Gadā Dhar Bhaṭṭ* (No. 512).

507. **ग्वाल कवि,** the poet and bard *Gwāl*, of *Mathurā*. Fl. 1815 A.D.

Sun. He was skilled in composition (साहित्य). His principal works were (1) *Sāhitya Dūkhan*, (2) *Sāhitya Dar'pan*, (3) *Bhakti Bhāw*, (4) *Sriṇgār Dōhā*, (5) *Sriṇgār Kābitta*. He also wrote minor works, such as a *Nakh'sikh* (see note to No. 87), *Gōpī Pachīsī*, *Jamunā Laharī* (written 1822 A.D.), etc. He was a rival of *Dēb Datt'* (No. 508) and of *Padmākar* (No. 506).

508. **देव दत्त,** *Dēb Datt'* the Brāhman, of *Sāṛhi*, district *Kānh'pur*. Fl. 1815 A.D.

He attended the court of Rājā *Khumān Siṇgh*, the Bundēlā of *Char'khārī*. He was a contemporary and rival of *Padmākar* (No. 506) and of *Gwāl* (No. 507). He is probably the same as the *Kabi Datt'* mentioned in Dig.

509. **भान दास कबि,** the poet and bard *Bhān Dās,* of *Char'-khārī,* in *Bundēl'khaṇḍ.* Fl. 1815 A.D.

He attended the court of Rājā *Khumān Siŋgh,* of *Char'khārī,* and wrote a prosody entitled *Rūp Bilās.*

510. **पजनेस कबि,** the poet *Paj'nēs,* of *Bundēl'khaṇḍ.* B. *1816* A.D.

Sriŋg. He resided in *Par'nā* (*Pannā*), and wrote a good work on vernacular composition (भाखा साहित्य), entitled *Madhu Priyā.* His poems are famous for their conceits and difficulties. The best specimen of his work is his *Nakh'sikh* (see note to No. 87). He was also a good Persian scholar.

511. **बलभद्र,** *Bal'bhadr'* the Kāyasth, of *Par'nā* (*Pannā*), in *Bundēl'khaṇḍ.* B. *1844.*

He attended the court of Rājā *Nar'pati Siŋgh,* the Bundēlā of *Par'nā* (*Pannā*).

Possibly the author of the *Bal'bhadra Charitra,* quoted by Garçin de Tassy, i, 104, from Ward, ii, 480.

512. **गदा धर भट्ट,** *Gadā Dhar Bhaṭṭ,* of *Bāndā.* B. *1855.*

Rāg. His paternal great-grandfather was the well-known *Mōhan Bhaṭṭ* (No. 502), whose son was *Padmākar* (No. 506), who had two sons, named *Mihī Lāl* (? No. 623) and *Ambā Par'sād.* The former's sons were *Bansī Dhar, Gadā Dhar, Chandr' Dhar,* and *Lachhmī Dhar.* The last had a son named *Bidyā Dhar.* These were all poets, but *Gadā Dhar* was the best and attended the court of Rājā *Bhawānī Siŋgh Datiyā,* son of *Bijāī Siŋgh Datiyā.* His best known work is the *Alaŋkār Chandrōday.*

513. **पहलाद,** the bard *Pah'lād,* of *Char'khārī,* in *Bundēl'-khaṇḍ.* Fl. 1810.

He attended the court of Rājā *Jagat Siŋgh,* of *Char'khārī.*

514. **विक्रम साहि,** Rājā *Bikram Sāhi alias Bijai Bahādur*, the Bundēlā, of *Char'khārī*, in *Bundēl'khaṇḍ*. Born 1785; D. 1828 A.D.

Rāg. The author of two much-admired works—(1) *Bikram Biradābalī*, (2) *Bikram Sat Saī*. Sib Siŋgh gives another Rājā *Bijai Bahādur*, a Bundēlā of *Ṭeh'rī*, about whom he mentions no particulars, giving the date as B. *1823*, which is the same as that which he wrongly gives for Bijai of Char'khārī. Ṭeh'rī and Char'khārī are both in Bundēl'khaṇḍ.

515. **बैताल कबि,** the poet and bard *Baitāl*. Fl. 1820 A.D.

He attended the court of *Bikrām Sāhi* (No. 514), and wrote moral and occasional pieces. A selection from his poems will be found in the *Bhkāhā Sār* of *Sāhib Prasād Siŋgh*. According to Garcin de Tassy, i, 118, his full name was *Santōkh Rāy Bētal*, and he wrote in Ūrdū. He appears to have been a contemporary and disciple of *Muḥammad Qiyām*.

516. **बीर कबि**, the poet *Bīr Bāj'pēyī alias Dāū Dādā*, of *Maṇḍilā*. Fl. 1820.

The author of a work entitled *Prēm Dīpikā*, written in answer to a challenge given by his brother *Bikram Sāhi* (No. 514).

517. **मान कबि,** the poet and bard *Mān*, of *Char'khārī*, in *Bundēl'khaṇḍ*. Fl. 1820 A.D.

He attended the court of *Bikram Sāhi* (No. 514). He is possibly the same as a *Mān Kabi* mentioned by Sib Siŋgh as a quietistic poet.

518. **बल देब कबि,** the poet *Bal Dēb*, of *Char'khārī*, in *Bundēl'khaṇḍ*. Fl. 1820.

He attended the court of *Bikram Sāhi* (No. 514). Cf. No. 543.

519. **बिहारी लाल,** the bard *Bihārī Lāl alias Bhōj Kabi*, of *Char'khārī*, in *Bundēl'khaṇḍ*. Fl. 1840 A.D.

He attended the court of Rājā *Ratan Siŋgh alias Rat'nēs* (cf. No. 149 Add. and No. 344 Add.), the Bundēlā of *Char'khārī*. His two principal works, the *Bhōj Bhūkhan* and the *Ras Bilās*, are much admired. His love for a courtezan named *Shar'fō* led him to compose a number of very popular verses in her honour.

520. अवधेस, *Awadhēs*, the Brāhman of *Char'khārī*, in *Bundēl'khaṇḍ*. Fl. 1840 A.D.

He was an old poet at the court of *Ratan Siŋgh*, of *Char'khārī*, the Bundēlā. His poems are said to possess taste, but Sib Siŋgh states that he has never been able to obtain copies of any complete work of his. Cf. No. 542.

521. राव राना कबि, the poet and bard *Rāw Rānā*, of *Char'khārī*, in *Bundēl'khaṇḍ*. Fl. 1840 A.D.

He was descended from ancient Bundēlā poets, and attended the court of Rājā *Ratan Siŋgh*, where he was shown great honour.

522. गोपाल बन्दीजन, the bard *Gōpāl*, of *Char'khārī*, in *Bundēl'khaṇḍ*. Fl. 1840 A.D.

He attended the court of Rājā *Ratan Siŋgh*, of *Char'khārī*.

523. बिहारी लाल चिपाठी, *Bihārī Lāl Trīpāṭhī*, of *Ṭik'māpur*, district *Kānh'pur*. Fl. 1840 A.D.

He is the most famous of the descendants of *Mati Rām Tripāṭhī* (No. 146). He was a greater poet than *Rām Dīn* (No. 524) or *Sītal* (No. 525).

524. राम दीन चिपाठी, *Rām Dīn Tripāṭhī*, of *Ṭik'māpur*, district *Kānh'pur*. Fl. 1840 A.D.

He was a descendant of *Mati Rām* (No. 146), and attended the court of Mahārāj *Ratan Siŋgh*, of *Char'khārī*.

525. सीतल चिपाठी, *Sītal Trīpāṭhī*, of *Ṭīk'māpur*, district *Kānh'pur*. Fl. 1840 A.D.

He was a descendant of *Mati Rām* (see No. 146) and father of the poet *Lāl* (No. ? 561, 919). He attended the courts at *Char'khārī* and other places in *Bundēl'khaṇḍ*.

526. **नवल सिङ्घ,** *Nawal Siṇgh* the Kāyasth, of *Jhānsī*. B. *1841*.

Sriṇg. He was a servant of the Rājā of *Santhar*. He had a great reputation, and was the author of (1) *Nām Rāmāyan* and (2) *Hari Nāmābalī*.

527. **अस्कन्द गिरि,** *Askand Girī*, of *Bāndā*. B. (? Fl.) *1859* A.D.

This poet belonged to the family of *Himmatí Bahādur* (No. 378), and was an excellent love-poet. His best work is the *Askand-Binōd*, dealing with that subject.

528. **समऽनेस कवि,** the poet *Sam'nēs*, a Kāyasth of *Bānhō* (*Rīwā̃*), in *Baghēl'khaṇḍ*. Fl. 1810.

He attended the court of Māhārāj *Jāī Siṇgh* (succeeded 1809, abdicated 1813), father of Mahārāj *Biswanāth Siṇgh*, of *Bāndhō*. He was author of a work entitled *Kābya Bhūkhan*.

529. **बिस्वनाथ सिङ्घ,** Mahārāj *Biswanāth Siṇgh*, of *Bāndhō* (*Rīwā̃*), in *Baghēl'khaṇḍ*. Reigned 1813—1834 A.D.

Rāg. The descendant of a line of kings famous for its patronage of poets. His ancestor *Nējā Rām Siṇgh*, who was a contemporary of *Ak'bar*, gave the poet *Hari Nāth* (No. 114) a hundred thousand rupees for a single *dōhā*. This king not only sustained the traditional liberality of his family, but was also the author of a Sanskrit work entitled *Sarvasaṇgraha*. He also wrote vernacular commentaries on the *Bījak* of *Kabīr* (see Nos. 13, 14), and on the *Binay Pattrikā* of *Tul'sī Dās* (No. 128). Another good vernacular work of his is entitled *Rām Chandr' kī Sawārī*.

530. **अजबेस नबीन भाट,** *Ajabēs*, the modern bard of that name. Fl. cir. 1830 A.D.

Sun. He attended the court of Mahārāj *Biswanāth Siŋgh* (No. 529), of *Bāndhō* (*Rīwā̃*) (1813—1834)—see *Ajabēs* (No. 24). I question the existence of this earlier poet. Not impossibly, the poem referred to him in No. 24 is by the poet now under consideration.

531. **गोपाल कवि**, the poet *Gōpāl*, a Kāyasth of *Bāndhō* (*Rīwā̃*), in *Baghēl'khaṇḍ*. Fl. cir. 1830 A.D.

He was minister of Mahārāj *Biswanāth Siŋgh* (No. 529) of *Bāndhō* (*Rīwā̃*) (1813—1834). His principal work is the *Gōpāl Pachīsī*.

532. **रघु राज सिङ्ग**, Mahārāj *Raghu Rāj Siŋgh*, the Baghēl of *Bāndhō* (*Rīwā̃*), in *Baghēl'khaṇḍ*. B. 1824, succeeded 1834, alive in 1883.

Sun. The author of a much-admired translation of the *Bhāgavata Purāṇa*, entitled *Ānandāmbudhi*; also of a history of Hanumān entitled *Sundar Satak* (written 1847 A.D.), and other works.

ADDENDA TO CHAPTER X, PART I.

533. **परम कवि**, the poet *Param*, of *Mahōbā*, in *Bundēl'khaṇḍ*. B. *1814* A.D.

The author of a *Nakh'sikh* (see note to No. 87).

534. **रसिक लाल कवि**, the poet *Rasik Lāl*, of *Bāndā*. B. *1823*.

An erotic poet.

535. **गुन सिन्धु कवि**, the poet *Gun Sindhu*, of *Bundēl'khaṇḍ*. B. *1825* A.D.

A clever erotic poet.

536. **खण्डन कवि**, the poet *Khaṇḍan*, of *Bundēl'khaṇḍ*. B. *1827* A.D.

He has written an excellent treatise on lovers. Sib Siŋgh states that copies of the work exist in *Jhā̃nsī*, and gives the names of the possessors.

537. **मदन मोहन कवि**, the poet *Madan Mōhan*, of *Char'khārī*, in *Bundēl'khaṇḍ*. B. *1823* A.D.

Rāg. A minister of the Rājā of *Char'khārī*. He was an erotic poet.

538. **राम किशुन चौबे**, *Rām Kishun Chaūbē*, of *Kāliñjar*, district *Bāndā*. B. *1829*.

The author of a quietistic work entitled *Binay Pachīsī*. He is probably the same as a *Rām Kishun Kabi* mentioned by Sib Siŋgh without particulars.

539. **हरि दास कवि**, the poet and bard *Hari Dās*, of *Bāndā*. B. *1834* A.D.

He was father of the poet *Nāne* (No. 545). He wrote an erotic poem entitled *Rādhā Bhūkhan*.

540. गङ्ग राम कबि, the poet *Gaṇg Rām*, of *Bundēl'khaṇḍ*. B. *1837*.

A commonplace poet.

541. परमानन्द लल्ला पुरानीक, *Par'mānand Lallā Purānīk*, of *Ajāigaṛh*, in *Bundēl'khaṇḍ*. B. *1837* A.D.

The author of a *Nakh'sikh* (see note to No. 87).

542. अवधेस, *Awadhēs*, the Brāhman, of *Bhūpā*, in *Bundēl'khaṇḍ*. B. *1838* A.D.

This poet is said to have been skilled in composing many beautiful poems, but Sib Siṇgh states that he has never been able to obtain copies of any complete work of his. Cf. No. 520.

543. बल देव कबि, the poet *Bal Dēb*, of *Char'khārī*, in *Bundēl'khaṇḍ*. B. *1839* A.D.

Probably the same as No. 518.

544. भोला सिङ्घ कबि, the poet *Bhōlā Siṇgh*, of *Par'nā* (*Pannā*), in *Bundēl'khaṇḍ*. B. *1839*.

545. नोने कबि, the poet and bard *Nōnē* of *Bāndā*, in *Bundēl'khaṇḍ*. B. *1844* A.D.

He was son of the poet *Hari Dās* (No. 539). He was learned in vernacular composition (भाखा साहित्य).

546. हरि दास कबि, the poet *Hari Dās*, a Kāyasth of *Par'nā* (*Pannā*), in *Bundēl'khaṇḍ*. B. *1844* A.D.

The author of a work on vernacular composition (भाखा साहित्य) entitled *Ras Kāumudī*. He also wrote twelve other similar works.

547. हिरन्देस कबि, the poet and bard *Hir'dēs*, of *Jhānsī*, in *Bundēl'khaṇḍ*. B. *1844* A.D.

Sriṇg. The author of a work entitled *Sriṇgār Nab Ras*.

548. नील सखी, *Nīl Sakhī*, of *Jāit'pur* in *Bundēl'khaṇḍ*. B. *1845*.

549. बन्स गोपाल, the bard *Bans Gōpāl*, of *Jālāun*, in *Bundēl'khaṇḍ*. B. *1845* A.D.

No particulars. He is possibly the same as a *Bans Gōpāl* mentioned by Sib Siṇgh without date as a bard.

550. नैसुक कबि, the poet *Nāisuk*, of *Bundēl'khaṇḍ*. B. *1847* A.D.

An erotic poet.

551. अम्बर भाट, the bard *Ambar* of *Chāujīt'pur*, in *Bundēl'khaṇḍ*. B. *1853* A.D.

552. दीन नाथ, the poet *Dīn Nāth*, of *Bundēl'khaṇḍ*. B. *1854* A.D.

553. पञ्चम कबि, the poet and bard *Pañcham*, the younger, of *Bundēl'khaṇḍ*. B. *1854* A.D.

He attended the court of Rājā *Gumān Siṇgh*, of *Ajāigaṛh*.

554. राधे लाल, *Rādhē Lāl*, a Kāyasth of *Rāj'gaṛh*, in *Bundēl'khaṇḍ*. B. *1854* A.D.

555. कुञ्ज लाल कबि, the poet and bard *Kuñj Lāl*, of *Mau Rānīpurā*, district *Jhānsī, in Bundēl'khaṇḍ*. B. *1855* A.D.

Some detached verses by him are known.

556. जनकेस, the bard *Jan'kēs*, of *Mau Rānīpurā*, district *Jhānsī*, in *Bundēl'khaṇḍ*. B. *1855* A.D.

He was a member of the suite of the Rājā of *Chhattr'pur*. His poems are said to be sweet.

557. कान्ह कबि, the younger poet *Kānh alias Kanhāī Lāl*, Kāyasth of *Rāj'nagar*, in *Bundēl'khaṇḍ*. B. *1857* A.D.

He has written some admired poems. His *Nakh'sikh* (see note, No. 87) is said to be worth looking at.

558. जवाहिर कबि, the poet and bard *Jawāhir*, of *Srīnagar*, in *Bundēl'khaṇḍ*. B. *1857* A.D.

Part II.—Banaras.

559. रघु नाथ कबि, the poet and bard *Raghu Nāth,* of *Banāras.* Fl. 1745 A.D.

Sriŋg. He was a fellow pupil of *Mukund Lāl* (No. 560), and father of *Gōkul Nāth* (No. 564), the translator of the *Mahābhārata.* He was court poet to Mahārāj *Baribanḍ Siŋgh,*[1] of Banāras, and lived at *Chāūrāgāw,* which is within the *Pañchakrōsh* or five-kōs circle round Banāras. He is counted as one of the masters of vernacular composition. He wrote (1) the *Rasik Mōhan,* (2) *Jag Mōhan,* (3) *Kābya Kalādhar* (written 1745 A.D.), (4) *Ishk Mahōtsab,* and a commentary on the *Sat Saī* of *Bihārī Lāl* (No. 196). These are all especially admired.

560. मुकुन्द लाल कबि, the poet *Mukund Lāl,* of *Banāras.* B. (? Fl.) *1746* A.D.

Sat. He was a fellow pupil of the poet *Raghu Nāth* (No. 559). Possibly the same as *Lāl Mukund* (No. 391).

561. लाल कबि, the poet and bard *Lāl,* of *Banāras.* Fl. cir. 1775 A.D.

Sun. He attended the court of Rājā *Chēt Siŋgh* (1770—1781), of Banāras. He wrote a treatise on lovers (see note to No. 87) entitled *Ānand Ras,* and a commentary on the *Sat Saī* of *Bihārī Lāl* (No. 196) entitled *Lāl Chandrikā.* Cf., however, No. 629.

562. हरि परःसाद, *Hari Par'sād,* of *Banāras.* Fl. cir. 1775 A.D.

He translated the *Sat Saī* of *Bihārī* (No. 196) into elegant Sanskrit verse at the instance of Rājā *Chēt Siŋgh* (1770—1781), of Banāras.

563. बलःबान सिङ्ह, Prince *Bal'bān Siŋgh,* of *Banāras.* Fl. cir. 1800 A.D.

He was son of Rājā *Chēt Siŋgh* (D. 1810). The Sib Siŋgh Sarōj names him as an author, but does not mention what he wrote.

[1] So Sib Siŋgh, but I can find no trace of any Rājā of Banāras of this name. Possibly *Bal'want Siŋgh* (reigned 1740—1770) is meant.

564. गोकुल नाथ बन्दीजन, the bard *Gōkul Nāth*, of *Banārsa*. Fl. cir. 1820.

Rāg., Sun. He was son of the poet *Raghu Nāth* (No. 559), of Banāras. His home was in the village of *Chāūrāgā̃w*, which is in the *Pañchakrōsh* or five-kōs circle round Banāras. His *Chēt-Chandrikā* is a work of great authority amongst poets. He has described in it the family history of Rājā *Chēt Siŋgh* (Fl. 1776, D. 1810) of Banāras, who was his patron. Another excellent work of his is the *Gōbind Sukhad Bihār*. The *Mahābhārata* (Rāg.) was translated into the vernacular at the instance of Rājā *Udit Nārāyan* (1795—1835), of Banāras, and in this work *Gōkul Nāth*, together with his son *Gōpī Nāth* (No. 565), and the latter's pupil, *Mani Dēb* (No. 566), had a principal share. The full name of the translation is the *Mahābhārat Dar'pan*, and of its supplement the *Haribans Dar'pan*, published in Calcutta in 1829 A.D. Garcin de Tassy (i, 158) says:—"There are other Hindustānī translations of the Mahābhārata; those with which I am acquainted are—

(1) *Kitāb-i-Mahābhārata*, or book of the Mahābhārata, of which a portion is contained in the Farzada Cieli collection.

(2) The copy of which Sir E. Ouseley has also only a portion.

(3) There is also among the manuscripts of Sir W. Ouseley a volume which contains a portion of the Mahābhārata in Sanskrit and Hindustānī.

(4) Among the numbers of the Hindustānī manuscripts of the Prince of Borgia described by Paulin de Saint Barthélemy there is a portion of the Mahābhārata entitled *Bālak Purān*, or the Legend of the Child (Krishna). The original manuscript is accompanied by an Italian translation by P. Marcus a Tomba.

Besides the Persian translation of the Mahābhārata attributed to *Abū'l Fazl*, minister of *Ak'bar*, there is another more recent one by *Najīb Khān ban 'Abdū'l Latīf*, made at the command of, and in the palace of, Nawāb *Mahāldār Khān Nazā* in the year 1782-83 A.D. The translator says that it was made according to the verbal interpretation of the Sanskrit text given to him in Hindūstānī by many Brāhmans.

Among the Persian manuscripts of the Asiatic Society of Bengal is found a third Persian translation by the Hindū *Bapās*."

To these may be added (1) the *Bijai Muktābalī* of the poet *Chhattr'* (No. 75), which is a condensed abstract of the Mahābhārata;

(2) *Sabal Siŋgh*, the Chauhān (No. 210), who translated 24,000 verses of the same work; and (3) *Chirañjīb* (No. 607), who is said to have done the same to the whole.

565. गोपी नाथ बन्दीजन, the bard *Gopī Nāth*, of *Banāras*. Fl. cir. 1820 A.D.

At the instance of Rājā *Udit Nārāyan*, of Banāras, the whole *Mahābhārata* was translated into the vernacular. *Gōpī Nāth* (who was son of *Gōkul Nāth*) (No. 564), and his pupil *Mani Dēb* (No. 566), took an important part in this work. The greater part of *Gōpī Nāth's* life was spent in this work. The rest of his time was spent in composing short pieces of various kinds. He is, however, most famous for the translation.

566. मनि देव, the bard *Mani Dēb*, of *Banāras*. Fl. cir. 1820 A.D.

Sun. He was a pupil of *Gōpī Nāth* (No. 565), and with him and *Gōkul Nāth* (No. 564) took a prominent part in the famous translation of the *Mahābhārata*.

567. पराग कबि, the poet *Parāg*, of *Banāras*. Fl. cir. 1820 A.D.

He attended the court of Rājā *Udit Nārāyan Siŋgh* (1795—1835), of *Banāras*. He translated the *Amara Kōça* (? Rāg. Cf. Nos. 170, 589, 761) into the vernacular.

568. राम सहाय, *Rām Sahāy*, a Kāyasth of *Banāras*. Fl. cir. 1820.

Rāg. He attended the court of Rājā *Udit Nārāyan Siŋgh* (1795—1835), of Banāras. He wrote a treatise on prosody entitled *Brittataraŋginī Sat Saī*.

569. देव कबि, the poet *Dēb*, of *Banāras*, *alias Kāshṭh Jihwā Swāmī*. Fl. cir. 1850 A.D.

Sun., Sriŋg. He studied Sanskrit in Banāras. On one occasion he quarrelled with his preceptor, and afterwards, to show his penitence, cut out his tongue, inserted a false wooden one instead, and carried on communications with others by means of a board, on which he wrote. He was an instructor of Mahārāj *Īswarī Nārāyan Siŋgh* (succeeded 1835, alive in 1883), of Banāras, who settled him in *Rām'nagar,* where he composed the *Binayāmrit* (a collection of hymns), the *Rāmāyan Parichāryā* (*see Harishchandr', Prasiddh Mahātmāō kā Jīban Charitr',* ii, 30), and other works. His hymns are still sung at the Banāras court.

570. **ठाकुर परसाद त्रिपाठी,** *Ṭhākur Par'sād Tripāṭhī,* of *Kishun'dās'pur,* district *Rāy Barēlī.* B. *1825;* Fl. 1863 A.D.

He was learned in Sanskrit composition, and in 1863 A.D. completed a work of great labour, entitled the *Ras Chandrōday,* a collection of poems by 242 poets, which he had collected mainly by house-to-house visitation in *Bundēl'khaṇḍ.* He afterwards went to *Banāras,* where he became a friend of the poets *Ganēs* (No. 573) and *Sar'dār* (No. 571), and received much honour from the nobles of *Āudh.* He died in 1867, leaving a large and valuable library, which was sold by his sons.

571. **सरदार कबि,** the poet and bard *Sar'dār,* of *Banāras.* Alive in 1883.

Sun., Sriŋg. He attended the court of Mahārāj *Īswarī Nārāyan Siŋgh,* of Banāras, and was son of the poet *Hari Jan* (No. 575). He has a great name. He was a friend of *Ṭhākur Par'sād Tripāṭhī* (No. 570), and a teacher of *Nārāyan Rāy* (No. 572). He is author of (1) *Sāhitya Sarasī,* (2) *Hanumat Bhūkhan,* (3) *Tul'sī Bhūkhan,* (4) *Mānas Bhūkhan,* (5) a commentary to the *Kabi-priyā* (No. 134), (6) a commentary to the *Rasik-priyā* (No. 134), (7) a commentary to the *Sat Saī* of *Bihārī* (No. 196), (8) *Sriŋgār Saŋgrah,* and (9) a commentary on 380 emblematic couplets by *Sūr Dās* (No. 37). No. 8 (printed by Nawal Kishōr, at *Lakh'naū*), is a deservedly popular work on rhetoric, and deals with all the branches of the art of poetical composition. It was written in 1848 A.D., and is quoted in this work as 'Sriŋg.' It contains quotations from the following poets:—

Chatur'bhuj (No. 40).
Nārāyan Dās (No. 51).
Parasū Rām (No. 55).
Ras Khān (No. 67).
Keh'rī (No. 70).
Par'bat (No. 74).

Krish'n Jīban (? Nos. 77, 438).
Sib (? No. 88).
Am'rēs (No. 90).
Ak'bar (No. 104).
Brahm (No. 106).
Rahīm (No. 108).
Khān'khānā (No. 108).
Gang (No. 119).
Nidhi (No. 131).
Kēsab Dās (No. 134).
Balibhadr' (No. 135).
Par'bīn Rāī (No. 137).
Sundar (No. 142).
Chintāmani (No. 143).
Bhūkhan (No. 145).
Mati Rām (No. 146).
Nrip Sambhu (No. 147).
Nīl Kanṭh (No. 148).
Par'tāp (No. 149).
Srīpati (No. 150).
Sib Nāth (No. 152).
Manḍan (No. 154).
Ratan (No. 155).
Mur'lī (No. 156).
Srī Dhar (No. 157).
Kālidās (No. 159).
Kabirāj (No. 160).
Sēnāpati (No. 165).
Ṭhākur (No. 173).
Kāsī Rām (No. 175).
Iswar (No. 177).
'Ālam (No. 181).
Par'sād (No. 183).
Niwāj (? Nos. 198, 448).
Hari Kēs (No. 203).
Srī Gōbind (No. 211).
Mōtī Rām (No. 216).
Par'mēs (? Nos. 222, 616).
Abhimanyu (No. 229).
Ghāsī Rām (No. 230).
Sēkh (No. 236).
Ballabh (No. 239).
Bēnī (? Nos. 247, 484).
Hari Jan (No. 249).
Rām Jū (? No. 252).
Bhū Dhar (? Nos. 256, 336).
Sirōmani (No. 262).
Bal Dēb (? Nos. 263, 359).
Tōkh (No. 265).
Mukund (No. 266).
Rūp Nārāyan (No. 268).
Bhar'mī (No. 273).
Kul'pati (No. 282).
Sūrati (No. 326).
Kripā Rām (? Nos. 328, 797).
Bhag'want (No. 333).
Uday Nāth (No. 334).
Kabīndr' (No. 334).
Giri Dhar Dās (No. 345).
Ghan Ānand (No. 347).
Dūlah (No. 358).
Dās (? No. 369).
Kishōr (No. 385).
Tārā (No. 419).
Pūkhī (No. 442).
Bōdhā (No. 449).
Krish'n Lāl (No. 456).
Mak'rand (No. 457).
Dhīr (No. 461).
Bhañjan (No. 468).
Santan (No. 472).
Singh (? No. 474).
Datt' (No. 475).
Mani Rām (No. 477).
Sangam (No. 480).
Ūdhō (No. 495).
Padmākar (No. 506).
Paj'nēs (No. 510).
Nawal (No. 526).
Hir'dēs (No. 547).

Raghu Nāth (No. 559).
Dēb (No. 569).
Sar'dār (No. 571).
Sib Datt' (No. 588).
Giri Dhārī (No. 625).
Chāin Rāy (No. 627).
Deokī Nandan (No. 630).
Gur Datt' (No. 631).
Dinēs (No. 633).
Gulāl (No. 657).
Bali Rām (No. 768).
Dhurandhar (No. 782).
Nāyak (No. 783).
Mahārāi (No. 793).
Rikhi Nāth (No. 794).
Dayā Dēb (No. 836).
Dēbī Siŋgh (No. 843).
Nabī (No. 848).
Nāth (cf. No. 850).
Man'sā Rām (No. 885).
Mīran (No. 892).
Rajjab (No. 898).
Ramāpatí (No. 900).
Sasi Nāth (No. 931).
Sib Rāj (No. 932).
Hari Lāl (No. 946).
Hēm (No. 950).
Bhīm (?).
Chhatt' (?).
Dēban (?).
Dhanēs (?).
Dhar'm (?).
Mak'sūdan (?).
Man Rāj (?).
Mithilēs (?).
Rati Nāth (?).
Sāhab Rām (?).
Samādhān (?).
Tulā Rām (?).

572. नारायन राय, the bard *Nārāyan Rāy,* of *Banāras.* Alive in 1883.

He was a pupil of the poet *Sar'dār* (No. 571). He wrote a metrical commentary on the *Bhākhā Bhūkhan* (No. 377) and a gloss on the *Kabi-priyā* (No. 134). He is also author of a number of erotic verses.

573. गनेस कवि, the poet and bard *Ganēs,* of *Banāras.* Alive in 1883.

He attended the court of Mahārāj *Īswarī Nārāyan Siŋgh*. He was a friend of *Ṭhākur Pār'sad* (No. 570), the author of the *Ras Chandrōday*.

574. बन्सी धर कवि, the poet *Bansī Dhar,* of *Banāras.* B. *1844* A.D.

He was son of the bard *Ganēs* (No. 573), who was alive in 1883. He is author of a work on composition entitled *Sāhitya Bansīdhar,* and of a translation of the *Rājanīti of Chāṇakya* entitled *Bhākhā Rāj'nīti* (? Rāg. Cf. Nos. 840 and 919). He is also the author of two works on morals, entitled *Bidur Prajāgar* and *Mitra Manōhar*. He is possibly the same as a *Bansī Dhar* and as a *Bansī Dhar Kabi* mentioned by Sib Siŋgh, both without date.

575. हरि जन कबि, the poet *Hari Jan*, of *Lalit'pur*. B. (? Fl.) *1851*.

He wrote a commentary to the *Rasik-priyā* (No. 134) under the name of Mahārāj *Īswarī Nārāyan Siŋgh*, of *Banāras*. He was father of the poet *Sar'dār* (No. 571).

576. बन्दन पाठक, *Bandan Pāṭhak*, of *Banāras*. Alive in 1883.

He wrote one of the best existing commentaries on the *Rāmāyan* of *Tul'sī Dās* (No. 128), at the suggestion of Mahārāj *Īswarī Nārāyan Siŋgh*, of *Banāras*. It is entitled *Mānas Saŋkābalī*.

577. जानकी पर॰साद कबि, the poet *Jānakī Par'sād*, of *Banāras*. Fl. 1814 A.D.

In 1814 A.D. he wrote a commentary on the *Rām-chandrikā* of *Kēsab Dās* (No. 134). He also wrote a work entitled the *Jukti Rāmāyan*, on which the poet *Dhanī Rām* (No. 578) wrote a commentary. Either he or the other *Jānakī Par'sād* (No. 695) may possibly be the same as a third poet of the same name mentioned by Sib Siŋgh without date.

578. धनी राम कबि, the poet *Dhanī Rām*, of *Banāras*. B. *1831* A.D.

At the request of Bābū *Deokī Nandan*, brother of the Mahārāj of *Banāras*, he translated the *Bhāṣā Prakāça* from Sanskrit into the vernacular, and wrote a commentary to the *Rām-chandrikā* of *Kēsab Dās* (No. 134). He also wrote a commentary to the *Jukti Rāmāyan* of the poet *Jānakī Par'sād* (No. 577).

579. सेवक कबि, the poet and bard *Sēbak*, of *Banāras*. Alive in 1883 A.D.

Sun. An erotic poet, who attended the court of Bābū *Deokī Nandan,* brother of the Mahārāj of *Banāras.* Possibly the same as No. 677.

580. गोपाल चन्द्र साहू, *Gōpāl Chandr' Sāhū, alias Giri Dhar Banār'sī, alias Giri Dhar Dās.* B. 1832 A.D.

Sun. He was son of *Kālī Harakh Chandr'* and father of the famous poet *Harishchandr'* (No. 581), of *Banāras.* His principal works are the *Dasābatār* and the *Bhāratī Bhūkhan.* The last is a commentary on the *Bhākhā Bhūkhan* (No. 377). *Harishchandr'* only died in the year 1885. Cf. Garcin de Tassy, i, 191.

581. हरिश्चन्द्र, Bābū *Harishchandr',* of *Banāras.* Born 9th September 1850.

Sun. The most celebrated of the native poets of the present day. He has done more for the popularisation of vernacular literature than almost any living Indian. He himself was a prolific author in many styles, and he excelled in all. He conducted for many years an excellent vernacular magazine entitled the *Harishchandrikā.* He was son of *Gōpāl Chandr' Sāhū alias Giri Dhar Banār'sī* (No. 580), who was a prolific author, but who died at the early age of 27, in the year 1859, leaving Harishchandra an orphan only 9 years old. The boy was educated at Queen's College, Banāras, and commenced to write at an early age. In the year 1880, so greatly had his fame extended that he was given the title of *Bhāratēndu,* or Moon of India, by the unanimous consent of all the editors of the vernacular papers of India. He died in the year 1885, universally regretted, being by general consent one who was *'ajāta-çatru.'* He is best known (see also No. 706) for the *Sundarī Tilak* (quoted in this work as 'Sun.'), published in 1869 (Sam. 1926), which is an anthology of poems in the Sawaīyā metre from the works of 69 poets. This work is by some said to have been compiled under his instructions by *Purukhōttam Sukal,* and has been frequently printed. One of his latest works was a series of excellent lives of great men, European and Indian, entitled *Prasiddh Mahātmāõ kā Jīban Charitr'.* He was certainly the best critic which Northern India has as yet produced. A short account of his life is given in the *Chandrāst* of *Byās Rām Shaŋkar Sharmā,* printed at the Hari Par'kās Press in Banāras in 1885, after the poet's death. Also at the end of *Harishchandr's Kāshmīr Kusum* (or history of Kāshmīr)[1] there is a short account of the author, and a list of about a hundred works by him. One work, not mentioned in this list, is a play entitled *Kāshī kā Chhayā-chittra*, in which there are several examples of the peculiar slang of Banāras. Another very popular work of his is the *Kabi Bachan Sudhā*, which is a collection of poems dealing with the rainy season. A complete collection of this author's works is now in course of publication by Bābū *Rām Dīn Singh*, of the Khadga Bilās Press, Bankīpur, under the title of the *Harishchandra Kalā*.

The following is a list of the poets quoted in the Sundarī Tilak :—

Ajabēs (Nos. 24, 530).
'Ālam (No. 181).
Alīman (No. 784).
Anant (No. 250).
Bal Dēb (No. 263).
Bēnī (Nos. 247, 484, 671).
Bēnī Par'bīn (No. 608).
Bhag'want (No. 333).
Bōdhā (No. 449).
Brahm (No. 106).
Chand (No. 6 or ? No. 93).
Chhitipāl (No. 332).
Dās (No. 369).
Dayā Nidhi (? Nos. 365, 787).
Dēb (No. 569).
Deokī Nandan (No. 630).
Gang (No. 119).
Ghan Ānand (No. 347).
Ghan Syām (No. 92).
Gōkul Nāth (No. 564).
Gopāl Chandr' alias *Giri Dhar Banār'sī* (No. 580).
Gwāl (No. 507).
Hanumān (No. 796).
Hari Kēs (No. 203).
Harishchandra (No. 581).
Kabirāj (No. 661).
Kālikā (No. 780).
Kishōr (No. 385).
Lāl (No. 561).
Mahā (No. 403).
Mah'rāj (No. 793).
Mak'rand (No. 457).
Mandan (No. 154).
Mani Dēb (No. 566).
Mannā Lāl alias *Dwij* (the *Sundarī Tilak Nāmābalī* gives *Munnā Lāl*) (No. 583).
Mān Singh alias *Dwij Dēb* (No. 599).
Mati Rām (No. 146).
Mubārak (No. 94).
Mur'lī Dhar (No. 156).
Nabīn (No. 790).
Nab Nidhi (No. 789).
Najīb Khān alias *Rasiyā* (No. 788).
Narēndra Singh (No. 690).
Narēs (No. 791).
Nāth (? Nos. 68, 147, 162, 440, 632, 850).
Nawāz (No. 198).
Nrip Sambhu (No. 147).
Padmākar (No. 506).

[1] Banāras. Mallika Chandra & Co. 1884.

Pāras (No. 792).
Par'mēs (? Nos. 222, 616).
Prēm (No. 351).
Raghu Nāth of *Jōdh'pur* (No. 193).
Raghu Rāj (No. 532).
Rām Nāth (No. 785).
Ras Khān (No. 67).
Rikhi Nāth (No. 794).
Sambhu (? No. 147).
Sar'dār (No. 571).
Sēbak (Nos. 579, 677).
Sēkhar (No. 795).
Sib (No. 88).
Srī Dhar (No. 157).
Srī Pati (No. 150).
Sukh Dēb Misar (No. 160).
Sumerū Siŋgh (No. 759).
Sundar Dās (No. 142).
Ṭhākur (No. 173).
Tōkh (No. 265).
Tul'sī Srī Ōjhā (No. 786).

582. दीन दयाल गिरि, *Dīn Dayāl Girī*, of *Banāras.* Fl. 1855.

Besides being learned in Sanskrit, he wrote a treatise on composition (साहित्य) in the above year, entitled *Anyōkti-Kalpadrum.* He is also the author of two works, entitled *Anurāg Bāg* and *Bāg Bahār* respectively.

583. मन्ना लाल, Paṇḍit *Mannā Lāl*, of *Banāras, alias Dwij Kabi.* Alive in 1883.

Sun. He is possibly the same as *Mān Siŋgh Shāk'dwīpī* (No. 599). At least both take the *nom de guerre* of *Dwij.* On the other hand, however, he is called *Munnā Lāl* in the *Sundarī Tilak Nāmābalī* of *Gōbardhan Nāth.*

ADDENDA TO CHAPTER X, PART II.

584. मनियार सिङ्घ, *Maniyār Siŋgh*, the Chhattrī, of *Banāras*, B. *1804*.

His best works are the *Hanumat Chhabīsī* and the *Bhākhā Sāundar'j Lah'rī.*

585. गजःराज उपाध्या, *Gaj'rāj Upādhyā*, of *Banāras.* B. *1817*.

He has written a prosody entitled *Brittahār*, and a *Rāmāyan*.

586. बन्स रूप कबि, the poet *Bans Rūp*, of *Banāras.* B. *1844*.

A panegyrist of the Mahārāj of Banāras.

587. माधबानन्द भारती, *Mādhabānand Bhāratī*, of *Banāras.* B. *1845* A.D.

The author of a translation of the *Çaŋkara Digvijaya* into the vernacular.

588. सिब दत्त, *Sib Datt'*, a Brāhman, of *Banāras.* B. *1854* A.D.

Sriŋg. Possibly the same as another *Sib Datt' Kabi* mentioned by Sib Siŋgh without particulars.

Part III.—Audh.

589. सुबन्स सुकल, *Subans Sukal*, of *Bigah'pur*, district *Unão*. B. *1777* A.D.

Rāg., Bid. He at first attended the court of Rājā *Um'rāw Siŋgh Bandhal'gōtī*, of *Amēṭhī*, district *Farukhābād*, and there translated from the Sanskrit the *Amara Kōça* (? Rāg. Cf. Nos. 170, 567, 761), *Rasataraŋgiṇī*, and *Rasamañjarī* into the vernacular. He then went to Rājā *Subbā Siŋgh* (No. 590) of *Ōel*, and assisted him in the compilation of the *Bidwan Mōd Taraŋginī*.

590. सुब्बा सिङ्घ, Rājā *Subbā Siŋgh*, the Chaūhān, *alias* the poet *Srī Dhar*, of *Ōel*, district *Khīrī*. Fl. 1817 A.D.

He was author of an important work on vernacular composition entitled *Bidwan Mōd Taraŋginī* (written 1817 A.D., and quoted in this work as 'Bid.'), which deals with the whole subject-matter of lovers, confidants, messengers, the seasons, the various styles, etc. But the most important aspect of the work is that it forms an anthology of extracts from works by the author's preceptor, *Subans Sukal* (No. 589), and forty-four other poets.

591. धौँकल सिङ्घ, *Dhaūkal Siŋgh*, the Bais, of *Nyāwā*, district *Rāy Barēlī*. B. *1803*.

He wrote a number of short works, of which the best known is the *Ramal Prashna*, a report of conversations on geomancy between Umā and Çambhu.

592. सहज राम, *Sahaj Rām*, a Baniyā of *Pãtēpur*, district *Sītāpur*. B. *1804* A.D.

He wrote a *Rāmāyan*, which is a translation of the *Raghuvamça* and of the *Hanuman Nāṭaka* (? Rāg.).

593. रिखि राम मिसर, *Rikhi Rām Misar*, of *Paṭṭī*. B. (? Fl.) *1844* A.D.

He attended the court of *Bāl Krish'n*, Dīwān of *Audh*, and was author of a work entitled *Bansī Kalpalatā*.

594. **जीब नाथ,** the bard *Jīb Nāth*, of *Nawal'gañj*, district *Unāo*. B. *1815* A.D.

He belonged to the family of *Bāl Krish'n*, Dīwān of *Āudh*. He wrote a work of merit entitled the *Basant Pachīsī*.

595. **सिब सिङ्ह,** *Sib Siŋgh, Sĕgar*, of *Kānthā*, district *Unāo*. B. *1821* A.D.

He is the author of the *Sib Siŋgh Sarōj*, on which this work is principally founded. He also translated the *Bṛihachchhivapurāṇa* both into the vernacular and into Ūrdū, and the *Brahmōttarakhaṇḍa* into the vernacular. He has a great collection of Arabic, Persian, Sanskrit, and vernacular manuscripts, which he delights in cataloguing. He was son of Mahārāj-kumār Ṭhākur *Ran'jīt Siŋgh, Sĕgar*, Ta'alūq'dār of Kānthā, and is himself an Inspector of Police.

596. **मदन गोपाल सुकल,** *Madan Gōpāl Sukal*, of *Phatūhābād* (*Fatuhābād*). B. *1819* A.D.

He attended the court of Rājā *Ar'jun Siŋgh*, of *Balirām'pur* (district *Gōḍā*), for many years. At his suggestion he wrote two works—the *Arjun Bilās* and a simple treatise on medicine entitled *Baidya Ratan*. Sib Siŋgh mentions two other poets—(1) *Madan Gōpāl* of *Char'khārī*, in *Bundĕl'khaṇḍ*, and (2) *Madan Gōpāl*, without any particulars. Neither of these are dated by him.

597. **गङ्गा पर॰साद,** *Gaŋgā Par'sād*, commonly known as *Gaŋg Kabi*, or the poet *Gaŋg*, the Brāhman of *Supāulī*, district *Sītāpur*. B. *1833* A.D.

He was given the village *Supāulī* rent-free on account of his poems. His son is also a poet, and is now alive in *Tihar'nā*. Gaŋgā Par'sād wrote a work entitled *Dūtī Bilās*, in which the various kinds of lovers' go-betweens (*dūti*) are described in a series of punning verses.

598. **जै कबि,** the poet and bard *Jai*, of *Lakh'naū*. Fl. 1845 A.D.

He was a pensioner of Nawāb *Wājid 'Ālī* (1847—1856), of *Lakh'-naū*. He wrote many poems in *Ūrdū* and in the vernacular. He is esteemed by all for his poems on morals (नीति), his occasional (सामयिक) pieces, his didactic poems (चेतावनी), etc. He had many religious controversies with the Musal'māns.

599. मान सिङ्ह, Mahārāj *Mān Singh*, the *Shāk'dwīpī*, *alias Dwij Dēb*, of *Āudh*. Fl. 1850.

Sun. He was skilled in Sanskrit, in the vernacular, in Persian, and in English. About the year 1850 A.D. he composed a work entitled *Sringār Latikā*, together with a commentary to it. In his latter years he gave up poetry and studied English law. He died in 1873. Amongst others, *Ṭhākur Par'sād* (No. 600), *Jagannāth* (No. 601), and *Bal Dēb Singh* (No. 602) attended his court. His poetical *nom de guerre* was *Dwij Dēb*, and he is possibly the same as *Mannā Lāl* (No. 583), who also wrote under the title *Dwij*. According to Ṭhākur Par'sād, he had a son named *Dar'san Singh*.

600. ठाकुर पर॰साद पयासी मिसर, *Ṭhākur Par'sad Payāsī Misar alias Paṇḍit Par'bīn*, of *Āudh*. Fl. 1850 A.D.

He wrote under the name of *Paṇḍit Par'bīn*. He attended the court of Mahārāj *Mān Singh* (No. 599), and lived near *Paliyā Shāh'gañj*.

601. जगन्नाथ कवि अवस्थी, the poet *Jagannāth Abasthī*, of *Sumērupur*, district *Unāo*. Alive in 1883.

He formerly attended the court of Mahārāj *Mān Singh* (No. 599), of *Āudh*. He subsequently obtained the patronage of Mahārāj *Sib Dīn Singh*, of *Al'war*. He has a great name for his knowledge of Sanskrit composition (साहित्य). He has written detached verses in the vernacular.

602. बल देव सिङ्ह, *Bal Dēb Singh*, the Chhattrī, of *Āudh*. Fl. 850 A.D.

He attended the court of Mahārāj *Mān Singh* (No. 599), and was the teacher of Rājā *Mādhab Singh* (? No. 604) in composition (साहित्य).

603. **चण्डी दत्त कवि,** the poet *Chaṇḍī Datt'*. B. *1841* A.D.

He attended the court of Mahārāj *Mān Siŋgh* (No. 599), of *Āudh*.

604. **माधव सिङ्घ,** Rājā *Mādhab Siŋgh*, of *Gōchī Amēṭhī*, district *Sul'tān'pur*. Alive in 1883.

He belongs to a family whose members have always been great patrons of learning. He is so himself. Among his ancestors may be named *Himmat Siŋgh* (cf. Nos. 160 and 334), *Gur Duṭṭ' Siŋgh* (No. 332), *Um'rāw Siŋgh* (cf. No. 589). He is author of the *Manōj Latikā*, the *Dēbī-charitr' Sarōj*, and the *Tridīp* (a vernacular translation of the *Bhar'tharī* (*Bhartṛihari*) *Shatak*). He appears to be the son of *Mān Siŋgh* (No. 599). (See No. 602.)

605. **क्रिश्न दत्त सिङ्घ,** *Krish'n Datt' Siŋgh*, the *Bisēn Rāj'put*, Rājā of *Bhin'gā*, district *Bahirāich*. B. *1852* A.D.

This Rājā was not only a skilled poet himself, but also encouraged the patronage of poets in his dominions. A member of his family was the famous *Jagat Siŋgh* (No. 340), and the poet *Sib Dīn* (No. 606) and others less known attended his court. At the present day members of his family are great patrons of poets.

606. **सिब दीन कवि,** the poet *Sib Dīn*, of *Bhin'gā*, district *Bahirāich*. B. *1858* A.D.

He attended the court of Rājā *Krish'n Datt' Siŋgh*, of *Bhin'gā*, and in his name wrote a work on poetry entitled *Krish'n Datt' Bhūkhan*.

ADDENDA TO CHAPTER X, PART III.

607. **चिरञ्जीव,** *Chirañjīb*, the Brāhman, of *Bais'wārā*. B. *1813* A.D.

? Rāg. He is said to have translated the *Mahābhārata* into the vernacular

608. **बेनी परबीन,** *Bēnī Par'bīn*, *Bāj'pēyī* of *Lakh'naū*. B. *1819*. A.D.

Sun. The author of several works. His best, a treatise on lovers. (See note to No. 87.)

609. **अङ्गन लाल,** the bard *Aṅgan Lāl alias* the poet *Rasāl,* of *Bil'grām,* district *Har'dōī.* B. *1823* A.D.

The author of a treatise on rhetoric entitled *Bar'wāī Alaṅkār.*

610. **मकरन्द राय,** the bard *Mak'rand Rāy,* of *Puwāwā̃,* district *Shāh-Jahān-pur.* B. *1823* A.D.

A descendant of *Chandan Rāy* (No. 374), and was the author of an admired work entitled *Hāsya Ras.*

611. **भौन कबि,** the poet and bard *Bhāūn* of *Bētī,* district *Rāy Barēlī.* B. *1824* A.D.

An admired erotic poet, who was the author of a treatise on rhetoric entitled *Sriṅgār Ratnākar.* His son, the poet *Dayāl* (No. 720), was alive in 1883.

612. **बादे राय कबि,** the poet and bard *Bādē Rāy,* of *Ḍal'maū,* district *Rāy Barēlī.* B. *1825.*

He attended the court of *Dayā Kishun,* Dīwān of *Lakh'naū.*

613. **सङ्कर कबि त्रिपाठी,** the poet *Saṅkar Tripāṭhī,* of *Bis'wā̃,* district *Sītāpur.* B. *1834* A.D.

In conjunction with his son, the poet *Sālik,* he wrote a *Rāmāyan* in *Kabitta* metres. He is possibly the same as another Saṅkar mentioned by Sib Siṅgh, without date, as an erotic writer.

614. **लोने सिङ्घ,** *Lōnē Siṅgh,* of *Bāchhil Tītāūlī,* district *Khīrī.* B. *1835* A.D.

He translated the tenth book of the *Bhāgavata Purāṇa* (Rāg.) into the vernacular.

615. **सीतल राय,** the bard *Sītal Rāy* of *Bāūrī,* district *Bahirāich.* B. *1837.*

He attended the court of Rājā *Gumān Siṅgh, Jan'wār,* of *Ekāūnā,* district *Bahirāich.*

616. **परमेस,** the bard *Par'mēs,* of *Satāwā̃,* district *Rāy Barēlī.* B. *1839* A.D.

Sun. (? Cf. No. 222.)

617. **बन्सी धर बाजपेयी,** *Bansī Dhar Bāj'pēyī,* of *Chintā Khērā,* district *Rāy Barēlī.* B. *1844* A.D.

A prolific author of many works. His vedantic dōhās are much admired.

618. **भवानी परसाद पाठक,** *Bhawānī Par'sād Pāṭhak alias Bhawān Kabi,* of *Māūrāwā,* district *Unāo.* B. *1844* A.D.

He is the author of an admired treatise on poetry called *Kābya Sirōmani,* or *Kābya Kalpadrum.* It treats of poetry, rhetoric, lovers, go-betweens, the passions, seasons, etc.

619. **महानन्द बाजपेयी,** *Mahānand Bāj'pēyī,* of *Bais'wārā.* B. *1844* A.D.

Rāg. He was a votary of Çiva worship, and translated the *Bṛihach-chhiva Purāṇa* into the vernacular.

620. **रस रङ्ग कबि,** the poet *Ras Raṅg,* of *Lakh'naū.* B. *1844* A.D.

An erotic poet.

621. **सम्भु नाथ मिसर कबि,** the poet *Sambhu Nāth Misar,* of *Bais'wārā.* B. *1844* A.D.

He attended the court of Rānā *Jadu Nāth Siṅgh, Bāīs,* of *Khajūr'gāw̃.* While still young he wrote a history entitled *Bāīs Bansābalī,* and translation of the fourth chapter of the *Çiva Purāṇa.*

622. **अजोध्या परसाद सुकल,** *Ajodhyā Par'sād Sukal,* of *Gōlā Gokaran-nāth,* district *Khīrī.* B. *1845* A.D.

Not a poet of high rank, but a voluminous writer. He wrote under the name of *Jōdhī.* He was much esteemed in the court of a Rājā *Būṛ*.

623. मिही लाल, the bard *Mihī Lāl alias Malind*, of *Ḍal'maū*, district *Rāy Barēlī*. B. *1845* A.D.

Cf. No. 512. He praised one *Bhūpāl Siŋgh.*

624. राम नाथ परधान, *Rām Nāth Par'dhān*, of *Āudh*. B. *1846* A.D.

The author of the *Rām Kalēwā* and other books.

625. गिरि धारी, *Giri Dhārī* the Brāhman, a Bais'wārā of *Satan'pur*. B. *1847* A.D.

Sriŋg. His poems either deal with Kriṣṇa's sports or are in the quietistic style. He was not a learned poet, but wrote elegantly.

626. हिमाचल राम कवि, the poet *Himāchal Rām*, a Brāhman of *Bhaṭāulī*, district *Fāīzābād*. B. *1847* A.D.

A simple writer.

627. चैन सिङ्घ, *Chāīn Siŋgh alias Har Charan*, the Khattrī, of *Lakh'naū*. B. *1853* A.D.

Sriŋg. He has written the *Bhārat Dīpikā* and the *Sriŋgār Sārābalī*. He is possibly the same as another *Chāīn Kabi* mentioned by Sib Siŋgh.

Part IV.—Miscellaneous.

628. जै चन्द, *Jāī Chand*, of *Jāīpur*. Fl. 1806.

Author of a Sanskrit and vernacular work dealing with the doctrines of the Jāin community, written in Sambat 1863 (1806 A.D.), and entitled *Swāmi Kārttikēyānuprēkṣa.*

629. लल्लू जी लाल, *Lallū Jī 'Lāl* of *Guj'rāt*, Āg'rāwalā. Fl. 1803 A.D.

The well-known author of—

(1) The *Prēm Sāgar* (Rāg.), which was written in the above year under the Marquis of Wellesley's Government, and under Dr. John Gilchrist's direction. In the preface he says it is a translation into Hindī from the Braj Bhākhā version of the 10th book of the *Bhāgavata Purāṇa.* The Braj version was by *Chatur'bhuj Misar* (? No. 40). The Prēm Sāgar was not printed till 1809, in Lord Minto's Government, under the direction of Mr. Abraham Lockitt. It has frequently been printed since, the best edition being Eastwick's (Hertford, 1851), which has an excellent vocabulary.

(2) The *Laṭāīf-i-Hindī*, a collection of 100 stories in Ūrdū, Hindī, and Braj Bhākhā. According to Garcin de Tassy (i, 306) it was printed in Calcutta under the title of "The new Cyclopædia Hindustanica, etc.," and Carmichael Smith reprinted a large portion of it in London under its true name.

(3) The *Rāj'nīti*, or *Bārttik Rāj'nīti*, a Braj Bhākhā translation of the *Hitōpadēça*. It was written in Sambat 1869 (A.D. 1812), and should be distinguished from translations of *Chāṇakya's Rājanīti*. (Cf. Nos. 574, 840, 919.)

(4) The *Sabhā Bilās* (Rāg.), a collection of poetical extracts from famous writers in the Braj Bhākhā dialect.

(5) The *Mādhab Bilās* (? Rāg.). Cf. No. 896.

(6) The *Lāl Chandrikā*, an excellent commentary on the *Sat Saī* of *Bihārī Lāl*, frequently printed. Cf., however, No. 561.

(7) The *Maçārdir-i-Bhākhā*, a grammatical work on the Hindī language, in prose and in the Nāgarī character. Garcin de Tassy says that a copy exists in the Library of the Asiatic Society of Bengal.

(8) The *Siṇghāsan Battīsī* (Rāg.), which was translated in 1804 by him and *Mirzā Kāẓim 'Alī* from an older Braj Bhākhā translation by *Sundar Dās* (No. 142).

(9) The *Baītāl Pachīsī* (Rāg.). Garcin de Tassy gives the following particulars concerning this work, which I have not been able to check, as in the copies now available in the bazār the preface is not printed. This work has also been translated from Sanskrit into Braj Bhākhā by *Sūrati Misar* (No. 326). Lallū translated this version into Hindūstānī, assisted by *Maẓ'har 'Alī Khān Wilā*; or rather, it was Wilā who was assisted by the former. Mr. James Mouat, then Professor of Hindūstānī in the College of Fort William, charged *Tāriṇī Charaṇa Mittra* with the task of looking over the work and expunging the Braj Bhākhā words not current in ordinary Hindūstānī.

I may mention, in addition to the above, that other translations of the same work, and bearing the same name, were made by *Sambhu Nāth* (No. 366) and by *Bhōlā Nāth* (No. 883).

(10) The novel of *Mādhōnal* or *Mādhabānal* (cf. No. 872), in the editing of which he was again assisted by Maẓ'har 'Ali Khān Wilā (see Garcin de Tassy, l.c.). This was translated from the work by *Mōtī Rām* (No. 216), bearing the same name. The legend of *Mādhavānala* and *Kāma Kandalā* is a very old one. There is a copy of the Sanskrit version in the Library of the Bengal Asiatic Society, which was written as far back as Sambat 1587, or 1530 A.D. (Rājēndra Lāl Mittra, *Notices of Sanskrit Manuscripts*, ii, 137.) The story is as follows. In *Puphāvatīnagarī* (the old name of *Bilharī*, in the Central Provinces) reigned Rājā *Gobind Rāo* in the Sambat year 919, or A.D. 862. He had a very handsome Brāhman attendant named *Mādhavānal*, who was specially skilful in singing and dancing, as well as an adept in

all arts and sciences, so that all the women fell in love with him. The husbands complained to the Rājā, and Mādhavānal was banished from Puphāvatī. He retired to *Kām'vati,* the capital of Rājā *Kām Sēn,* who was fond of music and singing, and gave the Brāhman a place in his court. This Rājā had a most beautiful woman (a *vēçya*) named *Kām Kandalā,* with whom Mādhavānal fell in love, for which he was expelled from Kām'vatī. He then went to *Ujāin,* and asked a boon from Rājā *Vikramāditya,* who was famed for granting every request that was made to him. The promise was duly made, and the Brāhman claimed to have Kām Kandalā given up to him. Vikramāditya accordingly besieged Kām'vatī and captured Kām Kandalā, who was at once made over to Mādhavānal. After some time, with Vikrama's permission, the happy pair retired to Puphāvatī, where Mādhavānal built a palace for Kām Kandalā, the ruins of which are still shown. (See *Rep. Arch. Surv. Ind.* ix, 37.)

(11) The novel of *Sakuntalā,* in the editing of which he was associated with *Kāẓim 'Alī Jawan* (see Garcin de Tassy, l.c.).

In connexion with the *Prēm Sāgar,* the following note on Hindī translations of the *Bhāgavata Purāṇa* may be of use. *Sūr Dās* (No. 37) is said to have translated the whole, but his translation has not come down to us. According to Ward, *View,* etc., ii, 481, *Priyā Dās* (cf. No. 319) was the author of a *Bhāgavad* in the dialect of *Bundēl'khaṇḍ* (see Garcin de Tassy, i, 405). The last-named author (i, 121) also mentions a *Bhūpati* (cf. No. 332), a Kāyasth, who 'was author of a *Bhāgavat* in Hindī verse entitled *Srī Bhāgavat.* There is a copy of it in the Library of the Asiatic Society of Bengal, and Ward quotes from it. I do not know if this copy is the same as one which exists in the British Museum, in Halhed's collection, No. 5620. The last is composed of verses of nine lines each, and is written in the Persian character. The dialect is unintelligible. There is also a *Bhāgavat* in Hindī verse in the India Office Library, entitled *Pōthī Bhāgavat,* but according to the catalogue it is only a portion of the Bhāgavata Purāṇa translated from the Sanskrit.' Mahārāj *Raghu Rāj Siṅgh* (No. 532) of *Baṅdhō* (*Rīwā̃*) was author of a much-admired translation of the *Bhāgavata Purāṇa,* entitled *Ānandāmbudhi. Kripā Rām* (No. 797) may also be mentioned as having translated the whole Purāṇa into *dōhās* and *chaupāīs* in simple language.

The tenth book of the Purāṇa, dealing with Kṛiṣṇa's life, is the most popular, and has been frequently translated. The *Prēm Sāgar* is the best known version, and those of *Chatur'bhuj Misar* (? No. 40) and

Nand Dās (No. 42) may also be mentioned. The latter is known as the *Dasam Skandh*. The *Krish'n Kallōl* of the poet *Mān* (No. 372) also appears to belong to this group. Another translation is by *Lōnē Siŋgh* (No. 614). Garcin de Tassy (i, 121) says a work entitled *Pōthī Dasam Iskandh* is mentioned in the catalogue of the Library belonging to a person named *Farzāda Qulī*, a copy of which is in the Fort William College Library. 'In the same Library there is a third copy, entitled *Srī Bhāgawat Dasam Iskandh*; and a fourth, in *Bhākhā*, exists in the India Office Library under the same title' According to the same author (i, 404), *Prēm Kēswar Dās* (No. 859) translated the twelfth book of the Purāṇa, a copy of the work being in the India Office Library. A commentary on this Purāṇa was written by *Balibhadr'* (No. 135).

630. देवकी नन्दन सुकल, *Deokī Nandan Sukal*, of *Mak'rand'pur*, district *Kānh'pur*. B. *1813* A.D.

Sun., Sriŋg. He was brother of *Gur Datt' Sukal* (No. 631) and of *Sib Nāth* (No. 632). The first is author of the *Pachchhī Bilās*, and *Deokī* of a *Nakh'sikh* (see note to No. 87) and of a number of short poems, of which two or three hundred are extant. None of Sib Nāth's poems have as yet been identified.

631. गुर दत्त सुकल, *Gur Datt' Sukal*, of *Mak'rand'pur*, district *Kānh'pur*. B. *1807*.

Sriŋg. He was brother of *Deokī Nandan* (No. 630) and *Sib Nāth* (No. 632). All three were good poets. His principal work was the *Pachchhī Bilās*.

632. सिब नाथ सुकल, *Sib Nāth Sukal alias Sambhōg Nāth*, of *Mak'rand'pur*, district *Kānh'pur*. B. *1813* A.D.

? Sun. He was brother of *Gur Datt'* (No. 631) and *Deokī Nandan* (No. 630), and was an admired poet. It is difficult to identify his poems owing to his habit of signing himself simply *Nāth*.

633. दिनेस कबि, the poet *Dinēs*, of *Ṭikārī*, in district *Gayā*. Fl. 1807.

Sriŋg. In the above year he wrote a well-known and much-admired *Nakh'sikh* (see note to No. 87), entitled *Ras Rahasya.* (Printed by *Rām Dīn Siŋgh,* Khadga Bilās Press, *Bāŋkipur.*)

634. बखतावर, *Bakh'tāwar,* of *Hāth'ras,* district *Alīgaṛh.* Fl. 1817 A.D.

A religious mendicant, author of an atheistical work in Hindī verse, entitled *Sūnīsār,* the essence of emptiness, the purport of which is to show that all notions of man and God are fallacies, and that nothing is. His patron was *Dayā Rām,* Rājā of *Hāth'ras,* when that fortress was destroyed by the Marquis of Hastings. See Wilson, *Religious Sects of the Hindus,* i, 360, and Garcin de Tassy, i, 102.

635. दलपति राय, *Dal'pati Rāy,* of *Am'dābād.* B. (? Fl.) *1828* A.D.

In conjunction with another Brāhman named *Bansī Dhar Srī Mālī* (No. 636) he wrote an excellent commentary on the *Bhākhā Bhūkhan* (No. 377).

636. बन्सी धर स्री माली, *Bansī Dhar Srī Mālī,* of *Am'dābād.* B. (? Fl.) *1828* A.D.

In conjunction with another Brāhman named *Dal'pati Rāy* (No. 635) he wrote an excellent commentary on the *Bhākhā Bhūkhan* (No. 376).

637. गुर दीन पाँड़े कबि, the poet *Gur Dīn Pāṛē.* B. (? Fl.) *1834* A.D.

He wrote an important work, entitled the *Bāk Manōhar Piŋgal* (written 1803 A.D.), which treats not only of prosody, but of rhetoric, the six seasons, *Nakh'sikh* (see note to No. 87), and composition.

638. क्रिश्नानन्द ब्यास देब, *Krish'nānand Byās Dēb.* Fl. 1842 A.D.

He is best known for his *Rāg-Sāgarōdbhab Rāg-Kalpadrum* (quoted in this work as 'Rāg.'), which is an anthology of selections from the works of more than two hundred poets who were followers of Krisṇa.

It was finished in Sambat 1900 (A.D. 1843),[1] and was written in emulation of Rājā Sir *Rādhākānta Dēb's* well-known Sanskrit Encyclopædia entitled the *Çabda-Kalpadruma*. Some years ago this work, which was printed in Calcutta, sold for a hundred rupees a copy, but it is now out of print.

Dr. Rājendra Lāl Mittra, who as a boy was personally acquainted with him, gives me the following information regarding this author:—'The book was in three volumes. The author, I remember, told me that he would make his work extend to seven volumes, the same as Rājā *Rādhākānta Dēb's Çabda-Kalpadruma*, but I do not think he had materials ready at hand for the purpose. He carried about with him a huge bundle of MS. notes, but I never had an opportunity to examine them, and I was too young then to care for them. The author was a Brāhman, and his great pretension was that he could sing in three octaves, the ordinary compass of the human voice being two and a half octaves. He pretended also that he could sing in all the *Rāgas* and *Rāgiṇīs* with absolute accuracy, and without ever mixing up the latter; but I never studied music myself, and in my youth cared nothing about it, so I never could get any proof of the man's pretensions. He was always singing, but was not a professional musician, that is, he never let himself out on hire. He received presents from the rich people of the town frequently, but never accepted anything as wages or remuneration for singing.'

It would be a work of too great labour to collect the names of all the poets whose works are quoted in this great work. The author, however, in his preface gives a list of all the poets with whom, and all the works (Hindī, Kar'nāṭī, Marāṭhī, Telugu, Gujrātī, Baŋgālī, Uṛiyā, English, Arabic, Peguan (sic), Persian, and Sanskrit) with which he is acquainted. From this preface the names of the following Hindī authors and works are abstracted. Several I have been unable to identify, and especially several works mentioned herein are not referred to elsewhere in this book:—

A.—HINDŪSTĀNĪ AUTHORS.

Chand (No. 6).
Pirthwī Rāj (cf. Nos. 6, 73).
Rāmānand (No. 10).
Kabīr (No. 13).
Kamāl (No. 16).
Bidyāpati (No. 17).
Mīrā Bāī (No. 20).
Rājā *Karan* (? No. 21).
Nānak (No. 22).
Nām Dēb (cf. No. 22).

[1] The first chapter is dated 19th March 1842; the second chapter, 1843.

Charan Dās (No. 23).
Gadādhar Misar (No. 25).
Mādhab Dās (No. 26).
Bhag'wān Dās (No. 29).
Ballabhāchār'j (No. 34).
Madh'wāchār'j (cf. No. 34).
Krish'n Dās (No. 36).
Sūr Dās (No. 37).
Par'mānand Dās (No. 38).
Kumbhan Dās (No. 39).
Chatur'bhuj Dās (No. 40).
Chhīt Swāmī (No. 41).
Nand Dās (No. 42).
Gōbind Dās (No. 43).
Agr' Dās (No. 44).
Kēwal Rām (No. 45).
Kalyān Dās (No. 48).
Kānhar Dās (No. 52).
Srī Bhaṭṭ (No. 53).
Byās Swāmi (No. 54).
Nīmāditya (cf. No. 54).
Hit Haribans (No. 56).
Dhrub Dās (No. 58).
Hari Dās (No. 59).
Tān Sēn (No. 60).
Abhay Rām (No. 64).
Chatur Bihārī (No. 65).
Mānik Chand (No. 78).
Ūdhō Dās (Nos. 79, 495).
Dāmōdar Dās (No. 84).
Chand Sakhī (No. 93).
Nāgarī Dās (? No. 95).
Rām Dās (No. 112).
Nar'hari Dās (? No. 113).
The Holy Master (*Tul'sī Dās*) (No. 128).
Braj Nidhi (? No. 131).
Dhīraj (? No. 136).
Bhūkhan (No. 145).
Mati Rām (No. 146.)
The Holy Master *Purukhōttam* (No. 200).
Bihārī (No. 226).
Ballabh Dās (? No. 239).
Malūk Dās (No. 243).
Madan Mōhan (No. 253).
Kul'pati Misar (No. 282).
Gopāl Dās (No. 297).
Jugul Dās (No. 313).
Braj Jīban Dās (? No. 315).
Syām Dās (No. 316).
Giri Dhar (No. 345).
Ānand Ghān (No. 347).
Man Bhāwan (No. 375).
Rasik Bihārī (No. 405).
Rām Par'sād (No. 444).
Padmākar (No. 506).
Gadā Dhar Bhaṭṭ (No. 512).
Bikram (No. 514).
Rājā *Biswanāth Siṅgh* (No. 529).
Gōkul Nāth (No. 564).
Rām Sahāy (No. 568).
Jānakī Dās (No. 577).
Mannū Lāl (Nos. 583, 599).
Subans (No. 589).
Jagannāth (? No. 601, 764).
Chir Jū (? No. 607).
Mahānand (No. 619).
Gyān Dās (? No. 651).
Brindāban Jīban (? No. 722).
Lachhirām (? No. 723).
Lōk Nāth (No. 753).
Jug Rāj Dās (? No. 765).
Dhōdhē (No. 766).
Bali Rām Dās (? No. 768).
Bish'n Dās (No. 769).
Lachchhan Dās (? No. 775).
Baksū (? No. 861).
The Holy Master *Brajādhīs* (? No. 878).

Hit Ānand (? No. 947).
Āsu Tōkh.
Bāijū Bāwarē.
Bhar'tharī.
Dayā Sakhī.
Dēb 'Ālam.
The Holy Master *Giri Dhar.*
Gōpāl Nāyak.
Jitaū.
Kālī Mir'jā.
Kam'lākar (? *Padmākar,* No. 506).
Kar'tāliyā.
Karunā Nidhān.
Krish'n Jīban.
Mōhan Dās.
Nar'sī Mah'tā.
Nar'siŋgh Dayāl.
Nasī Rām.
Nīl Mani.
Nīl Ratan.
Raghu Mahāsay.
Rām Gulām.
Rām Jas.
Raŋgīlā Prītam.
Raŋgīlī Sakhī.
Rasik Gōbind.
Rasik Rāy.
Rāy Mōhan.
Rūp Sanātan.
Sah'jō Bāī.
Sāmā Sakhī.
Saūdā.
Sāwarī Sakhī.
Sib Chandr'.
Sōnā Dāsī.
Syām Sundar.
Ṭhaṇḍī Dās.

B.—HINDŪSTĀNĪ WORKS.[1]

Prithī Rāj Rāy'sā (No. 6).
The *Bījak of Kabīr* (No. 13).
The *Granth* of the Sīkhs (No. 22).
Padminī Kathā (? No. 31).
Padmāwat (No. 31).
Sudāmā Charitr' (No. 33).
The twelve books of the *Bhāgavata Purāṇa* (Nos. 37, 40, 532, 614, 629, 797, 859).
Sūr Sāgar (No. 37).
Rukminī Maŋgal (No. 42).
Rās Pañchādhyāyī (? No. 42).
Bhakt Mālā (No. 51).
Saŋgīt Sār of *Tān Sēn* (No. 60).
Rāmāyan of *Tul'sī Dās* (No. 128).
Gītābalī (No. 128).
Kabitta Rāmāyan (No. 128).
Dōhābalī (No. 128).
Rām Sat Saī (No. 128).
Pañch Ratan (No. 128).
Bar'wē Rāmāyan (No. 128).
Binay Pattrikā (No. 128).
Hanumān Bāhuk (No. 128).
Rām Salākā (No. 128).
Srī Krish'nābalī (No. 128).
Kabi-priyā (No. 134).
Rasik-priyā (No. 134).
Rām-chandrikā (No. 134).
Ashṭa-jām (No. 140; cf. No. 694).
Bhākhā Piŋgal (No. 141).
Siŋghāsan Battīsī (Nos. 142, 629).

[1] I would draw the attention of scholars to the huge list of Sanskrit works mentioned in the preface of this valuable work.

Bhākhā Amar Kōs (Nos. 170, 567, 589, 761).
The *Shāirs* of *Naẓīr* (No. 171).
Bihārī Sat Saī (No. 196).
Chhattra Par'kās (No. 202).
Khaṭ Ritu (by many poets) (Nos. 210, 479, 648).
Sib Swarōday (? No. 309).
Saras Ras (No. 326).
Bāitāl Pachīsī (Nos. 326, 366, 629, 883).
Kōk Sār (No. 347).
Rasārnab (No. 356).
Prabōdh Chandrōday (the play) (No. 369).
Braj Bilas (No. 369).
Bhākhā Bhūkhan (No. 377).
Sālihōtr' (Nos. 365, 376, 469, 657, 854, 949).
Rāg Mālā (Nos. 400, 904).
Anēkārth and *Nām Mālā* (No. 433).
Jagat Binōd (No. 506).
Ānand Ras (Nos. 561, 668).
The *Mahābhārata* in *Braj Bhākhā* (No. 564, etc.).
Rāj Nīti (Nos. 574, 629, 840, 919).
The *Shāirs* of *Mannū Lāl* (Nos. 583, 599).
Hanumān Nāṭak (No. ? 592).
Prēm Sāgar (No. 629).
Sabhā Bilās (No. 629).
Hitōpadēs (No. 629).
Mādhō Bilās (Nos. 629, 896).
Rāg-Sāgarōdbhab Rāg-Kalpadrum (No. 638).
Lilāvatī (translation) (No. 912).
Ābhās Rāmāyan (?).
Ab'tār Charitr'.
Awadh Bilās.
Bāidya Manōtsab.
The *Bhagavad Gītā* (translation).
Bēdararī Kathā.
Bhākhā Bāidak.
Bhākhā Chhand.
Bhākhā Indrajāl.
Bhākhā Kāyadā.
Bhākhā Kōkh.
Bhākhā Sābar.
Bhūgōl Brittānt.
Bidyābhyās kā phal.
Bikh Parīchhā.
Braj Jātrā.
Brindāban Sat.
Chār Dar'wēsh.
Ḍāktarī (doctery, *i.e.* the art of medicine ! !).
Dayā Bilās.
Dhyān Mañjarī.
Ganitāṅk.
Gar'bhābalī Rāmāyan.
The *Ghazals* of *Sāudā.*
Gōpī Chand Gān.
Gōrakh Machhēndr' Samāj.
Gyān Upadēs.
The *Hār Mālā* of *Nar'sī.*
Hātam Tāī.
Hīrā Rāñjhā.
Kāsī Khaṇḍ.
Kāutuk Ratnābalī.
Krish'n Gītābalī.
Lūnā Chamārī kā Mantr'.
Mān Mañjarī.
Manōrañjan Itihās.
Nāin Sukh.
Nīti Kathā.
Phar'mākōpīyā (! !).
Rājā Bhar'tharī Gān.

Rām Binōd.
Rām Charan Chinh.
Ras Rāj.
Rōgāntak Sār.
Sāmudrikā (translation).
Saŋgīta Darpaṇa (translation).
Saŋgīta Ratnākara (translation).
Saŋgīt Pachīsī.
Sarpādi Jantun kī Pōthī.
Sisu Bōdh.
Slōkābalī Rāmāyan (? by *Tul'sī Dās*).
Snēh Sāgar.
Strī Sichchhā Bidhāyak.
Sugā Bahattarī.
Up'dēs Kathā.

639. राम परऽसाद, *Rām Par'sād*, the *Agar'wālā*, of *Mīrāpur*. B. (? Fl.) *1844* A.D.

Rāg. Father of *Tul'sī Rām* (No. 640) and author of some quietistic poems (cf. No. 444). Garcin de Tassy (i, 420) mentions an author of this name who wrote a Vaishnava work entitled *Dharmatattwasār*. It was written at *Ahmadābād*.

640. तुलऽसी राम, *Tul'sī Rām*, the *Agar'wālā*, of *Mīrāpur*. Fl. 1854.

In the above year he translated the *Bhakt Mālā* of *Nābhā Dās* (No. 51) into Ūrdū. He was son of No. 639.

641. भानु नाथ झा, *Bhānu Nāth Jhā*. Fl. 1850 A.D.

He attended the court of Mahārāj *Mahēswar' Siŋgh*, of *Dar'bhaŋgā*. He wrote in Maithilī. See J. A. S. B., vol. liii, p. 86. His best known work is a play in Sanskrit, Prākrit, and Maithilī, entitled *Prabhāvatī Haraṇa*.

642. हरऽख नाथ झा, *Har'kh Nāth Jhā*, the Sōtī Brāhman, of *Dar'bhaŋgā*. B. 1847 A.D.

A Maithil poet of the first rank, who is chief Paṇḍit at the court of the Mahārāj of Dar'bhaŋgā. He is the author of numerous Maithilī songs and of more than one play (*Prabandha*) in mixed Sanskrit, Prākrit, and Maithilī. The best known of the last is the *Uṣā Haraṇa*. See J. A. S. B., vol. liii, p. 92.

He is also author of several Sanskrit works. He was a pupil of *Mōd Nāth Jhā* and *Gōpāl Ṭhākur*, and afterward studied at Banāras College. He was born at *Ujāin*, in the Dar'bhaŋgā district.

643. सिब पर॰कास सिङ्ह, Bābū *Sib Par'kās Siŋgh,* of *Ḍum'rāw,* district *Shāhābād.* B. *1844* A.D.

The author of a commentary on the *Binay Pattrikā* of *Tul'sī Dās* (No. 128), entitled *Rām Tattwa Bōdhanī.*

644. कामन्ता पर॰साद, *Kām'tā Par'sād,* the *Asōthar,* of *Lakh'purā,* district *Fatih'pur.* B. *1854* A.D.

Ras. He belonged to the family of *Bhag'want Rāy,* the *Khīchī,* of *Asōthar* (No. 333), and is said to have been learned in the study of composition (साहित्य). He wrote in Sanskrit, in Prākṛit, in the vernacular, and in Persian. Sib Siŋgh in his *Sarōj* (p. 57) gives a specimen of his powers, which consists of a verse of four lines—the first in Sanskrit, the second in Prākṛit, the third in vernacular, and the fourth in Persian. Sib Siŋgh mentions a good *Nakh'sikh* (see note to No. 87) by a poet of this name, who is probably the same person.

ADDENDA TO CHAPTER X, PART IV.

645. भूप नारायन, the bard *Bhūp Nārāyan,* of *Kākūpur,* district *Kānh'pur.* B. *1801* A.D.

He wrote a metrical genealogy of the Chandēlā Chhattrī kings of *Sib'rāj'pur.*

646. दुर॰गा कबि, the poet *Dur'gā.* B. *1803* A.D.

647. चूड़ामनि कबि, the poet *Chūṛāmani.* B. *1804* A.D.

A poet who praised in his works two patrons, named *Gumān Siŋgh* and *Ajīt Siŋgh.*

648. आजम कबि, the poet *Ājam* (*A'zam*). B. *1809* A.D.

This Musalmān was a friend of other good poets, and himself composed poems. His best works are a *Nakh'sikh* (see note to No. 87) and the *Khaṭ Ritu* (Rāg.) (or description of the six seasons).

649. मेधा कबि, the poet *Mēdhā.* Fl. 1810 A.D.

The author of a work entitled *Chittrabhūkhan,* written in the above year.

650. कमल॰लेस कबि, the poet *Kam'lēs.* B. *1813* A.D.

Has written an excellent work on lovers. (See note to No. 87.)

651. ग्यान चन्द्र॰ जती, *Gyān Chandr' Jatī,* of *Rāj'putānā.* B. *1813* A.D.

? Rāg. He was Colonel Tod's preceptor.

652. सम्पति कबि, the poet *Sampati.* B. *1813* A.D.

653. भोज कबि, the poet *Bhōj* the elder. B. *1815* A.D.

654. रिखि जू कबि, the poet *Rikhi Jū.* B. *1815* A.D.

An erotic poet.

655. अम्बुज कबि, the poet *Ambuj*. B. *1818* A.D.

His poems on morals and his *Nakh'sikh* (see note to No. 87) are said to possess taste.

656. कबिराय कबि, the poet *Kabirāy*. B. *1818* A.D.

He has written some ingenious verses on morals (नीति)।

657. गुलाल कबि, the poet *Gulāl* B. *1818* A.D.

Sriṇg. His principal work is a *Sālihōtr'* (Rāg.), a treatise on veterinary surgery.

658. दीना नाथ अध्वर्य्य, *Dīnā Nāth Adhwarya*, of *Mōhār*, district *Fatih'pur*. B. *1819* A.D.

He wrote a vernacular commentary to the *Brahmōttara Khaṇḍa*.

659. बेनी परगट, *Bēnī Par'gaṭ*, a Brāhman, of *Nar'wal*. B. *1823* A.D.

660. *Anonymous.*

A rājā of *Uniyārā*. Fl. *1823* A.D. Sib Siṇgh states that he is the author of very excellent commentaries to the *Bhākhā Bhūkhan* (No. 376) and the *Nakh'sikh* of *Balibhadr'* (No. 135), and that the name of the author is missing in his copies. *Uniyārā* is a division of *Jaipūr*.

661. कबिराज कबि, the poet and bard *Kabirāj*. B. *1824* A.D.

Sun. A mediocre poet. Not to be confounded with *Sukh Dēb Misar* of *Kampilā* (No. 160), who sometimes describes himself as a *kabirāj* or poet-laureate.

662. मोग जी कबि, the poet and bard *Mōg Jī*, of *Rāj'putānā*. Fl. 1829 A.D.

The author of a genealogy and history of the kings of the *Khīchī* branch of the *Chauhāns*.—See Tod's *Rājasthān*, i, 81, and ii, 454; Calc. ed. i, 87, and ii, 499.

Sib Siṇgh calls him *Mūk Jī*.

663. गुर दत्त कबि, the poet *Gur Datt'* the elder. B. *1830* A.D.

He attended the court of *Sib Siṇgh Sawāī*, son of *Jai Siṇgh*. I do not know who these princes were.

664. हठी कबि, the poet *Haṭhī*, of *Braj*. B. *1830* A.D.

The author of a work entitled *Rādhā Satak*.

665. टेर कबि, the poet *Ṭēr*, of district *Main'purī*. B. *1831* A.D.

666. क्रिशन कबि, the poet *Krish'n*. B. *1831* A.D.

He has written some detached verses on morals (नीति).

667. आछे लाल भाट, the bard *Āchhē Lāl*, of *Kanauj*. B. *1832* A.D.

668. दया नाथ दुबे, *Dayā Nāth Dūbē*. Fl. 1832 A.D.

In the above year he commenced a work entitled *Ānand Ras* (Rāg.), dealing with the subject of lovers.

669. राम दीन, the bard *Rām Dīn*, of *Alīgañj*, district *Īṭā*. B. *1833* A.D.

670. माखन लखेरा, *Mākhan Lakhērā*. B. *1834* A.D.

No particulars. Probably the same as a *Mākhan Kabi* mentioned by Sib Siṇgh as born in *1813* A.D.

671. बेनी दास कबि, the poet and bard *Bēnī Dās*, of *Mēwār*. B. *1835* A.D.

? Sun. He was one of the public historians of *Mēwār*.

672. छेदी राम कबि, the poet *Chhēdī Rām*. Fl. 1837 A.D.

The author of a treatise on prosody, entitled *Kabi-nēh*, written in the above year.

673. अनुनैन कवि, the poet *Anunāin*. B. *1839* A.D.

The *Nakh'sikh* (see note to No. 87) by him is said to be a good poem.

674. औध कवि, the poet *Āudh*. B. *1839* A.D.

Sib Siṅgh knows nothing about this poet, a specimen of whose poetry he gives. He suspects that he may be the same as *Ajodhyā Par'sād Bāj'-pēyī* (No. 693).

675. नरोत्तम, *Narōttam*, of the *Dōāb*. B. *1839* A.D.

676. मनी राम मिसर, *Manī Rām Misar*, of *Saṭhī*, district *Kānh'pur*. B. *1839* A.D.

No particulars. He is possibly the same as a *Manī Rām Kabi* mentioned by Sib Siṅgh, without date, as an erotic poet.

677. सेवक कवि, the poet *Sēbak*. Fl. *1840* A.D.

? Sun. He attended the court of Rājā *Ratan Siṅgh*, of *Chakr'pur*. Possibly the same as No. 579.

678. फाल्का राव, *Phal'kā Raw*, of *Gwāliyar*. B. *1844* A.D.

He was minister of *Lachhiman Raw*, and wrote a good commentary to the *Kabi-priyā* (No. 134).

679. मीतू दास गौतम, *Mitū Dās Gāūtam*, of *Har'dhāūr'pur*, district *Fatih'pur*. B. *1844* A.D.

The author of numerous Vedantic works.

680. रघु नाथ उपाध्या, *Raghu Nāth Upādhyā*, of *Jāūn'pur*. B. *1844* A.D.

The author of a work entitled *Nir'nay Mañjarī*.

681. सुख दीन कवि, the poet *Sukh Dīn*. B. *1844* A.D.

An erotic poet.

682. सूखन कवि, the poet *Sūkhan*. B. *1844* A.D.

An erotic poet.

683. भवानी दास कवि, the poet *Bhawānī Dās*. B. *1845* A.D.

No particulars. *Jāī Krish'n* (No. 830) was the son of a *Bhawānī Dās*, but it is doubtful if it is this poet or not.

684. बल देव दास कवि, the poet *Bal Dēb Dās*, of *Jāūharī Hāth'ras*. B. *1846* A.D.

He translated the *Kriṣṇa Khaṇḍa*, line for line, into the vernacular.

685. अवध बकस, *Awadh Bakas* (*Bakhsh*). B. *1847* A.D.

His poems possess taste. Sib Siṅgh does not know the name of his country or village.

686. सहज राम सनाढ्य, *Sahaj Rām Sanāḍhya*, of *Bandhuā*. B. *1848* A.D.

The author of a history of Prahlāda entitled *Prahlād Charitr'*.

687. अनीस कवि, the poet *Anīs*. B. *1854* A.D.

Dig.

688. भूमी देव कवि, the poet *Bhūmī Dēb*. B. *1854* A.D.

689. भूसुर कवि, the poet *Bhūsur*. B. *1854* A.D.

690. जै नरिन्द सिङ्घ, Mahārāj *Jāī Narind Siṅgh alias Narēndra Siṅgh* of *Paṭiyālā*. Fl. 1857, D. 1862 A.D. Sun.

CHAPTER XI.

HINDŪSTĀN UNDER THE QUEEN. [1857—1887.]

THE present chapter concludes the proper historical portion of this work. It deals entirely with the "India of the Queen,"—with a period free from internal commotion, and in which every inducement and encouragement has been offered for the spread and for the acquisition of knowledge. One consequence of this has been the wide extension of the art of printing. Large Native publishing-houses have risen in Lakh'naū, Banāras, and Paṭ'nā, from which have issued floods of printed works, old and new, good, bad, and indifferent. At the same time a mushroom growth of smaller establishments has sprung up all over Hindūstān, and there is now scarcely a town of importance which does not possess its printing-press or two. Every scribbler can now see his writings in type or lithographed for a few rupees, and too often he avails himself of the power and the opportunity.

The rise of the Vernacular Press has been a prominent feature of the period under review. Hundreds of sheets have sprung into an ephemeral existence and have died in turn, while a few have lived through their childhood and deservedly survive as exceptions to the general fate. This is not the place to allude to the tone of the Indian Vernacular Press, and I purposely avoid doing so, beyond calling attention to the fact that as a rule the Hindī newspapers offer a favourable comparison with the more disloyal and scurrilous contemporaries which disgrace Baŋgālī journalism.

It has been impossible for me, face to face with such a mass of literature, to attempt to describe it with anything like completeness. I have only selected a few names which appeared to me worthy of notice, and even this selection I cannot pretend to be satisfactory. Hindūstān at present is practically without any independent review which I could take as a guide, and I have been compelled to trust to my own, necessarily limited, reading, aided by the lists of names given in the Sib Siŋgh Sarōj. For earlier periods I have had the winnowing basket of time, which has dissipated the chaff and collected the grains ready for examination; but for the present not only is the proportion of chaff to grain infinitely greater, but the two are as yet unseparated.

Such as it is I give the following list, which contains all the names mentioned in the Sib Siŋgh Sarōj, together with those of other writers whom I have met in the course of my reading, and which I think worthy of preservation. I must add that many writers belonging to this period as well as to the preceding one (some of whom are happily still alive) will be found entered in the last chapter. Some of these, *e.g.* Harishchandr', really belong to the post-Mutiny days, but have been deliberately included in the earlier period in order to complete the convenient consideration of groups or families of authors.

691. उमापति त्रिपाठी, Paṇḍit *Umāpati Tripāṭhī*, of *Ajodhyā*, district *Faizābād*. D. *1874*.

He was a deeply-read paṇḍit in all branches of Sanskrit learning. He at first lived in *Banāras*, but afterwards settled in *Ajodhyā* (*Āudh*), where he occupied himself with compositions and teaching. He died A.D. 1874. His most celebrated works are in Sanskrit, but he wrote a few short books in the vernacular, such as the *Dohābalī*, *Ratnābalī*, etc. He wrote under the *nom de guerre* of *Kōbid*.

692. रघु नाथ दास, Mahant *Raghu Nāth Dās*, of *Ajodhyā*, district *Faizābād*. Alive in *1883* A.D.

He was originally a Brāhman of *Pāitēpur*, district *Fatih'pur*, but, abandoning all worldly possessions, he became a devotee of Rām, and wrote hundreds of admired hymns in that deity's honour. See No. 693.

693. अजोध्या परसाद बाजपेयी, *Ajodhyā Par'sād Bāj'pēyī*, of *Sātan'pur'wā*, district *Rāy Barēlī*. Alive in *1883*.

This poet is well known as being extremely learned both in Sanskrit and the vernacular. His poems are said to be full of taste, and of uncommon excellence. Amongst his works may be mentioned—

(1) *Chhandānand*.
(2) *Sāhitya Sudhāsāgar*.
(3) *Rām Kabittābalī*.

Sib Siŋgh says he generally resides with *Raghu Nāth Dās*, the Mahant (No. 692), or with Rājā *Jag'mōhan Siŋgh* in *Chandāpur*. (Cf. No. 709.) He wrote under the name of *Āudh* (cf. No. 674).

694. **गोकुल परसाद,** Lālā *Gōkul Par'sād*, a Kāyasth, of *Balirām'pur*, district *Gōḍā*. Alive in *1883*.

He wrote in the year 1868 A.D., in honour of the late Rājā *Dig-bijāi Siŋgh* (succeeded 1836), an anthology entitled *Dig-bijāi Bhūkhan* (quoted in this work as 'Dig.'), containing selections from the works of 192 poets. He is also author of works entitled *Ashṭa-jām* (Rāg.), *Chitrakalādhar*, *Dūtī Dar'pan*, and others. He wrote under the *nom de guerre* of *Braj*.

695. **जानकी परसाद,** the bard *Jānakī Par'sād*, of *Jōhabēnakaṭī*, district *Rāy Barēlī*. Alive in *1883*.

He is son of *Ṭhākur Par'sād* (No. ? 570), and is learned both in Persian and in Sanskrit. In Ūrdū he has written a history of India entitled *Shād Nāmā*. In the vernacular he is author of (1) *Raghubīr Dhyānābalī*, (2) *Rām Naba-ratan*, (3) *Bhag'batī Binay*, (4) *Rām-nibās Rāmāyan*, (5) *Rāmānand Bihār*, (6) *Nīti-bilās*. This poet excels in picturesqueness and in the quietistic style. Either he or the other *Jānakī Par'sād* (No. 577) may possibly be the same as a third poet of the same name mentioned by Sib Siŋgh without date, who wrote an ingenious acrostic asking one *Siŋgh Rāj* for a shawl (*dusālā*).

696. **महेस दत्त** *Mahēs Datt'*, of *Ghanāulī*, district *Bārā-baŋkī*. Alive in *1883*.

He was author of a useful anthology named *Kābya Saŋgrah* (quoted in this work as 'Kāb.'), which was printed in Sambat 1932 (1875 A.D.). Possibly the same as a *Mahēs Kabi* mentioned by Sib Siŋgh as born in 1803 A.D.

697. **नन्द किशोर मिसर,** *Nand Kishōr Misar alias* the poet *Lēkh'rāj*, of *Gandhāuli*, district *Sītāpur*. Alive in *1883*.

The author of (1) *Ras Ratnākar*, (2) *Laghu Bhūkhan Alaŋkār*, (3) *Gaŋgā Bhūkhan*. He is *lambar'dār* of the village of Gandhāulī.

He is possibly the same as two other poets mentioned by Sib Siṅgh, viz. *Nand* Kabi and *Nand Kishōr* Kabi. The latter is author of a work entitled *Rām Krish'n Gun-Māl.*

698. माता दीन मिसर *Mātā Dīn Misar.* Alive in *1883.*

He translated the *Shāh Nāma* into the vernacular. In Sambat 1933 (A.D. 1876) he published the *Kabi Ratnākar* (quoted in this work as 'Kab.'), an anthology containing poems by twenty poets.

699. शिव प्रसाद्, Rājā *Śiva Prasād,*[1] C.S.I., of *Banāras.* B. 1823. Alive in 1887.

This gentleman, the well-known friend of education in India, is the grandson of Bībī *Ratan Kūar* (No. 376). He is also well-known for his efforts to popularise a style of the Hindūstānī language, which he calls the colloquial speech of Āg'rā, Dillī, and Lakh'naū, or of Hindūstān proper, midway between the Persian-ridden Ūrdū and the Sanskrit-ridden Hindī. These efforts have given rise to a lively and not yet decided controversy amongst the natives of India. He is a most prolific author of works on education, and a complete list of his books, communicated by himself, is appended to this section.

The following account of his life is compiled partly from the *Modern History of the Indian Chiefs, Rājās, Zamīndārs,* etc., by Lokenath Ghose, and partly from materials kindly furnished to the author by the Rājā himself. Towards the end of the 11th century there was a man named *Dhāndhal,* of the *Pāwar* (*Pramara*) tribe, in *Ran'thambhōr* (*Jāipur* territory). Having obtained a son through the blessing of a Jain pontiff, he embraced that religion and was included in the Ōs'wāl caste. Ran'thambhōr being taken and plundered by *Alāu'd-dīn Khiljī* late in the 13th century, the family migrated successively to *Ahmadābād* and *Champānēr,* and settled finally in *Khambhāt. Amar Datt',* twenty-sixth in descent from Dhandhal, presenting a diamond to *Shāh Jahān* (1628—1658), pleased him so much, that the emperor conferred on him the title of Rāy, brought him to *Dillī,* and made him court jeweller. Rāy Amar Datt' died leaving one son, who married a

[1] The name is transliterated thus because it is the way he spells it himself. According to the system of transliteration adopted in this book it would be *Çiva Prasāda, Sib Par'sād,* or *Siv Par'sād.*

sister of *Sēṭh Mānik Chand*, of *Murshidābād*. The youngest son of this marriage, *Jagat Sēṭh Fatah Chand*, was adopted by his uncle the Sēṭh, and two of his elder brothers having been killed in the sack of Dillī by *Nādir Shāh*, the family settled in Murshidābād. Fatah Chand's grandson *Jagat Sēṭh Mah'tāb Rāy* was arrested with his cousin Rājā *Dāl Chand* by Nawāb *Kāsim 'Alī Khān* for taking up the cause of the British and joining Lord Clive. Rājā *Dāl Chand* escaped and reached *Banāras*, where he ended his days under the protection of the Nawāb Wazīr of Āudh.

Rājā *Śiva Prasād* is the son of Bābū *Gōpī Chand* and great grandson of Rājā *Dāl Chand*. He lost his father when only eleven or twelve years of age, and was brought up by his mother and grandmother, the latter of whom, Bībī *Ratan Kūar* (No. 376), was one of the most learned women of her age. He partly owes his education, though very slightly, to Banāras College, then only an English Seminary; but he is emphatically an example of a self-made and self-instructed man. Of his grandmother he says, with characteristic modesty, "the best part of the little knowledge I may be credited with, I acquired from her." In his youth he was strongly anti-European in his ideas, and hence in his seventeenth year he accepted the post of Wakīl to the late Mahārāj of *Bharat' pur* to attend the court of Colonel Sutherland, the then Governor-General's Agent at Āj'mēr. He says :—"My expenses under the Maharajah were somewhat about Rs. 5,000 per mensem, but I found the Dar'bār there rotten to the core, and as hopeless as anything can be on earth. I became disgusted, resigned, returned, and wanted to become an ascetic; but my friends commenced taunting me. They called me a fool and a mad man. They said '*Patang achchhā chaṛhā thā, lēkin gōt khā gayā*,'—'a paper kite had got fine and high, but was swooping down again,' or '*Andhē kē hāth baṭēr lag gaī thī*,'—'a quail had fallen into the hand of a blind man.'[1] I could not bear this, and I made up my mind again to serve, but some one who was greater than the Maharajah of Bharat'pur. I joined Lord Hardinge's camp before Fīrōz'pur. Mud'kī had been fought, and Sobrāon was about to be fought. There the treatment I received opened my eyes. I vowed I would never serve a Native again." He rose to be Mīr Munshī of the Simla Agency when Mr. Edwards became Superintendent of the Protected Hill States there, and he looks back to that period as the best part of his life. When

[1] That is, excessive luck. It usually takes several men in full possession of their eyes to net a single quail.

Mr. Edwards in 1851 or 1852 went home on furlough, Rājā S'iva Prasād resigned, and on account of the old age of his mother, intended to live a private life in Banāras; but Mr. Tucker, the then Governor-General's Agent at Banāras, prevailed on him to accept the Mīr Munshīship of that Agency, and afterwards obtained for him the post of Joint-Inspector in the Department of Public Instruction. Sir W. Muir made him a full Inspector, and after serving the Government for thirty years he retired on a well-earned pension, and is now living at Banāras. He has received many honours from Government, amongst which may be mentioned the hereditary title of Rājā and the Companionship of the most exalted Star of India. The following extract from a letter written by him to the author will fitly conclude this notice:—"I have just written to a friend in England that if he ever has to name a man who at least claims to be contented, thankful, and happy, he can name S'iva Prasād. I have one son and three grandsons * * * My occupation now is culture of land and culture of mind."

The following is a list of Rājā S'iva Prasād's vernacular works:—

No.	Names of Books.	Subject.	Remarks.
	HINDI.		
1	*Bar'n Māla* ...	Primer	With stories and engravings.
2	*Bāl Bōdh* ...	Easy Reader	Originally written in English by Mr. W. Edwards.
3	*Bidyāŋkur* ...	An adoption of Chambers's Rudiments of Knowledge and a few pages of Introduction to Sciences.	With illustrations. Originally written for Mr. Edwards' schools in the hills. Its Ūrdū version is called *Huqāiqu-'l-māujūdāt.*
4	*Bāmā-man Rañjan*	Some celebrated women of the East and West.	Taken from English and Baŋgālī books for Mr. H. C. Tucker. Its Ūrdū version is called *Hikāyātu'l-Sālihāt.*
5	*Hindī Byākaran* ...	Hindī Grammar ...	Its counterpart in Ūrdū is called *Sarf-ō-Nahw-i-Ūrdū* (No. 19).

No.	Names of Books.	Subject.	Remarks.
	HINDI.		
6	*Bhūgōl Hastāmalak, Part I. (Asia.)*	Geography	Compiled from no less than a hundred books of reference, with coloured maps. Its Ūrdū version is called *Jām-i-Jahān Numā* (No. 20).
7	*Chhōṭa Bhūgōl Hastāmalak.*	Abridgment of the Bhūgōl Hastāmalak (No. 6).	Its Ūrdū version is called *Chhōṭā Jām-i-Jahān Numā.*
8	*Itihās Timir Nāshak* (in three parts).	History of India from the earliest ages to the Queen's Proclamation, 1858.	In English, History of Hindūstān; in Ūrdū, *Āina-i-Tārīkh Numā.*
9	*Guṭ'kā*	Selections.	
10	*Mānava Dharma-sār.*	Extracts from the Institutes of *Manu.*	With original Sanskrit.
11	*Ditto*	Ditto	With Sir William Jones's English translation.
12	*Sandford āūr Merton kī kahānī.*	Hindī version of Qissa-i-Sandford-o-Merton (No. 25).	(In the Press.)
13	*Sīkhō kā Uday Ast.*	Rise and fall of the Sīkh nation.	Compiled from authentic and official records. Its Ūrdū version, *Sīkhō kā Tulū' āūr Ghurūb,* is in the Press.
14	*Swayambōdh Ūrdū.*	Ūrdū Primer and Self-Instructor.	Out of print.
15	*Aṅgrēzī Achchharō kē sīkh'nē kī Upāy.*	Roman characters ...	Ditto.
16	*Bachchō kā In'ām.*	A little prize-book for children.	
17	*Rājā Bhōj kā Sap'nā*	A story	Written for Mr. H. C. Tucker.
18	*Bīr Siṅgh kā Brittānt.*	Against infanticide ...	Written for Mr. W. Edwards. Out of print.
	URDU.		
19	*Sarf-ō-Nahw-i-Ūrdū*	Ūrdū Grammar.	
20	*Jām-i-Jahān Numā*	Geography.	
21	*Chhōṭā Jām-i-Jahān Numā.*	Abridgment of Jām-i-Jahān Numā (No. 20).	

No.	Names of Books.	Subject.	Remarks.
	URDU.		
22	*Mazāmin*	Selections.	
23	*Kuchh Bayān ap'nī Zubān kā.*	A lecture on the vernaculars, delivered before the Banāras Institute.	
24	*Dil Bah'lāō* (in three parts).	Miscellany	Written for Mr. H. C. Tucker.
25	*Qissa-i-Sandford-o-Merton.*	Translation, or rather adaptation, of Sandford and Merton.	Ditto.
26	*Dunnallan* ...	Beauties of Christianity, or life of a Methodist Christian gentleman. Abridged from Grace Kennedy.	Translated for Mr. H. C. Tucker. Out of print.
27	*Gulāb āūr Chamēlī kā Qissā.*	Adaptation of the above.	
28	*Sachchī Bahādurī*	True heroism	Translated for Mr. H. C. Tucker.
29	*Miqra'atu'l-kāhilīn.*	Life in earnest	Written for Mr. H. C. Tucker.
30	*Shahādat-i-Qurānī bar Kutub-i-Rabbānī.*	Testimony borne by the Qurān to the Bible.	Written for a gentleman.
31	*Tārīkh-i-kalīsā* ...	History of the early church.	Ditto.
32	*Fārsī Sarf-ō-Nahw*	Persian Grammar in Ūrdū.	

700. **लक्ष्मी नाथ ठाकुर,** *Lachhmī Nāth Ṭhākur,* of *Mithilā.* Fl. 1870 A.D.

A prolific and much-admired writer in the Bais'wārī dialect.

701. **फतूरी लाल,** *Phatūrī* (or *Fatūrī*) *Lāl,* a Kāyasth, of *Tir'hut.* Fl. 1874 A.D.

The author of a very popular poetical account of the famine of 1873-74, entitled *Kabitt' Akālī,* written in the Maithilī dialect. See

J. A. S. B., extra No., 1881, p. 24 (*Maithil Chrestomathy*, by G. A. Grierson).

702. चन्द्र॰ झा, *Chandr' Jhā*. Alive in 1883.

A living poet of *Mithilā* of considerable eminence. He attends the court of Mahārāj *Lachh'mīshwar Siṇgh* Bahādur of *Dar'bhaṇgā*, and is author of a much-admired *Rāmāyan* in the Maithilī dialect of Bihārī.

703. जान साहिब, *Jān Sāhib*. Died about 1883 A.D.

This is the poetical name of Mr. *John Christian*, the only European writer with whom I am acquainted whose vernacular poetry has made its way to the masses. He was a prolific writer of Christian hymns, which are known to all the singers of Tir'hut, most of whom recite them without any idea of their original meaning. His most admired work is the *Mukti-Muktābalī*, a metrical life of Christ.

704. अम्बिका दत्त॰ व्यास, *Ambikā Datt' Byās*, of *Banāras*. Alive in 1888 A.D.

A rising author. He has written several plays, which will be found mentioned in No. 706. His *Bhārat Sāubhāgya* was written in honour of her Majesty's Jubilee. Amongst his other works may be mentioned *Madhumatī*, a translation of the well-known Baṇgālī novelette of that name.

705. छोटू राम तिवारी, Paṇḍit *Chhōṭū Rām Tiwārī*, of *Banāras*. B. cir. 1840 A.D.; D. 1887 A.D.

This gentleman was for many years Professor of Sanskrit at Paṭ'nā College, and it was the author's privilege to number him amongst his more intimate friends. His knowledge of the earlier vernacular poetry of his country was profound and accurate, and his reputation extended over a wide area. As a writer of his own language his fame rests on his *Rām Kathā*, of which, I believe, no authorised edition was ever published. It is admittedly a model of the very purest and best modern Hindī, free alike from vulgarisms and from pedantry. He kept the proofs of the work by him for several years, incessantly polishing it and repolishing it, till the day of his death. So much was the work admired that there was a large sale of these proof-sheets, which achieved great popularity, and extracts from them have been given prominent situations in the many Readers and Anthologies which have been issued of late years.

He was son of *Dēbī Dayāl Tripāṭhī*, and had two brothers—an elder, named *Sītal Par'sād*, author of a play entitled *Jānakī Maŋgal*, the first Hindī play ever acted, and a younger, called *Gōpī Nāth*, who was father of *Kālī Par'sād Tiwārī* (No. 739).

NOTE ON THE HINDĪ[1] AND ON THE BIHĀRĪ DRAMA.

706. The Hindī drama is a plant of very recent growth. It is true that some of the earlier writers wrote what they called *nāṭaks*, for instance *Niwāj* (No. 198) wrote a *Sakuntalā*, and *Braj Bāsī Dās* (No. 369) and others translations of the *Prabōdha Chandrōdaya;* but these were plays only in name, being without entrances and exits of the characters. Similarly, the *Dēb Māyā Prapañch* of the celebrated poet *Dēb* (No. 140), the *Prabhāwatī* written for the Mahārāj of Banāras, and the *Ānand Raghunandan* written for Mahārāj *Biswanāth Siŋgh* (No. 529) of *Rīwā*, are wanting in the essentials of dramatic poetry.

The first Hindī play in which there are regular exits and entrances for the characters was the *Nahukh Nāṭak* of *Giridhar Dās* (*Gōpāl Chandr'*) (No. 580), which deals with Indra's expulsion from his throne by Nahuṣa and his subsequent reinstatement. Harishchandr', the son of the author, was seven years old at the time it was written, which was therefore the year 1857.

The next Hindī play in a really dramatic form was the *Sakuntalā* of Rājā *Lachhman Siŋgh*, which has in later years been edited by Mr. Pincott. It was followed by *Harishchandra's* (No. 581) *Bidyā Sundar*, founded on the well-known Baŋgālī poem of that name, but happily free from its obscenities. The fourth was the *Taptā Sambaran* of *Srīnibās Dās*, the fifth *Harishchandra's Baidikī Hinsā*, and the sixth *Tōtā Rām's Kētō Kritānt*. These examples found many imitators.

The first Hindī play ever performed was the *Jānakī Maŋgal* of *Sītal Par'sād Tiwārī*, elder brother of *Chhōṭū Rām Tiwārī* (No. 705).

[1] Partly abridged from *Harishchandra's 'Nāṭak;' Shrī Harishchandra Kalā*, p. 38.

This took place in the *Banāras* theatre in the Sambat year 1925 (1868 A.D.), and was very successful. It was followed by the *Ran Dhīr Prēm Mōhinī* of *Srīnibās Dās* and the *Satya Harishchandr'* of *Harishchandr'* at *Allāhābād* and *Kānh'pur.*

In *Bihār,* on the contrary, a dramatic tradition has existed for nearly five centuries. *Bidyāpati Ṭhākur* (1400 A.D.) (No. 17) was the author of two plays—the *Pārijāt Haran* and the *Rukminī Swayambar.* Manuscripts of these plays exist, I believe, to the present day, but I have never seen them. *Lāl Jhā* (No. 363) was author of the *Gāurī Parinay.* At the beginning of the present century *Bhānu Nāth Jhā* (No. 641) wrote the *Prabhābatī Haran. Har'kh Nāth Jhā* (No. 642) is author of the *Ukhā Haran* or (in Sanskrit) *Uṣā Haraṇa.* All these poets were Maithil Brāhmans. It must be admitted that their works hardly come under the name of *vernacular* plays, as the characters speak in Sanskrit and in Prakrit, only the songs being in Maithilī.

The following is a list of Hindī plays given by Harishchandr', *l.c.*

Name of play.	Author.
Nahukh Nāṭak ...	*Giridhar Dās.*
Sakuntalā ...	*Lachhman Siŋgh.*
Mudrā Rāchhas ...	*Harishchandr'.*
Satya Harishchandr' ...	*Ditto.*
Bidyā Sundar ...	*Ditto.*
Andhēr Nagarī ...	*Ditto.*
Viṣasya Viṣamāuṣadham ...	*Ditto.*
Satī Pratāp ...	*Ditto*
Chandrābalī ...	*Ditto.*
Madhurī ...	*Ditto.*
Pākhaṇḍ Biṛamban ...	*Ditto.*
Nab Mallikā ...	*Ditto.*
Durlabh Bandhu ...	*Ditto.*
Prēm Jōginī ...	*Ditto.*
Jāisā Kām Wāisā Parinām ...	*Ditto.*
Karpūr Mañjarī ...	*Ditto.*
Nīl Dēbī ...	*Ditto.*
Bhārat Durdasā ...	*Ditto.*
Bhārat Jananī ...	*Ditto.*
Dhanañjay Bijay ...	*Ditto.*
Bāidikī Hinsā ...	*Ditto.*
Būṛh Mūh Muhāsē, Lōg Chalē Tamāsē ...	*Gōkul Chand.*

Name of play.		Author.
Adbhut Charitr', or Grih Chanḍī	...	*Srī Matī.*
Taptā Sambaran	...	*Srīnibās Dās.*
Ran Dhīr Prēm Mōhinī	...	*Ditto.*
Kētō Kritānt	...	*Tōtā Rām.*
Sajjād Sumbul	...	*Kēshō Rām Bhaṭṭ.*
Sham'shād Sāūsan	...	*Ditto.*
Jay Nar'siŋgh kī	...	*Deokī Nandan Tiwārī.*
Hōlī Khagēs	...	*Ditto.*
Chachchhu Dān	...	*Ditto.*
Pad'māwatī	...	*Bāl Krish'n Bhaṭṭ.*
Sarmishṭhā	...	*Ditto.*
Chandr' Sēn	...	*Ditto.*
Sarōjinī	...	*Ganēs Datt'.*
Sarōjinī	...	*Rādhā Charan Gosā̃ī.*
Mrichchhakaṭikā	...	*Gadā Dhar Bhaṭṭ.*
Bārāŋganā Rahasya	...	*Bad'rī Nārāyan Chāūdh'rī.*
Bigyān Bibhākar	...	*Jānī Bihārī Lāl.*
Lalitā Nāṭikā	...	*Ambikā Datt' Byās.*
Dēb Purukh Drishya	...	*Ditto.*
Bēnī Saŋghār	...	*Ditto.*
Gō Saŋkaṭ	...	*Ditto.*
Bhārat Sāūbhāgya	...	*Ditto.*
Jānakī Maŋgal	...	*Sītal Par'sād Tiwārī.*
Dukkhinī Bālā	...	*Rādhā Krish'n Dās.*
Padmāwatī	...	*Ditto.*
Mahā Rās	...	Mahārāj Kumār *Khaṛag Lāl Bahādur Mall.*
Rām Līlā	...	*Dāmōdar Shāstrī.*
Mrichchhakaṭikā	...	*Ditto.*
Bāl Khēl	...	*Ditto.*
Rādhā Mādhab	...	*Ditto.*
Wēnis kā Sāūdāgar (Merchant of Venice)	...	*Balēswar Par'sād.*
Mrichchhakaṭikā	...	*Ṭhākur Dayāl Siŋgh.*
Wēnis kā Sāūdāgar	...	*Ditto.*

ADDENDA TO CHAPTER XI.

707. पचम कवि, the poet and bard *Pañcham,* of *Ḍal'maū,* district *Rāy Barēlī.* B. (? Fl.) *1867* A.D.

708. फूल चन्द, *Phūl Chand,* a Brāhman, of *Bais'wārā.* B. (? Fl.) *1871* A.D.

Sib Singh gives two poets of this name ; the second without date.

709. सुदरसन सिङ्ह, Kumār *Sudar'san Singh*, of *Chandāpur*. (Cf. No. 693.) B. (? Fl.) *1873*.

He has published a collection of his own poems.

710. मानिक चन्द, *Mānik Chand* the Kāyasth, of district *Sītāpur*. B. (? Fl.) *1873* A.D.

711. अनन्द सिङ्ह, *Anand Singh alias Dur'gā Singh*, of *Ahawanadi Koliyā*, district *Sītāpur*. Alive in *1883* A.D.

712. ईस्वरी परसाद, त्रिपाठी *Īswarī Par'sād Tripāṭhī*, of *Pīr'nagar*, district *Sītāpūr*. Alive in *1883*.

He has written a translation of the *Rāmāyaṇa* of *Vālmīki* in the form of an epic poem in various metres under the name of the *Rām Bilās*.

713. उमराव सिङ्ह पँवार, the bard *Um'rāw Singh*, of *Sāīd'pur*, district *Sītāpur*. Alive in *1883*.

714. गुर दीन राय बन्दीजन, the bard *Gur Dīn Rāy*, of *Pāītēya*, district *Sītāpur*. Alive in *1883*.

He attended the court of Rājā *Ran Jīt Singh Sāh Jāg'rē* (No. 716), of *Īsānagar*, district *Khīrī*.

715. बल देव कवि अवस्थी, the poet *Bal Dēb Abasthī*, of *Dāsāpur*, district *Sītāpur*. Alive in *1883*.

Under the name of Rājā *Dal Thambhan Singh Gāūr Sawāīyā*, of *Hathiyā*, he wrote a work on lovers entitled *Sringār Sudhākar*.

716. रनजीत सिङ्ह साह जाँगरे, Rājā *Ran Jīt Singh Sāh Jāg'rē*, of *Īsānagar*, district *Khīrī*. Alive in *1883*.

The author of a translation of the *Hrivaṁça*.

717. ठाकुर परसाद त्रिबेदी, *Ṭhākur Par'sād Tribēdī*, of *Alīgañj*, district *Khīrī*. Alive in *1883*.

718. हजारी लाल त्रिबेदी, *Hajārī Lāl Tribēdī*, of *Alīgañj*, district *Khīrī*. Alive in *1883*.

A quietistic and moral poet.

719. गङ्गा दयाल दूबे, *Gangā Dayāl Dūbē*, of *Nis'gar*, district *Rāy Barēlī*. Alive in *1883*.

Said to be skilled in Sanskrit and the vernacular.

720. दयाल कबि, the poet and bard *Dayāl*, of *Bētī*, district *Rāy Barēlī*. Alive in *1883*.

He is son of the poet *Bhāūn* (No. 611).

721. बिस्वनाथ, the bard *Biswanāth*, of *Ṭikaī*, district *Rāy Barēlī*. Alive in *1883*.

He praised one *Ran'jīt Singh* (? No. 716). He is possibly the same as a *Biswanāth Kabi* mentioned by Sib Singh as born 1844 A.D., who has written a number of poems on the manners and customs of the people of *Lakh'naū*.

722. ब्रिन्दाबन, *Brindāban*, a Brāhman, of *Sem'rāūtā*, district *Rāy Barēlī*. Alive in *1883*.

? Rāg. No particulars. He is possibly the same as a *Brindāban Kabi* mentioned by Sib Singh.

723. लछिराम कबि, the poet and bard *Lachhirām*, of *Hōl'pur*, district *Bārābaṅkī*. Alive in *1883*.

He wrote a treatise on lovers (see note to No. 87) under the name of *Sib Singh* (the author of the anthology), and called it *Sib Singh Sarōj*. Cf. No. 126.

724. सन्त बकस, the bard *Sant Bak's*, of *Hōl'pur*, district *Bārābaṅkī*. Alive in *1883*.

Cf. No. 126.

725. समर सिङ्ह, *Samar Singh*, a Chhattrī, of *Haṛ'hā*, district *Bārābaṅkī*. Alive in *1883*.

The author of a *Rāmāyan*.

726. **सिव परन्सन्न कबि,** the poet *Sib Par'sann*, a Sāk'dwīpī Brāhman, of *Rām'nagar*, district *Bārābaṇkī*. Alive in *1883*.

727. **सीता राम दास,** *Sītā Rām Dās*, a Baniyā, of *Bīrāpur*, district *Bārābaṇkī*. Alive in *1883*.

728. **गुनाकर त्रिपाठी,** *Gunākar Tripāṭhī*, of *Kāntha*, district *Unāo*. Alive in *1883*.

He writes in Sanskrit and in the vernacular. His family is famed for its knowledge of astronomy.

729. **सुख राम,** *Sukh Rām*, a Brāhman, of *Chāuhattarī*, district *Unāo*. Alive in *1883*.

He is possibly the same as a *Sukh Rām Kabi* mentioned by Sib Siṇgh as B. (? Fl.) *1844* A.D. and as an erotic poet.

730. **देबी दीन,** the bard *Dēbī Dīn*, of *Bil'grām*, district *Har'dōī*. Alive in *1883*.

His best works are a *Nakh'sikh* (see note to No. 87) and the *Ras-dar'pan*.

731. **माता दीन सुकल,** *Mātā Dīn Sukal*, of *Aj'gara*, district *Par'tāp'gaṛh*. Alive in *1883*.

He attends the court of Rājā *Ajīt Siṇgh*, of *Par'tāp'gaṛh*. Some verses by him, entitled *Gyān Dōhābalī*, will be found in the *Bhākhā Sār* of *Sāhib Prasād Siṇgh*.

732. **कन्हैया बख्श,** *Kanhāiyā Bakhsh* the Bais, of *Baia'wārā* (*Āudh*). Alive in *1883*.

His best work is in the quietistic style.

733. **गिरि धारी भाट,** *Giri Dhārī Bhāṭ*, of *Maū Rānīpurā*, in district *Jhānsī*, *Bundēl'khaṇḍ*. Alive in *1883*.

734. **जबरेस,** the bard *Jab'rēs*, of *Bundēl'khaṇḍ*. Alive in *1883*.

735. **रन धीर सिङ्ह,** Rājā *Ran Dhīr Siṇgh*, *Sir'māūr*, of *Siṇg'rā Maū*. Alive in *1883*.

Besides being a patron of poets, he is author of the *Kābya Ratnākar* (written 1840 A.D.) and the *Bhūkhan Kāumudī* (written 1860 A.D.). There are many towns of the name of Maū in India, but I have been unable to identify that named as above by Sib Siṇgh.

736. **सिव दीन,** Paṇḍit *Sib Dīn alias Raghu Nāth*, a Brāhman, of *Rasūl-ābād*. Alive in *1883*.

The author of the *Bhābāmahimna* and other works. Possibly the same as a *Sib Dīn* Kabi mentioned by Sib Siṇgh without particulars. There are several towns of the name of Rasūlābād in India. I do not know which is the one above referred to.

737. **राम नारायन,** *Rām Nārāyan*, a Kāyasth. Alive in *1883*.

An erotic poet. He is Munshī to Mahārāj *Mān Siṇgh* (No. 599).

738. **अम्बिका परन्साद,** *Ambikā Par'sād*. Alive in 1883 A.D.

He belongs to the *Shāhābād* district, and is the author of numerous songs in the Bhoj'pūrī dialect, which are not of great merit, but are valuable as samples of the author's mother tongue. A number are given in Part II of *Seven Grammars of the Bihār Dialects*.

739. **काली परन्साद तिवारी,** *Kālī Par'sād Tiwārī*, of *Banāras*. Alive in 1888.

This gentleman is Head Paṇḍit of the Jhāūgañj City School, in *Paṭ'nā*. He is the author of several school-books, and of a *Bhākhā Rāmāyan*, in mixed Hindī prose and verse, in a simple style, which is much admired. He is nephew of Paṇḍit *Chhoṭū Rām Tiwārī* (No. 705).

740. बिहारी लाल चौबे *Bihārī Lāl Chaūbē*, Assistant Professor of Sanskrit at *Paṭ'nā* College, Alive in 1888.

This gentleman, besides writing a large number of useful school-books, is author of a useful work on rhetoric entitled *Bihārī Tul'sī Bhūkhan Bōdh.* He is also editing a good edition of the *Sat Saī* of *Tul'sī Dās* (No. 128) in the *Bibliotheca Indica.*

CHAPTER XII.

MISCELLANEOUS.

THE following chapter contains the names of a number of minor poets, whose dates I have not been able to fix.

I.—Poets mentioned in the Kabi-mala of Tul'si (No. 153), and therefore earlier than 1655 A.D.

741. सङ्ख कबि, the poet *Saṇkh*.

742. साहब कबि, the poet *Sāhab*.

743. सिद्ध कबि, the poet *Siddh*.

744. सुबुद्धि कबि, the poet *Subuddhi*.

745. स्री कर कबि, the poet *Srī Kar*.

746. स्री हठ कबि, the poet *Srī Haṭh*.

II.—Poets mentioned in the Hajara of Kalidas Tribedi (No. 159), and therefore earlier than 1718 A.D.

747. जसवन्त कबि, the poet *Jas'want* the younger.

748. तीखी कबि, the poet *Tīkhī*.

If I understand Sib Siṇgh aright, poems by him are included in Haj.

749. तेही कबि, the poet *Tēhī*.

If I understand Sib Siṇgh aright, poems by him are included in Haj.

750. दिला राम कबि, the poet *Dilā Rām*.

751. राम रूप कबि, the poet *Rām Rūp*.

I have collected several songs by him in Mithilā.

752. लोधे कबि, the poet *Lōdhē*.

III.—Poets mentioned in the Kabya-nir'nay of Bhikhari Das (No. 344), and therefore earlier than 1723 A.D.

753. लोक नाथ कबि, the poet *Lōk Nāth*.

Also in Rāg.

754. गुलाम नबी, Sayyad *Gulām Nabī alias* the poet *Ras Līn*, of *Bil'grām*, district *Har'dōī*.

Besides being learned in Arabic and Persian, he was also a master of the vernacular. He wrote a *nakh'-sikh* called *Aṇg Dar'pan* (dated 1637 A.D.), and a treatise on rhetoric, entitled *Ras Par'bōdh* (dated 1741 A.D.) There is something wrong about these dates. The latter is probably the correct one.

755. बलि कबि, the poet *Bali*.

An erotic poet.

756. रहीम कबि, the poet *Rahīm*.

He is distinct from *'Abdu'r Rahīm Khān'khānā* (No. 108). It is difficult to distinguish between the works of this poet and those of his illustrious namesake.

IV.—Poets mentioned by the poet Sudan (No. 367), and therefore earlier than 1753 A.D.

757. **सनेही कवि,** the poet *Sanēhī.*

758. **सिव दास कवि,** the poet *Sib Dās.*

Garcin de Tassy (I, 474) mentions an author of this name who came from *Jāipur,* to whom we owe the *Sib Chāupāī,* a work quoted by Ward in his *History of the Hindūs* (II, 481). He was also author of a book the name of which Garcin de Tassy gives as *Pōthī lōk ūkat ras jagat,* which he confesses he does not understand.

759. **सुमेरु सिङ्घ साहेबज्जादा,** Prince *Sumērū Singh.*

Also in Sun.

760. **सूरज कवि,** the poet *Sūraj.*

761. **हरि कवि,** the poet *Hari.*

The author of a commentary on the *Bhākhā Bhūkhan* (No. 377), entitled *Chamatkār Chandrikā,* and of a metrical commentary on the *Kabi-priyā* (No. 134) entitled *Kabi-priyābharan.* He also translated the *Amara Kōça* (? Rāg. cf. Nos. 170, 567, 589) into the vernacular.

762. **हित राम कवि,** the poet *Hit Rām.*

V.—Poets mentioned in the Rag-Sagarodbhab Rag-Kalpadrum of Krishnanand Byas Deb (No. 638), and therefore earlier than 1843 A.D.[1]

763. **छबीले कवि,** the poet *Chhabīlē,* of *Braj.*

764. **जगन्नाथ दास,** *Jagnnāth Dās.*

He is possibly the same as one *Jagannāth Kabi* the elder, mentioned by Sib Singh. Cf. No. 601.

765. **जुग राज कवि,** the poet *Jug Rāj.*

Said to be the author of some tasteful poems.

766. **धोँधे दास,** *Dhōdhē Dās,* of *Braj.*

767. **नाम देव,** *Nām Dēb.*

Poems by him are also included in the Sīkh *Granth* (see Nos. 22, 169).

768. **बलि राम दास,** *Bali Rām Dās,* of *Braj.*

Also Sring. Possibly the same as a *Bali Rām* quoted by Garcin de Tassy (I, 105) from Mack. (II, 108) as author of the *Chit Bilās,* a treatise on the creation of the world, in which are described the objects and end of human existence, the formation of gross and ethereal bodies, and the means of acquiring salvation.

769. **बिशन्न दास,** *Bish'n Dās.*

Also the name of the author of a number of emblematic dōhās.

770. **भगवान हित राम राय,** *Bhag'wān Hit Rām Rāy.*

771. **मन निधि कवि,** the poet *Man Nidhi.*

772. **मनि कण्ठ कवि,** the poet *Mani Kanth.*

773. **मुरारि दास,** *Murāri Dās,* of *Braj.*

774. **रसिक दास,** *Rasik Dās,* of *Braj.*

---

[1] See also many other names mentioned in the preface of the same work extracted out in No. 638.

775. राम राय, *Rām Rāy*, the Raṭhaūr.

776. लच्छन दास कबि, the poet *Lachchhan Dās.*

I have found a poem in the Braj dialect, and bearing his name, in Mithilā.

He was son of Rājā *Khēm Pāl* the Raṭhaūr.

777. लछुमन सरन दास, *Lachhuman Saran Dās.*

778. सगुन दास कबि, the poet *Sagun Dās.*

779. स्याम मनोहर कबि, the poet *Syām Manōhar.*

VI.—Poet mentioned in the Ras Chandroday of Thakur Par'sad (No. 570), and therefore earlier than 1863 A.D.

780. कालिका कबि, the poet and bard *Kālikā*, of *Banāras.* Alive in 1883. Also in Sun.

VII.—Poets mentioned in the Dig-bijai Bhukhan of Gokul Par'sad (No. 694), and therefore earlier than 1868 A.D.

781. खान कबि, the poet *Khān.*

782. धुरन्धर कबि, the poet *Dhurandhar.*

Also Sriṇg.

783. नायक कबि, the poet *Nāyak.*

Also Sriṇg.

VIII.—Poets mentioned in the Sundari Tilak of Harishchandr' (No. 581), and therefore earlier than 1869 A.D.

784. आलीमन कबि, the poet *Ālīman.*

785. कबि राम, *Kabi Rām alias Rām Nāth*, the Kāyasth.

Sib Siṇgh gives two poets of this name. One he puts down as alive in *1883*, and the other as born in *1841.* Probably they are the same.

786. तुलसी स्री ओझा जी, *Tul'sī Srī Ōjhā Jī*, of *Jōdh'pur* (*Mār'wār*).

He is said to be an elegant erotic poet.

787. दया निधि, *Dayā Nidhi*, a Brāhman, of *Paṭ'nā.*

Possibly the same as a *Dayā Nidhi Kabi* mentioned by Sib Siṇgh, also without date. Cf. No. 365.

788. नजीब खान, *Najīb Khān alias* the poet *Rasiyā*, councillor of the Mahārāj of *Paṭiyālā.*

789. नव निधि कबि, the poet *Nab Nidhi.*

790. नबीन कबि, the poet *Nabīn.*

An erotic poet.

791. नरेस कबि, the poet *Narēs.*

It appears from a reference in one of his detached poems that he was the author of a treatise on lovers (see note to No. 87).

792. पारस कबि, the poet *Pāras.*

793. महन्राज कबि, the poet *Mah'rāj.*

Also Sriṇg.

794. रिखि नाथ कबि, the poet *Rikhi Nāth.*

Also Sriṇg. An erotic poet.

795. सेखर कबि, the poet *Sēkhar.*

An erotic poet.

796. हनुमान कबि, the poet and bard *Hanumān*, of *Banāras.*

IX.—Poets mentioned in the Kabya Sangrah of Mahes Datt' (No. 696), and therefore earlier than 1875 A.D.

797. क्रिपा राम, *Kripā Rām*, the Brāhman, of *Narāinapur*, district *Gōḍā*.

He translated the whole *Bhāgavata Purāṇa* into simple language in *dōhās* and *chāupāis*. Cf. No. 328.

He is probably the same as a Kripā Rām Kabi (date unknown) who was the author of a poem in the Champū style, entitled *Mādhab Sulōchanā*, and as another Kripā Rām Kabi (date also unknown), author of an erotic poem in the *dōhā* metre, entitled *Hit Taraṅginī*.

798. नवल दास, *Nawal Dās*, the Chhattrī, of *Gūr Gāw*, district *Bārābaṅkī*.

He is the author of a work entitled *Gyān Sarōbar*. His date is (certainly incorrectly) put by Sib Siṅgh at Sambat 1316 (A.D. 1259).

X.—Miscellaneous poets whose dates I have been unable to fix. Collected from various sources, principally the Sib Singh Saroj.

799. अमर जी कबि, the poet *Amar Jī*, of *Rāj'putānā*.

According to Sib Siṅgh he is mentioned by Tod in his Rājasthān, but I have been unable to find the place.

800. कल्यान सिङ्घ भट्ट, *Kalyān Siṅgh Bhaṭṭ*.

801. काली चरन बाजप्पेयी, *Kālī Charan Bāj'pēyī*, of *Bigah'pur*, district *Unāo*.

Said to have been a skilled poet.

802. काली दीन कबि, the poet *Kālī Dīn*.

He translated poems in honour of Durgā.

803. कुञ्ज गोपी, *Kuñj Gōpī*, the Gāuṛ Brāhman, of *Jāipur*.

An erotic writer.

804. केसव्वर राम कबि, the poet *Kēs'war Rām*.

Author of a work entitled *Bhramar-gīt*, or songs of a bee, which however, according to Garcin de Tassy (I, 302), was written by *Krish'n Dās*, No. 806.

805. क्रिपाल कबि, the poet *Kripāl*.

An erotic writer.

806. क्रिश्न्न दास, *Krish'n Dās*.

Author of a commentary on the *Bhakt Mālā* (see No. 51). See Garcin de Tassy, I, 302. Garcin de Tassy makes him also possibly the author of a *Bhramar-gīt* (see No. 804), and of a religious treatise entitled *Prēm Sattwa Nirūp*.

807. खान मुलन्तान कबि, the poet *Khān Mul'tān*.

808. खुसाल पाठक, *Khusāl Pāṭhak*, of *Rāy Barēlī*.

He wrote on lovers (see note to No. 87).

809. खूब चन्द कबि, the poet *Khūb Chand*, of *Mār'wār*.

He composed a poem in honour of Rājā *Gambhīr Sāhī*, of *Īdar*.

810. खेतल कबि, the poet *Khētal*.

He wrote on lovers (see note to No. 87).

811. गङ्गा धर कबि, the poet *Gaṅgā Dhar*.

He has written a commentary on the *Sat Saī* of *Bihārī* (No. 196) in the *kuṇḍaliya* and *dōhā* metres, named the *Up'sat'sāiyā*.

812. गज सिङ्घ, *Gaj Siṇgh.*

The author of the *Gaj Siṇgh Bilās.* (Cf., however, No. 190.)

813. गीध कबि, the poet *Gīdh.*

Some detached *chhappās* and *dōhās* by him are extant.

814. गुमानी कबि, the poet *Gumānī*, of *Paṭ'nā.*

He wrote a number of verses, which are in every one's mouth in Bihār. The first three lines are in Sanskrit, and the fourth of each is a Hindī proverb. Specimens have been published in the *Indian Antiquary.* An example is

यावद्रामः ब्रह्मधारी
नायातीह लसंहारी
तावत्तस्मै देया नारी
ज्यों भीँजे त्यों कम्बल भारी

(Mandōdarī addresses Rāvaṇa). (*Sanskrit*) Before Rāma come armed here to fight with thee, do thou return his wife to him, for (*Hindī proverb*) 'The longer a blanket moisteneth (in the dew), the heavier it is.'

815. गुलाम राम कबि, the poet *Gulām Rām.*

His poems are said to be good.

816. गुलामी कबि, the poet *Gulāmī.*

His poems are said to be good.

817. गोसाँईं कबि, the poet *Gosāī*, of *Rāj'putānā.*

His occasional *dōhās* and those on morals are excellent.

818. गोपाल राय कबि, the poet *Gōpāl Rāy.*

He wrote some verses in praise of *Narēndr' Lāl Sāhī* and *'Ādil Khān.*

819. गोपाल सिङ्घ, *Gōpāl Siṇgh*, of *Braj.*

He wrote the *Tul'sī Sabdārth Par'kās.* In it he describes the *Ashṭa Chhāp* (see No. 35).

820. गोबिन्द राम, the bard *Gōbind Rām*, of *Rāj'putānā.*

He was author of a work entitled the *Hāṛāwatī*, which is a history of the Hāṛā family (cf. Tod's *Rājāsthān*, II, 454; Calc. ed. ii, 499).

821. घासी भट्ट, *Ghāsī Bhaṭṭ.*

822. चक्र पानि, *Chakr' Pānī.*

A Maithil poet (see J. A. S. B., vol. LIII, p. 91).

823. चतुरभुज, *Chatur'bhuj.*

A Maithil poet (see J. A. S. B., vol. LIII, p. 87).

824. चोखे कबि, the poet *Chōkhē.*

Sib Siṇgh says that his poems are clever (चोखी).

825. छत्तन कबि, the poet *Chhattan.*

826. जगन्नेस कबि, the poet *Jag'nēs.*

827. जनारदन भट्ट, *Janār'dan Bhaṭṭ.*

He wrote a treatise on medicine entitled *Bāidya Ratan.*

828. जयानन्द, *Jayānand.*

He was a Maithil poet, a Karan Kāyasth by caste (see J. A. S. B., vol. LIII, p. 85).

829. जुगुल परसाद चौबे, *Jugul Par'sād Chaubē.*

He has written a good *Dōhābalī.*

830. जै क्रिश्न कबि, the poet *Jāi Krish'n.*

He was son of the poet *Bhawānī Dās.* Cf. No. 683. He wrote a treatise on prosody entitled *Chhand Sār.*

831. जै सिङ्घ कबि, the poet *Jāi Siṇgh.*

An erotic writer.

832. टह्न्कन कबि, the poet *Tah'kan*, of the *Pañjāb*.

He has translated the episode of the Sacrifices of the Pāṇḍavas (*Pāṇḍavō kē yajña*) from Sanskrit into the vernacular.

833. ठाकुर राम कबि, the poet *Thakur Rām*.

A quietistic poet.

834. डाक, *Ḍāk*, an agricultural poet (see Ghāgh (No. 217) and cf. *Bihār Peasant Life*).

835. ढाकन कबि, the poet *Ḍhākan*.

836. दया देब कबि, the poet *Dayā Dēb*.

Sriṇg.

837. दान कबि, the poet *Dān*.

An erotic poet.

838. दिलीप कबि, the poet *Dilīp*.

839. देब नाथ कबि, the poet *Dēb Nāth*.

840. देब मनि कबि, the poet *Dēb Mani*.

He wrote a commentary in the vernacular to the first 16 *adhyāyas* of *Chāṇakya's Rājanīti* (Rāg. Cf. Nos. 574 and 919).

841. देबी कबि, the poet *Dēbī*.

An erotic poet. Probably the same as one of the many other poets whose names commence with *Dēbī*.

842. देबी दत्त कबि, the poet *Dēbī Datt'*.

A writer of quietistic and occasional pieces.

843. देबी सिङ्घ कबि, the poet *Dēbī Siṇgh*.

Sriṇg.

844. द्विज नन्द कबि, the poet *Dwij Nand*.

845. नजामी, *Najāmī*.

I know nothing about this poet, except one short poem in praise of Sib, bearing his name, in the Bais'wārī dialect, which I collected orally in Mithilā.

846. नन्द राम कबि, the poet *Nand Rām*.

A quietistic poet.

847. नन्दीपति, *Nandīpati*.

A Maithil poet. See J. A. S. B., vol. LIII, p. 79.

848. नबी कबि, the poet *Nabī*.

Sriṇg. The author of an excellent *Nakh'sikh* (see note to No. 87).

849. नवल किशोर कबि, the poet *Nawal Kishōr*.

No particulars. He is possibly the same as one of the other poets whose name commences with *Nawal*, and as a poet mentioned by Sib Siṇgh, without date, as *Nawal Kabi*.

850. नाथ, *Nāth*.

Sriṇg. Many poets, such as *Kāsī Nāth* (No. 139), *Uday Nāth* (No. 334), *Sib Nāth* (No. 632), &c., often call themselves, as *nom de guerre*, simply Nāth, which has given rise to great confusion. Cf. Nos. 68, 147, 162, 440, 632.

851. नेही कबि, the poet *Nēhī*.

852. नैन कबि, the poet *Nain*.

853. पखाने कबि, the poet *Pakhānē*.

854. परधान केसब राय कबि, the poet *Par'dhān Kēsab Rāy*.

He wrote a treatise on veterinary surgery entitled *Sālihōtr'* (Rāg). He is possibly the same as a *Par'dhān Kabi* mentioned by Sib Siṇgh, without date or particulars.

855. परमल्ल, *Par'mall*.

He was son of *Saṇkar*, and was author of a Jain work entitled *Srīpāl Charitr'*. See Garcin de Tassy, I, 401. Cf. id. I, 520.

856. पुरान कबि, the poet *Purān.*

857. पुष्कर कबि, the poet *Pushkar.*

The author of a work on composition (साहित्य) entitled *Ras-ratan.*

858. पूरन चन्द जूथ, *Pūran Chand Jūth.*

He wrote a work entitled the *Rām-rāhasya Rāmāyan.*

859. प्रेम केसर दास, *Prēm Kēswar Dās.*

Author of a translation into the vernacular of the 12th book of the *Bhāgavata Purāṇa.* The India Office Library is said by Garcin de Tassy (I, 404) to possess a copy.

860. फेरन कबि, the poet *Phēran.*

861. बकसी कबि, the poet *Bak'sī.*

Possibly the same as a *Bak'sū* mentioned in the preface to Rāg.

862. बजरङ्ग कबि, the poet *Baj'raṅg.*

863. बदन कबि, the poet *Badan.*

864. बन्सी धर मिसर, *Bansī Dhar Misar*, of *Sandīlā.*

A quietistic poet.

865. बरग राय, *Bar'g Rāy.*

Author of a work entitled *Gōpāchalakathā*, or History of *Gwāliyar.* See Garcin de Tassy, I, 518.

866. बाबू भट्ट कबि, the poet *Bābū Bhaṭṭ.*

867. बिदुख कबि, the poet *Bidukh.*

A poet who dealt with the sports of Kṛiṣṇa.

868. बिन्दा दत्त कबि, the poet *Bindā Datt'.*

An erotic poet.

869. बिसम्भर कबि, the poet *Bisambhar* or *Biswāmbar.*

An erotic poet.

870. बिसेसर कबि, the poet *Bisēsar.*

871. बुद्ध सेन कबि, the poet *Buddh Sēn.*

872. बुध सिङ्घ, *Budh Siṅgh*, the *Pañjābī.*

Author of an elegant translation into the vernacular of the story of *Mādhavānala* or *Mādhōnal.* (Cf. Nos. 216, 629.)

873. बुलाकी दास, *Bulākī Dās.*

A prolific writer of *ghāṭōs* or songs peculiar to the month of Chait in the Bhoj'pūrī dialect. See *Some Bhoj'pūrī Folk-songs*, J. R. A. S., vol. xviii.

874. बेनी माधव भट्ट, *Bēnī Mādhab Bhaṭṭ.*

875. बैन कबि, the poet *Bain.*

876. बोधी राम कबि, the poet *Bōdhī Rām.*

877. ब्रज मोहन कबि, the poet *Braj Mōhan.*

An erotic poet.

878. ब्रजेस कबि, the poet *Brajēs*, of *Bundēl'khaṇḍ.*

879. ब्रिन्द कबि, the poet *Brind.*

880. भगवान दास निरञ्जनी, *Bhag'wān Dās, Nirañjanī.*

He translated the *Bhartṛihari Çataka* into the vernacular under the name of *Bhrityahari Sat.*

881. भञ्जन, *Bhañjan.*

A Maithil poet. See J. A. S. B., vol. LIII, p. 90.

882. भड्डर, *Bhaḍḍar*, an agricultural poet. See *Ghāgh* (No. 217) and cf. *Bihār Peasant Life.*

He was by tradition a noted astrologer, and is said to have belonged to the Shāhābād district. Many folk-tales are current concerning him.

883. भोला नाथ, *Bhōlā Nāth*, a Brāhman, of *Kanauj.*

He wrote a metrical version of the *Baitāl Pachīsī* (Rāg.).

884. मङ्गद कवि, the poet *Maṅgad*.

885. मनःसा राम कवि, the poet *Man'sā Rām*.

Sriṅg. A writer on lovers (see note to No. 87). He is possibly the same as a *Man'sā Kabi* mentioned by Sib Siṅgh as a great master of alliteration.

886. मनी राय कवि, the poet *Manī Rāy*.

An erotic poet.

887. मन्यठ कवि, the poet *Manya*.

An erotic poet.

888. मनोहर दास निरञ्जनी, *Manōhar Dās, Nirañjanī*.

The author of a Vedantic work entitled *Gyān-chūran Bachanikā*.

889. मह:ताब कवि, the poet *Mah'tāb*.

The author of an admired *Nakh'-sikh* (see note to No. 87).

890. महिपति, *Mahipati*.

A Maithil poet. See J. A. S. B., vol. LIII, p. 84.

891. मानिक दास कवि, the poet *Mānik Dās*, of *Mathurā*.

The author of a work entitled *Mānik-bōdh*, treating of Kriṣṇa's sports.

892. मीरन कवि, the poet *Mīran*.

Sriṅg. The author of an admired *Nakh'sikh* (see note to No. 87).

893. मुनि लाल कवि, the poet *Muni Lāl*.

894. मुसाहिब, *Musāhib*, Rājā of *Bijāur*.

He wrote commentaries on the *Binay Pattrikā* (see No. 128) and on the *Ras Rāj* (see No. 146).

895. मून, *Mūn*, the Asōthar, a Brāhman, of *Ghāzīpur*.

The author of many works. Amongst them the *Rām Rāban kā juddh* may be mentioned.

896. रघु राम, *Raghu Rām*, the Guj'rātī, of *Ah'madābād*.

The author of a play entitled *Mādhab Bilās* (? Rāg. Cf. No. 629).

897. रघु लाल कवि, the poet *Raghu Lāl*.

An erotic poet.

898. रज्जब कवि, the poet *Rajjab*.

Sriṅg. An esteemed author of *dōhās*.

899. रतन पाल कवि, the poet *Ratan Pāl*.

The author of various *dōhās* on morals.

900. रमापति, the poet *Ramāpati*.

? Sriṅg. A Maithil poet. See J. A. S. B., vol. LIII, p. 83.

901. रस पुञ्ज दास, *Ras Puñj Dās*, the Dādū Panthī.

The author of two good works on prosody, entitled *Prastār Prabhākar* and *Brittya Binōd*.

902. राम चरन, *Rām Charan*, a Brāhman of *Ganēs'pur*, district *Bārābaṅkī*.

The author of a Sanskrit work entitled *Kāyastha-kula Bhāskara*, and of a vernacular work entitled *Kāyasth-dhar'm Dar'pan*.

903. राम दत्त: कवि, the poet *Rām Datt'*.

904. राम दया कवि, the poet *Rām Dayā*.

The author of a work entitled *Rāg Mālā* (Rag.). Cf. No. 400.

905. राम देव सिङ्घ, *Rām Dēb Siṅgh*, a Chhattrī of the Solar race, of *Khaṇḍāsā*.

906. राम नाथ मिसर, *Rām Nāth Misar*, of *Āzam'gaṛh*.

907. राम बख्श, *Rām Bakhsh alias Rām Kabi.*

He attended the court of the Rānā of *Sir'māūr.* He is the author of a treatise on vernacular composition (साहित्य) and of a commentary to the *Sat Saī* of *Bihārī Lāl* (No. 196).

908. राम लाल कवि, the poet *Rām Lāl.*

909. राम सेख कवि, the poet *Rām Sēkh,* a Brāhman.

The author of a play entitled *Nritya Rāghab Milan.*

910. राम सेवक कवि, the poet *Rām Sēbak.*

The author of a work entitled *Dhyān Chintāmani.*

911. रामा कान्त, *Rāmā Kant.*

I have collected songs in the Braj dialect in Mithilā, purporting to be by this poet.

912. राय चन्द कवि, the poet *Rāy Chand,* of *Nāgar,* in *Guj'rāt.*

According to Sib Siṇgh he attends the dar'bār of Rājā *Dāl Chand, Jagat Sēṭh* in *Murshidābād,* and is the author of two displays of learning, entitled (1) *Gīt'gōbindādarshan* (a translation of the *Gīta Gōvinda*) and (2) *Līlāvatī* (Rāg.). There was a Rājā *Dāl Chand* of Murshidābād who was great-grandfather of Rājā *Śiva Prasād* (No. 699, *q.v.*), who may possibly be the person referred to by Sib Siṇgh.

913. राय जू कवि, the poet *Rāy Jū.*

An erotic poet. Possibly the same as a *Rāy Kabi* mentioned by Sib Siṇgh, also as an erotic poet.

914. लछुमन कवि, the poet *Lachhuman.*

He wrote a *Sālihōtr',* or treatise on veterinary surgery.

915. लछुमन सिङ्घ, *Lachhuman Siṇgh.*

An erotic poet.

916. लछ्मी कवि, the poet *Lachhmī.*

Sib says he is mentioned by *Saran* (?)

917. ललित राम कवि, the poet *Lalit Rām.*

918. लाजब कवि, the poet *Lājab.*

919. लाल कवि, the poet *Lāl.*

He translated *Chāṇakya's Rājanīti* (Rāg.) into the vernacular. Cf. Nos. 525, 574, and 840.

920. लाल चन्द कवि, the poet *Lāl Chand.*

The author of emblematic *kabittas* and *kuṇḍaliyās.*

921. लोक मनि कवि, the poet *Lōk Manī.*

Sib Siṇgh says that he is mentioned by *Saran* (?)

922. लोने कवि, the poet and bard *Lōnē,* of *Bundēl'khaṇḍ.*

An erotic poet.

923. वजन्हन, *Waz'han.*

A quietistic Vedantic author of *dōhās.*

924. वहाब, *Wahāb.*

The author of a well-known *Bārā Māsā,* or song descriptive of the 12 months.

925. वाहिद कवि, the poet *Wāhid.*

An erotic poet.

926. सत्रु जीत सिङ्घ, Rājā *Satru Jit Siṇgh,* the Bundēlā of *Datiyā,* in *Bundēl'khaṇḍ.*

The author of a treatise on rhetoric, &c., under cover of a commentary to the *Ras Rāj* (No. 146).

927. सबल स्याम कवि, the poet *Sabal Syām.*

928. सम्भु नाथ मिसर, *Sambhu Nāth Misar,* of *Murādābād,* district *Unāo.*

929. सम्भु परःसाद कबि, the poet *Sambhu Par'sād.*

An erotic poet.

930. सरस राम, *Saras Rām.*

A Maithil poet, who attended the court of a King *Sundar.* See J. A. S. B., vol. LIII, p. 87. Possibly this King was the Rājā *Sundar Ṭhākur* of *Tir'hut,* who came to the throne 1641 A.D. and died 1666 A.D.

931. ससिनाथ कबि, the poet *Sasi Nāth.*

Sriṅg. An erotic poet.

932. सिब राज, *Sib Rāj* of *Jaipur.*

? Sriṅg. A writer of whom Garcin de Tassy (I, 476) speaks as follows:—"We owe to him a work entitled *Ratan-mālā,* quoted by Ward in his *History of the Hindūs,* II, 481. I do not know if it is the same work which Mr. Wilson has made use of for his dictionary. This last is a list of the names of vegetable and mineral drugs in Sanskrit and Hindī. We owe to the same author the *Sib-Sāgar,* a work also cited by Ward." The author is also mentioned in the *Sib Siṅgh Sarōj.*

933. सुजान कबि, the poet *Sujān.*

An erotic poet.

934. सुन्दर कबि, the poet and bard *Sundar,* of *As'nī,* district *Fatih'pur.*

The author of a work entitled *Ras Par'bōdh.*

935. सुलःतान कबि, the poet *Sul'ṭān.*

An erotic poet.

936. सोभ कबि, the poet *Sōbh.* An erotic poet.

937. सोभ नाथ कबि, the poet *Sōbh Nāth.*

938. हनुमन्त कबि, the poet *Hanumant.*

He attended the court of Rājā *Bhānu Par'tāp Siṅgh.*

939. हर चरन दास कबि, the poet *Har Charan Dās.*

The author of a good work on vernacular composition (साहित्य) entitled *Brihat Kabi-ballabh.*

940. हर जीवन कबि, the poet *Har Jīban.*

941. हर दयाल कबि, the poet *Har Dayāl.*

An erotic poet.

942. हरि चन्द कबि, the poet *Hari Chand,* of *Bar'sāna,* in *Braj.*

The author of a prosody entitled *Chhand Swarūpinī.*

943. हरि देब कबि, the poet *Hari Dēb,* a Baniyā, of *Brindāban,* in *Braj.*

The author of a prosody entitled *Chhand Payōnidhi.*

944. हरि बल्लभ कबि, the poet *Hari Ballabh.*

A quietistic poet.

945. हरि भानु कबि, the poet *Hari Bhānu.*

The author of a treatise on vernacular composition (साहित्य) entitled *Narind Bhūkhan.*

946. हरि लाल कबि, the poet *Hari Lāl.*

Sriṅg. Possibly the same as another *Hari Lāl Kabi,* also mentioned by Sib Siṅgh without date, as an erotic poet.

947. हित नन्द कबि, the poet *Hit Nand.*

Possibly the same as a *Hit Ānand* mentioned in the preface to Rāg.

948. **हीरा लाल कवि,** the poet *Hīrā Lāl*.

An erotic poet.

949. **हुलास राम कवि,** the poet *Hulās Rām*.

The author of a treatise on veterinary surgery entitled *Sālihōtr'* (Rāg). Possibly the same as a *Hulās Kabi* mentioned by Sib Singh as an erotic poet.

950. **हेम कवि,** the poet *Hēm*. Sring. An erotic poet.

951. **हेम गोपाल कवि,** the poet *Hēm Gōpāl*.

The author of an emblematic verse, which is all that is known to have survived of his work.

952. **हेम नाथ कवि,** the poet *Hēm Nāth*.

He attended the court of *Kalyān Singh*, of *Keh'rī*.

INDICES.

N.B.—The figures refer to sections of the work.

INDEX No. I.

NAMES OF PERSONS.

M 2

INDEX No. II.

NAMES OF WORKS.

INDEX No. III.

NAMES OF PLACES.

Bengal Secretariat Press—Reg. No. 4077J—702—24-7-89.